References for the Rest of Us!®

BESTSELLING BOOK SERIES FROM IDG

Are you intimidated and confused by computers? Do you find that traditional manuals are overloaded with technical details you'll never use? Do your friends and family always call you to fix simple problems on their PCs? Then the *...For Dummies®* computer book series from IDG Books Worldwide is for you.

...For Dummies books are written for those frustrated computer users who know they aren't really dumb but find that PC hardware, software, and indeed the unique vocabulary of computing make them feel helpless. *...For Dummies* books use a lighthearted approach, a down-to-earth style, and even cartoons and humorous icons to diffuse computer novices' fears and build their confidence. Lighthearted but not lightweight, these books are a perfect survival guide for anyone forced to use a computer.

> *"I like my copy so much I told friends; now they bought copies."*
> — Irene C., Orwell, Ohio

> *"Quick, concise, nontechnical, and humorous."*
> — Jay A., Elburn, Illinois

> *"Thanks, I needed this book. Now I can sleep at night."*
> — Robin F., British Columbia, Canada

Already, millions of satisfied readers agree. They have made *...For Dummies* books the #1 introductory level computer book series and have written asking for more. So, if you're looking for the most fun and easy way to learn about computers, look to *...For Dummies* books to give you a helping hand.

PALMPILOT™ FOR DUMMIES®

PALMPILOT™ FOR DUMMIES®

by Bill Dyszel

IDG Books Worldwide, Inc.
An International Data Group Company

Foster City, CA ♦ Chicago, IL ♦ Indianapolis, IN ♦ New York, NY

PalmPilot™ For Dummies®

Published by
IDG Books Worldwide, Inc.
An International Data Group Company
919 E. Hillsdale Blvd.
Suite 400
Foster City, CA 94404
www.idgbooks.com (IDG Books Worldwide Web site)
www.dummies.com (Dummies Press Web site)

Copyright © 1998 IDG Books Worldwide, Inc. All rights reserved. No part of this book, including interior design, cover design, and icons, may be reproduced or transmitted in any form, by any means (electronic, photocopying, recording, or otherwise) without the prior written permission of the publisher.

Library of Congress Catalog Card No.: 98-87910

ISBN: 0-7645-0381-2

Printed in the United States of America

10 9 8 7 6 5 4 3 2 1

1B/RU/RQ/ZY/IN

Distributed in the United States by IDG Books Worldwide, Inc.

Distributed by Macmillan Canada for Canada; by Transworld Publishers Limited in the United Kingdom; by IDG Norge Books for Norway; by IDG Sweden Books for Sweden; by Woodslane Pty. Ltd. for Australia; by Woodslane (NZ) Ltd. for New Zealand; by Addison Wesley Longman Singapore Pte Ltd. for Singapore, Malaysia, Thailand, Indonesia and Korea; by Norma Comunicaciones S.A. for Colombia; by Intersoft for South Africa; by International Thomson Publishing for Germany, Austria and Switzerland; by Toppan Company Ltd. for Japan; by Distribuidora Cuspide for Argentina; by Livraria Cultura for Brazil; by Ediciencia S.A. for Ecuador; by Ediciones ZETA S.C.R. Ltda. for Peru; by WS Computer Publishing Corporation, Inc., for the Philippines; by Unalis Corporation for Taiwan; by Contemporanea de Ediciones for Venezuela; by Computer Book & Magazine Store for Puerto Rico; by Express Computer Distributors for the Caribbean and West Indies. Authorized Sales Agent: Anthony Rudkin Associates for the Middle East and North Africa.

For general information on IDG Books Worldwide's books in the U.S., please call our Consumer Customer Service department at 800-762-2974. For reseller information, including discounts and premium sales, please call our Reseller Customer Service department at 800-434-3422.

For information on where to purchase IDG Books Worldwide's books outside the U.S., please contact our International Sales department at 650-655-3200 or fax 650-655-3297.

For information on foreign language translations, please contact our Foreign & Subsidiary Rights department at 650-655-3021 or fax 650-655-3281.

For sales inquiries and special prices for bulk quantities, please contact our Sales department at 650-655-3200 or write to the address above.

For information on using IDG Books Worldwide's books in the classroom or for ordering examination copies, please contact our Educational Sales department at 800-434-2086 or fax 317-596-5499.

For press review copies, author interviews, or other publicity information, please contact our Public Relations department at 650-655-3000 or fax 650-655-3299.

For authorization to photocopy items for corporate, personal, or educational use, please contact Copyright Clearance Center, 222 Rosewood Drive, Danvers, MA 01923, or fax 978-750-4470.

LIMIT OF LIABILITY/DISCLAIMER OF WARRANTY: AUTHOR AND PUBLISHER HAVE USED THEIR BEST EFFORTS IN PREPARING THIS BOOK. IDG BOOKS WORLDWIDE, INC., AND AUTHOR MAKE NO REPRESENTATIONS OR WARRANTIES WITH RESPECT TO THE ACCURACY OR COMPLETENESS OF THE CONTENTS OF THIS BOOK AND SPECIFICALLY DISCLAIM ANY IMPLIED WARRANTIES OF MERCHANTABILITY OR FITNESS FOR A PARTICULAR PURPOSE. THERE ARE NO WARRANTIES WHICH EXTEND BEYOND THE DESCRIPTIONS CONTAINED IN THIS PARAGRAPH. NO WARRANTY MAY BE CREATED OR EXTENDED BY SALES REPRESENTATIVES OR WRITTEN SALES MATERIALS. THE ACCURACY AND COMPLETENESS OF THE INFORMATION PROVIDED HEREIN AND THE OPINIONS STATED HEREIN ARE NOT GUARANTEED OR WARRANTED TO PRODUCE ANY PARTICULAR RESULTS, AND THE ADVICE AND STRATEGIES CONTAINED HEREIN MAY NOT BE SUITABLE FOR EVERY INDIVIDUAL. NEITHER IDG BOOKS WORLDWIDE, INC., NOR AUTHOR SHALL BE LIABLE FOR ANY LOSS OF PROFIT OR ANY OTHER COMMERCIAL DAMAGES, INCLUDING BUT NOT LIMITED TO SPECIAL, INCIDENTAL, CONSEQUENTIAL, OR OTHER DAMAGES. FULFILLMENT OF EACH COUPON OFFER IS THE RESPONSIBILITY OF THE OFFEROR.

Trademarks: All brand names and product names used in this book are trade names, service marks, trademarks, or registered trademarks of their respective owners. IDG Books Worldwide is not associated with any product or vendor mentioned in this book.

 is a trademark under exclusive license to IDG Books Worldwide, Inc., from International Data Group, Inc.

About the Author

Bill Dyszel writes frequently for leading magazines such as *Success Magazine, PC Magazine,* and *Computer Shopper,* while also working as a consultant to many of New York City's leading firms in the securities, advertising, and publishing businesses. His list of current and former clients includes Salomon Brothers, First Boston, Goldman Sachs, Ogilvy & Mather, KMPG Peat Marwick, and many others. He is also the author of *Microsoft Outlook 98 For Dummies*.

The world of high technology has led Bill to grapple with such subjects as multimedia (or how to make your $2,000 computer do the work of a $20 radio), personal information managers (how to make your $3,000 laptop computer do the work of a $3 datebook), and graphics programs (how to make your $5,000 package of computers and peripheral devices do the work of a 50-cent box of crayons). All joking aside, he has found that after you've figured out the process, most of this stuff can be useful, helpful, and, yes, even cool.

Like many public figures with skeletons in their closets, this author has a secret past. Before entering the computer industry, Bill sang with the New York City Opera and worked regularly on the New York stage as a singer and an actor in numerous plays, musicals, and operas. He also wrote the opera spoof *99% ARTFREE!,* which won critical praise from *The New York Times,* the *New York Daily News,* and the Associated Press when he performed the show off-Broadway.

ABOUT IDG BOOKS WORLDWIDE

Welcome to the world of IDG Books Worldwide.

IDG Books Worldwide, Inc., is a subsidiary of International Data Group, the world's largest publisher of computer-related information and the leading global provider of information services on information technology. IDG was founded more than 25 years ago and now employs more than 8,500 people worldwide. IDG publishes more than 275 computer publications in over 75 countries (see listing below). More than 90 million people read one or more IDG publications each month.

Launched in 1990, IDG Books Worldwide is today the #1 publisher of best-selling computer books in the United States. We are proud to have received eight awards from the Computer Press Association in recognition of editorial excellence and three from *Computer Currents*' First Annual Readers' Choice Awards. Our best-selling *...For Dummies*® series has more than 50 million copies in print with translations in 38 languages. IDG Books Worldwide, through a joint venture with IDG's Hi-Tech Beijing, became the first U.S. publisher to publish a computer book in the People's Republic of China. In record time, IDG Books Worldwide has become the first choice for millions of readers around the world who want to learn how to better manage their businesses.

Our mission is simple: Every one of our books is designed to bring extra value and skill-building instructions to the reader. Our books are written by experts who understand and care about our readers. The knowledge base of our editorial staff comes from years of experience in publishing, education, and journalism — experience we use to produce books for the '90s. In short, we care about books, so we attract the best people. We devote special attention to details such as audience, interior design, use of icons, and illustrations. And because we use an efficient process of authoring, editing, and desktop publishing our books electronically, we can spend more time ensuring superior content and spend less time on the technicalities of making books.

You can count on our commitment to deliver high-quality books at competitive prices on topics you want to read about. At IDG Books Worldwide, we continue in the IDG tradition of delivering quality for more than 25 years. You'll find no better book on a subject than one from IDG Books Worldwide.

John Kilcullen
CEO
IDG Books Worldwide, Inc.

Steven Berkowitz
President and Publisher
IDG Books Worldwide, Inc.

Eighth Annual
Computer Press
Awards ≥1992

Ninth Annual
Computer Press
Awards ≥1993

Tenth Annual
Computer Press
Awards ≥1994

Eleventh Annual
Computer Press
Awards ≥1995

IDG Books Worldwide, Inc., is a subsidiary of International Data Group, the world's largest publisher of computer-related information and the leading global provider of information services on information technology. International Data Group publishes over 275 computer publications in over 75 countries. More than 90 million people read one or more International Data Group publications each month. International Data Group's publications include: **ARGENTINA:** Buyer's Guide, Computerworld Argentina, PC World Argentina; **AUSTRALIA:** Australian Macworld, Australian PC World, Australian Reseller News, Computerworld, IT Casebook, Network World, Publish, Webmaster; **AUSTRIA:** Computerwelt Osterreich, Networks Austria, PC Tip Austria; **BANGLADESH:** PC World Bangladesh; **BELARUS:** PC World Belarus; **BELGIUM:** Data News; **BRAZIL:** Annuário de Informática, Computerworld, Connections, Macworld, PC Player, PC World, Publish, Reseller News, Supergamepower; **BULGARIA:** Computerworld Bulgaria, Network World Bulgaria, PC & MacWorld Bulgaria; **CANADA:** CIO Canada, Client/Server World, ComputerWorld Canada, InfoWorld Canada, NetworkWorld Canada, WebWorld; **CHILE:** Computerworld Chile, PC World Chile; **COLOMBIA:** Computerworld Colombia, PC World Colombia; **COSTA RICA:** PC World Centro America; **THE CZECH AND SLOVAK REPUBLICS:** Computerworld Czechoslovakia, Macworld Czech Republic, PC World Czechoslovakia; **DENMARK:** Communications World Danmark, Computerworld Danmark, Macworld Danmark, PC World Danmark, Techworld Danmark; **DOMINICAN REPUBLIC:** PC World Republica Dominicana; **ECUADOR:** PC World Ecuador; **EGYPT:** Computerworld Middle East, PC World Middle East; **EL SALVADOR:** PC World Centro America; **FINLAND:** MikroPC, Tietoverkko, Tietoviikko; **FRANCE:** Distributique, Hebdo, Info PC, Le Monde Informatique, Macworld, Reseaux & Telecoms, WebMaster France; **GERMANY:** Computer Partner, Computerwoche, Computerwoche Extra, Computerwoche FOCUS, Global Online, Macwelt, PC Welt; **GREECE:** Amiga Computing, GamePro Greece, Multimedia World; **GUATEMALA:** PC World Centro America; **HONDURAS:** PC World Centro America; **HONG KONG:** Computerworld Hong Kong, PC World Hong Kong, Publish in Asia; **HUNGARY:** ABCD CD-ROM, Computerworld Szamitastechnika, Internetto online Magazine, PC World Hungary, PC-X Magazin Hungary; **ICELAND:** Tolvuheimur PC World Island; **INDIA:** Information Communications World, Information Systems Computerworld, PC World India, Publish in Asia; **INDONESIA:** InfoKomputer PC World, Komputek Computerworld, Publish in Asia; **IRELAND:** ComputerScope, PC Live!; **ISRAEL:** Macworld Israel, People & Computers/Computerworld; **ITALY:** Computerworld Italia, Macworld Italia, Networking Italia, PC World Italia; **JAPAN:** DTP World, Macworld Japan, Nikkei Personal Computing, OS/2 World Japan, SunWorld Japan, Windows NT World, Windows World Japan; **KENYA:** PC World East African; **KOREA:** Hi-Tech Information, Macworld Korea, PC World Korea; **MACEDONIA:** PC World Macedonia; **MALAYSIA:** Computerworld Malaysia, PC World Malaysia, Publish in Asia; **MALTA:** PC World Malta; **MEXICO:** Computerworld Mexico, PC World Mexico; **MYANMAR:** PC World Myanmar; **NETHERLANDS:** Computer! Totaal, LAN Internetworking Magazine, LAN World Buyers Guide, Macworld Netherlands, Net, WebWereld; **NEW ZEALAND:** Absolute Beginners Guide and Plain & Simple Series, Computer Buyer, Computer Industry Directory, Computerworld New Zealand, MTB, Network World, PC World New Zealand; **NICARAGUA:** PC World Centro America; **NORWAY:** Computerworld Norge, CW Rapport, Datamagasinet, Financial Rapport, Kursguide Norge, Macworld Norge, Multimediaworld Norge, PC World Ekspress Norge, PC World Nettverk, PC World Norge, PC World ProduktGuide Norge; **PAKISTAN:** Computerworld Pakistan; **PANAMA:** PC World Panama; **PEOPLE'S REPUBLIC OF CHINA:** China Computer Users, China Computerworld, China InfoWorld, China Telecom World Weekly, Computer & Communication, Electronic Design China, Electronics Today Weekly, Game Software, PC World China, Popular Computer Week, Software Weekly, Software World, Telecom World; **PERU:** Computerworld Peru, PC World Profesional Peru, PC World SoHo Peru; **PHILIPPINES:** Click!, Computerworld Philippines, PC World Philippines, Publish in Asia; **POLAND:** Computerworld Poland, Computerworld Special Report Poland, Cyber, Macworld Poland, Networld Poland, PC World Komputer; **PORTUGAL:** Cerebro/PC World, Computerworld/Correio Informático, Dealer World Portugal, Mac*In/PC*In Portugal, Multimedia World; **PUERTO RICO:** PC World Puerto Rico; **ROMANIA:** Computerworld Romania, PC World Romania, Telecom Romania; **RUSSIA:** Computerworld Russia, Mir PK, Publish, Seti; **SINGAPORE:** Computerworld Singapore, PC World Singapore, Publish in Asia; **SLOVENIA:** Monitor; **SOUTH AFRICA:** Computing SA, Network World SA, Software World SA; **SPAIN:** Comunicaciones World España, Computerworld España, Dealer World España, Macworld España, PC World España; **SRI LANKA:** Infolink PC World; **SWEDEN:** CAP&Design, Computer Sweden, Corporate Computing Sweden, Internetworld Sweden, it.branschen, Macworld Sweden, MaxiData Sweden, MikroDatorn, Natverk & Kommunikation, PC World Sweden, PCaktiv, Windows World Sweden; **SWITZERLAND:** Computerworld Schweiz, Macworld Schweiz, PCtip; **TAIWAN:** Computerworld Taiwan, Macworld Taiwan, NEW ViSiON/Publish, PC World Taiwan, Windows World Taiwan; **THAILAND:** Publish in Asia, Thai Computerworld; **TURKEY:** Computerworld Turkiye, Macworld Turkiye, Network World Turkiye, PC World Turkiye; **UKRAINE:** Computerworld Kiev, Multimedia World Ukraine, PC World Ukraine; **UNITED KINGDOM:** Acorn User UK, Amiga Action UK, Amiga Computing UK, Apple Talk UK, Computing, Macworld, Parents and Computers UK, PC Advisor, PC Home, PSX Pro, The WEB; **UNITED STATES:** Cable in the Classroom, CIO Magazine, Computerworld, DOS World, Federal Computer Week, GamePro Magazine, InfoWorld, I-Way, Macworld, Network World, PC Games, PC World, Publish, Video Event, THE WEB Magazine, and WebMaster; online webzines: JavaWorld, NetscapeWorld, and SunWorld Online; **URUGUAY:** InfoWorld Uruguay; **VENEZUELA:** Computerworld Venezuela, PC World Venezuela; and **VIETNAM:** PC World Vietnam. 5/7/98

Author's Acknowledgments

Thanks to the many people who have made this book possible, most of all my indefatigable project editor Ted Cains, without whom much of this book would have been impossible. Thanks also to Sherri Morningstar, my acquisitions editor; technical reviewers Gayle Ehrenman and Shawn Morningstar; copy editors Gwenette Gaddis, Kim Darosett, and Constance Carlisle; and to Jennifer Ehrlich, Mike Kelly, Mary Bednarek, Diane Steele, and everyone else at IDG Books, as well as to my agent Gloria Norris. And special thanks to the good folks at A & R Partners, Inc., for lending PalmPilots to IDG Books during the development and production of this book.

Publisher's Acknowledgments

We're proud of this book; please register your comments through our IDG Books Worldwide Online Registration Form located at http://my2cents.dummies.com.

Some of the people who helped bring this book to market include the following:

Acquisitions, Editorial, and Media Development

Project Editor: Ted Cains

Acquisitions Editor: Sherri Morningstar

Copy Editors: Kim Darosett, Gwenette Gaddis

Technical Editors: Gayle Ehrenman, Shawn Morningstar

Media Development Editor: Marita Ellixson

Media Development Coordinator: Megan Roney

Associate Permissions Editor: Carmen Krikorian

Editorial Manager: Colleen Rainsberger

Media Development Manager: Heather Heath Dismore

Editorial Assistant: Jamila Pree

Production

Project Coordinator: Valery Bourke

Layout and Graphics: Lou Boudreau, Linda M. Boyer, Angela F. Hunckler, Jane E. Martin, Brent Savage, Kate Snell

Proofreaders: Christine Berman, Kelli Botta, Michelle Croninger, Nancy Price, Rebecca Senninger, Christine Snyder, Janet M. Withers

Indexer: Sharon Duffy

Special Help

Constance Carlisle, Kristin A. Cocks, Jennifer Ehrlich, Wendy Hatch, Darren Meiss

---

General and Administrative

IDG Books Worldwide, Inc.: John Kilcullen, CEO; Steven Berkowitz, President and Publisher

IDG Books Technology Publishing: Brenda McLaughlin, Senior Vice President and Group Publisher

Dummies Technology Press and Dummies Editorial: Diane Graves Steele, Vice President and Associate Publisher; Mary Bednarek, Director of Acquisitions and Product Development; Kristin A. Cocks, Editorial Director

Dummies Trade Press: Kathleen A. Welton, Vice President and Publisher; Kevin Thornton, Acquisitions Manager

IDG Books Production for Dummies Press: Michael R. Britton, Vice President of Production and Creative Services; Cindy L. Phipps, Manager of Project Coordination, Production Proofreading, and Indexing; Kathie S. Schutte, Supervisor of Page Layout; Shelley Lea, Supervisor of Graphics and Design; Debbie J. Gates, Production Systems Specialist; Robert Springer, Supervisor of Proofreading; Debbie Stailey, Special Projects Coordinator; Tony Augsburger, Supervisor of Reprints and Bluelines

Dummies Packaging and Book Design: Robin Seaman, Creative Director; Kavish + Kavish, Cover Design

♦

The publisher would like to give special thanks to Patrick J. McGovern, without whom this book would not have been possible.

♦

Contents at a Glance

Introduction 1

Part I: Getting to Know Your PalmPilot 9
Chapter 1: What Can a PalmPilot Do? 11
Chapter 2: Going in Stylus 33
Chapter 3: Making Your PalmPilot Your Own 47
Chapter 4: Saving Time with PalmPilot Timesavers 65

Part II: Getting Down to Business 71
Chapter 5: Names and Addresses in a ZIP 73
Chapter 6: To Do's That YOU Do! 89
Chapter 7: Memo Mania 109
Chapter 8: The Date Game 121
Chapter 9: Beaming PalmPilot Data through the Air with Infrared 137
Chapter 10: Special Delivery: Using PalmPilot Mail 145

Part III: PalmPilot and the Outside World 165
Chapter 11: Installing and HotSyncing to the Desktop Programs for
Windows and Mac 167
Chapter 12: Operating the PalmPilot Desktop Program for Windows and Mac ... 181
Chapter 13: Using the PalmPilot Modem 223

Part IV: Extending the Life of Your PalmPilot 241
Chapter 14: Upward Mobility — Upgrading Your PalmPilot 243
Chapter 15: PalmPilot Software by Profession 253

Part V: The Part of Tens 265
Chapter 16: Ten Things You Can't Do with a PalmPilot . . . Yet 267
Chapter 17: Ten Nifty PalmPilot Accessories 271
Chapter 18: Ten Ultracool Commercial Software Programs for the PalmPilot 275

Appendix A: Internet Resources for the PalmPilot 285

Appendix B: Troubleshooting Tips 289

Appendix C: About the CD 293

Index 303

IDG Books Worldwide End-User License
Agreement 332

Installation Instructions 334

Book Registration Information .... Back of Book

Cartoons at a Glance

By Rich Tennant

page 9

page 265

page 71

page 241

page 165

Fax: 978-546-7747 • E-mail: the5wave@tiac.net

Table of Contents

Introduction *1*
Who Should Buy This Book 1
Pilot, PalmPilot, Palm III — Make Up Your Mind 2
How This Book Is Organized 3
    Part I: Getting to Know Your PalmPilot 3
    Part II: Getting Down to Business 3
    Part III: PalmPilot and the Outside World 4
    Part IV: Extending the Life of Your PalmPilot 4
    Part V: The Part of Tens 4
    Appendixes 4
Conventions Used in This Book 5
    How much do you need to know? 5
    Some helpful terms 5
Icons Used in This Book 7
Getting Started 8

Part I: Getting to Know Your PalmPilot *9*

Chapter 1: What Can a PalmPilot Do? 11
What Is This Thing, Anyway? 12
What's on the Outside of Your PalmPilot 13
    Application hard buttons 14
    Scroll buttons 15
    Power button 16
    Contrast wheel 16
    Reset button 16
The Screen 17
    The display 17
    Soft buttons 19
        Applications 20
        Menu 21
        Calculator 21
        Find 22
    The Graffiti area 23
Which PalmPilot Do I Have? 23
What Do the Standard Applications Do? 24
HotSyncing Is Definitely Hot Stuff 30
Batteries Are Included, but. 30

Chapter 2: Going in Stylus 33
Graffiti 33
  Graffiti letters and numbers 34
  Moving the Graffiti cursor 36
  Making capital letters without a shift key 38
  Punctuating your text 40
  Graffiti whiz secrets 40
  The amazing Graffiti fish loop 42
  The Graffiti ShortCut symbol 43
The On-Screen Keyboard 44
Other Text Entry Tricks 45
  The T9 system 46
  GoType 46

Chapter 3: Making Your PalmPilot Your Own 47
Setting General Preferences 47
  Setting the time 48
  Setting the date 49
  Setting the Auto-off interval 50
  Setting the sound volume 51
  Turning off beaming 53
Setting Button Preferences 53
Setting Format Preferences 55
Using the Security Application 56
  Setting your password 57
  Deleting a forgotten password 58
  Hiding private items 59
Setting Up ShortCuts 60
  Adding a new ShortCut 61
  Editing a ShortCut 62
  Deleting a ShortCut 63
Hacking Up Your PalmPilot 63

Chapter 4: Saving Time with PalmPilot Timesavers 65
General Timesavers 65
  Using ShortCuts 66
  Beaming a business card quickly 66
  Using your finger instead of the stylus 66
  Checking the time 66
  Reassigning a hard button to your favorite program 67
Application Timesavers 67
  Pressing hard buttons to change categories 67
  Viewing different dates by pressing buttons 67
  Uncluttering your Date Book 68
  Drag and drop to change appointment times 68
  Cut, copy, and paste 69
  Adding multiple items to a category 69

    Graffiti Timesavers 70
        Start writing to create new items 70
        Opening Graffiti Help with a single stroke 70

Part II: Getting Down to Business 71

Chapter 5: Names and Addresses in a ZIP 73

    Accessing Your Address Book 73
    Putting Names into Your PalmPilot 74
        Adding a new name 75
        What's in a name? Editing an address record 78
        Attaching a note to an address record 79
        Marking your business card 81
    Using the Names You've Entered 82
        Finding Mr. Right (or whoever) 82
        Deleting a name 84
        Deleting a note from an address record 85
        Setting Address Book preferences 86
        Setting up custom fields 87

Chapter 6: To Do's That YOU Do! 89

    Adding New To Do's 90
        Creating a To Do item 90
        Entering details for a To Do item 91
        Attaching notes to items 93
    Viewing Items by Category 95
        Adding categories 96
        Deleting categories 96
        Renaming categories 97
    What to Do with the To Do's You Do 98
        Have I got a job for you? Beaming To Do's! 98
        Changing To Do's 99
        Undoing a mistake 101
        Marking the To Do's that you've done 102
        Deleting a To Do 102
        Deleting a note 103
        Setting preferences for your To Do List 104
        Looking up an address and phone number 106
        Purging To Do's that you've done 107

Chapter 7: Memo Mania 109

    Take a Memo 110
        Adding items 110
        Reading memos 111
        Changing items 112
        Categorizing items 114
        Making a memo private 115

PalmPilot For Dummies

Using What You Have 116
    Deleting items 116
    Viewing memos by category 117
    Changing fonts 118
    Setting preferences to organize your memos 118
    Beaming your memos 120

Chapter 8: The Date Game 121

Date Book Views 122
    The Daily view 122
    The Week view 123
    The Month view 124
Making Dates 125
    Adding appointments the simple way 126
    Adding appointments the complete way 127
    No Time Events 128
    Alarms 128
    Adding notes to appointments 130
    Address Book Lookup 130
    Repeating appointments 130
    Private items 132
Putting Appointments in the Past 133
    Deleting appointments 133
    Setting preferences 134
    Purging your Date Book 136

Chapter 9: Beaming PalmPilot Data through the Air with Infrared 137

The Beaming Thing 137
    Sending an item 138
    Receiving an item 139
    Sending a category 140
    Receiving a category 141
    Sending an application 142
    Receiving an application 143
Beaming into the Future 144

Chapter 10: Special Delivery: Using PalmPilot Mail 145

Making Sense of the PalmPilot Postal System 146
Working with Your Messages 146
    Creating a message 147
    Reading a message 149
    Replying to a message 150
    Forwarding a message 152
    Deleting a message 153
    Purging deleted messages 154
    Saving drafts 155
    Sending a blind copy 155
    Sorting messages 157

Customizing Your PalmPilot E-Mail 158
    Setting HotSync options 158
    Filtering messages 160
    Using signatures 161
    Setting truncating options 162

Part III: PalmPilot and the Outside World 165

Chapter 11: Installing and HotSyncing to the Desktop Programs for Windows and Mac 167

Installing Palm Desktop for Windows 167
    Connecting the cradle to your PC 168
    Now, you get to install Palm Desktop 169
Installing the Pilot Desktop for Macintosh 172
    Connecting the cradle to your Mac 172
    Now, on to installing Pilot Desktop 173
    Setting up your Mac to HotSync 177
To HotSync or Not to HotSync . . . Just Do It 178

Chapter 12: Operating the PalmPilot Desktop Program for Windows and Mac 181

Palm Desktop Basics 182
    Understanding the Palm Desktop interface 182
    Arranging your Date Book 183
        Adding appointments 185
        Repeating appointments 186
        Making appointments private 188
        Deleting appointments 188
    Arranging your Address Book 189
        Adding a new Address Book entry 189
        Editing an address record 191
        Attaching a note to an address record 191
        Finding the name you want 192
        Deleting a name 193
        Setting up custom fields 193
    Doing stuff with your To Do's 194
        Creating a To Do item 194
        Setting the priority for a To Do item 194
        Assigning a category to a To Do item 195
        Adding categories 196
        Deleting categories 197
        Renaming categories 198
        Assigning a due date to a To Do item 199
        Marking a To Do item private 200
        Attaching notes to To Do items 201
        Viewing items by category 202

           Deleting a To Do item 202
           Setting preferences for your To Do List 203
      Working with Memos 204
           Creating a memo 205
           Reading a memo 206
           Printing a memo 206
           Editing a memo 207
           Categorizing a memo 207
           Making a memo private 208
           Deleting a memo 210
      What does that Expense button do? 210
      The Drag To icons 211
  Furnishing Your PalmPilot 211
      Checking memory 212
      Installing applications 213
           Using Palm Desktop for Windows 213
           Using Pilot Desktop for Macintosh 214
      Deleting applications 215
           Deleting applications on a Palm III 216
           Deleting applications on a PalmPilot Professional 217
  Protecting Your Turf 218
      Restoring PalmPilot data 218
      Backing up your data 219
  Archiving Your PalmPilot Stuff 219
      Viewing archived items 220
      Returning an archived item to your PalmPilot 221
  Accommodating Multiple Users 222

Chapter 13: Using the PalmPilot Modem 223

  PalmPilot Modem Basics 223
      Setting up your modem 224
      Setting up your PalmPilot to use the modem 225
  Setting Up Your PalmPilot for a Modem HotSync 227
      Entering the Modem HotSync phone number 228
      Disabling call waiting 229
      Setting up Palm Desktop for a Modem HotSync 230
  PalmPilot on the Internet 232
      Setting up your Internet connection 233
      Sending and receiving REAL e-mail 235
      Setting up a PalmPilot Internet e-mail program 236
      Sending and receiving PalmPilot Internet e-mail 239
      Browsing the Web 239
  Sending a Fax with Your PalmPilot 240

Part IV: Extending the Life of Your PalmPilot 241

Chapter 14: Upward Mobility — Upgrading Your PalmPilot 243
Upgrading Made Easy 243
Upgrading Your PalmPilot 244
    Installing a new version of the Palm OS 245
    Installing a new memory card into a pre-Palm III model 246
    Upgrading a Palm III 248
Upgrading the PalmPilot Desktop Program 251

Chapter 15: PalmPilot Software by Profession 253
Architect/Building Professional 253
Athletic Coach 254
Bartender 254
Couch Potato 254
Electrical Engineer 255
Help Desk Technician 255
Lawyer 256
Manager 256
Minister 256
Molecular Biologist 257
Musician 257
New York City Taxi Driver 258
Parent 258
Physician 259
Pilot 259
Psychic 260
Salesperson 261
Stock Broker/Investor 261
Teacher 261
Telemarketer 262
Travel Agent 262
Writer 263

Part V: The Part of Tens 265

Chapter 16: Ten Things You Can't Do with a PalmPilot . . . Yet 267
Run on AC Power 267
Recharge Batteries in the Cradle 268
View Two Programs at the Same Time 268
Link Items between Programs 268
Search and Replace Text 268
Record Voice Notes 269
Create an Appointment That Spans Two or More Dates 269
Use Superscripts and Subscripts 269
Create Recurring To Do Items 269

Assign Multiple Categories to One Item 270
Categorizing Dates 270
Other Things a PalmPilot Can't Do 270

Chapter 17: Ten Nifty PalmPilot Accessories 271

WriteRight 271
Brain Wash 272
Karma Cloth 272
Extra Styluses 272
Card Scanner 273
UniMount 273
SuperPilot Memory Board 273
DeLorme TripMate GPS Receiver 273
Minstrel Wireless Modem 274
Cases 274

Chapter 18: Ten Ultracool Commercial Software Programs for the PalmPilot 275

T9 276
QuickSheet 276
FlashBuilderIII 277
Forms Programs 277
Actioneer for the Palm Computing Environment 279
Delorme Street Atlas 280
CardScan 280
Small Talk 281
HandFax 281
Synchronization Programs 282

Appendix A: Internet Resources for the PalmPilot 285

The PalmPilot Web Ring 285
Calvin's PalmPilot FAQ 285
InSync Online 286
Palm Central 286
PalmOS.com 286
The PalmPilot Newsgroups 286
PalmPower Magazine 287
PDA Dash 287
Pilot Gear H.Q. 287
Pilot Zone 288
3Com 288

Appendix B: Troubleshooting Tips 289

Screen Taps Don't Work 289
My Screen Is Blank 289
The Menu Button Doesn't Work 290

My PalmPilot Won't Turn Off	290
The Hard Buttons Stick	290
Graffiti Is Always Wrong	290
My Screen Is Too Dark	291
My PalmPilot Won't Start	291
Beaming Fails	291
I Got a "Fatal Exception" Error	292

Appendix C: About the CD 293

System Requirements	293
Using the CD	294
How to use the CD using the Mac OS	294
What You'll Find	295
Financial tools	295
FCPlus Professional	295
Qmate	295
Time Expense Auto Keeper (TEAK)	295
Fun and games	296
Blackjack	296
Eliza, Pilot Psychologist	296
Jpack	296
Klondike	296
Language Dictionary	296
Words Per Minute	296
Internet tools	297
AvantGo Desktop and Web Client	297
HandMail	297
HandWeb	297
Microsoft Internet Explorer	297
MindSpring Internet Access	297
Netscape Communicator	298
Palmeta Mail	298
Multimedia	298
AportisDoc	298
Image Viewer	298
TealPaint	298
Organizational tools	299
Action Names	299
Actioneer	299
AreaCoder	299
BrainForest	299
BugMe!	299
PhoneLog	299
Punch List	299
TealGlance	299
ThoughtMill	300
TimeReporter	300
World Time	300

Synchronization tools 300
    Desktop to Go 300
    PROFS-AutoPilot 300
    UnDupe 300
Utilities 300
    FlashBuilder III for the Palm III 300
    HandFax 301
    MakeDoc 301
    PalmPrint 301
    Satellite Forms 301
    TealEcho 301
    TealMagnify 301
If You've Got Problems (Of the CD Kind) 301

Index 303

IDG Books Worldwide End-User License Agreement 332

Installation Instructions 334

Book Registration Information .... Back of Book

Introduction

*B*e warned, the PalmPilot is addictive! You may not believe that you can become so wrapped up in a little block of plastic, but the experiences of millions of crazed PalmPilot users indicate otherwise. I know that you won't find anything nasty like tar or nicotine in a PalmPilot, but once you're hooked, you'll have a tough time living without it. After you've enjoyed the convenience of carrying a little bit of computing power in your pocket or purse, you'll want more and more.

For me, the most subversive effect of using a PalmPilot is the way that it's spoiled me against the way other computers work. I just can't wait patiently anymore for a regular computer to "boot up"; I'm too accustomed to my PalmPilot turning on instantly. I also get a little annoyed waiting for a regular computer to find and open the last document that I was working on, because I'm used to having my PalmPilot jump right to the last item I worked on. And I certainly get peeved when my laptop runs out of juice after an hour or so because my PalmPilot runs for a month on a set of AAA batteries.

Sadly, I can't dispense with my regular computer just yet. The PalmPilot isn't meant to replace conventional computers; it's intended to give you a handy and portable window for accessing information, much of which you keep on your computer. But don't be fooled — the PalmPilot is a really powerful little machine in itself.

Who Should Buy This Book

The PalmPilot is the most successful new electronic product in history. In the first two years following the PalmPilot's introduction, nearly 2 million units were sold. That's hot. No gadget has ever sold so quickly, including hit products like the VCR, the Sony Walkman, and the answering machine. In 1997, the sales for handheld units using the PalmPilot system were greater than the sales for handhelds using the once-popular Macintosh system. Chances are strong that if you don't have a PalmPilot yourself, someone you know either has one or wants one. As you read this book, you'll find out how a PalmPilot works and what it can do for you. You'll also get a taste of what peripherals you can add to a PalmPilot to make it suit your needs a bit better. If you fit in any of the following categories, this book is meant for you:

- You're planning to buy a PalmPilot, and you want to know what you can do with it and what it can do for you.
- You already own a PalmPilot, and you want to get the most from it quickly.
- You're looking for a gift to give someone who already has a PalmPilot. PalmPilots are very popular gifts. You can send me one anytime.
- You own one of those Windows CE machines and have realized the error of your ways (say it isn't so!).

Even if you're just curious about the PalmPilot phenomenon, this book is aimed at showing you what all the excitement's about. Nearly anyone in any walk of life can receive some benefit from a PalmPilot, even if all that person wants is a little fun.

Pilot, PalmPilot, Palm III — Make Up Your Mind

I find it exciting to be a PalmPilot owner because improvements for the PalmPilot come along so quickly. But the rapid pace can also be confusing, because some of the features that are available for the current PalmPilots weren't available on PalmPilots that were sold only six or eight months ago. Also, I don't know which PalmPilot model you're using, so I have to qualify everything I write here to avoid confusing people who have older PalmPilots (older than 6 to 12 months).

Because this is the first *PalmPilot For Dummies* book, I try to cover the whole range of products based on the design from 3Com. When the first handheld units were produced, they were simply called Pilots. When the little Pilots became popular, the Palm people changed the name to PalmPilot to avoid confusion with the popular Pilot brand pens. Then the Palm people decided to drop the Pilot thing altogether and call their product Palm III (the latest version at the time of this writing).

In this book, I strike a happy medium and call the thing a PalmPilot whenever I'm talking about something that could apply to any model. When I discuss a feature that appears only on the Palm III, I say so. (For general information on what each model does, see Chapter 1.) But if you find the model differences too confusing, you can always upgrade whatever model you have to a Palm III; just see Chapter 14 for details.

You may also be using another product that's based on Palm Computing technology but has a different name, like the IBM WorkPad (Sheesh! What a drab name! I wish they'd call it the IBM FunPad!). The information in this book applies to the WorkPad, too. Other products based on the Palm Computing design are in the pipeline as well, and the general principles in this book should work for those products, too.

How This Book Is Organized

To help you more easily find out how to do what you want to do, I divided this book into parts. Each part covers a different aspect of using your PalmPilot. The first couple of parts focus on the PalmPilot itself — what you can do if you just have that. In later parts, I discuss add-ons for your PalmPilot, as well as the desktop computer program that comes with your PalmPilot. (Yes, your PalmPilot can actually talk to your desktop computer. If this possibility really floats your boat, then jump right into Part III.)

Here's a quick-and-dirty outline of the book — just enough to whet your whistle and make you want to buy it!

Part I: Getting to Know Your PalmPilot

"Getting to know you, getting to know all about you...." Ahem, sorry — I can't resist a little show tune every now and again. Anyway, nothing about using the PalmPilot is difficult, but many features and options aren't exactly obvious. The first part of this book describes what you have to work with on your PalmPilot and how you work with what you've got. I explain what all those funny-looking buttons and other doodads do on the outside of your PalmPilot, and I give you a lesson in Graffiti — and no, not so you can join a gang and practice spray-can art. Graffiti is the special alphabet that you can use for entering information into your PalmPilot. And if you're in the secret agent biz (or if you're just security-minded), you can find out how to keep confidential information on your PalmPilot safe from prying eyes.

Part II: Getting Down to Business

Yes, Virginia, the PalmPilot is a computer. It doesn't act grouchy and forbidding like other computers, but it can do many of the jobs that are typically performed by enormous desktop units (ironically called microcomputers, of all things). The PalmPilot comes with a set of pre-installed programs when you buy it. Those programs act as a personal information manager (PIM) to help you keep track of your schedule, address book, and To Do list. If you've ever used a computer for personal organizing, the methods of the PalmPilot may seem familiar. There's also a Memo Pad for jotting down random notes to yourself or others, and you can even copy your e-mail to your PalmPilot and read it while you're sitting by the pool. (Sorry, the pool isn't included.)

The very latest PalmPilot — the Palm III — features infrared beaming, a method for sending information between two Palm IIIs through the air using an invisible beam of light. How cool is that?

Part III: PalmPilot and the Outside World

No computer is an island, especially the tiny PalmPilot. If it were, you'd be in trouble at high tide. The Palm people always figured that folks would use their PalmPilots in conjunction with some other computer, simply because there's no denying the physical limitations of a tiny computer when entering data and connecting to other resources like the Internet or a CD-ROM. This part tells you all that you need to know about HotSyncing (the process through which your PalmPilot and your Windows PC or Macintosh talk to each other) and walks you through installing and operating the desktop programs that come with your PalmPilot. And when you're out and about and you want to use the PalmPilot Modem to HotSync to your computer . . . well, I show you how to do that, too. How's that for a bargain?

Part IV: Extending the Life of Your PalmPilot

Like any appliance, the day may come when you need more from your PalmPilot, and the Maytag repairman is nowhere in sight. Or perhaps you need to make your PalmPilot do something new. In this part, I show you some options for making your little PalmPilot do big things. I cover upgrading your PalmPilot and software add-ons that may impress your peers in your particular profession. Whether you're a doctor or a bartender, there's add-on software out there for you.

Part V: The Part of Tens

Why ten? Beats me! All the other ...*For Dummies* books get a Part of Tens, so I'll be darned if mine doesn't have one, too! Here, you find out what your PalmPilot *can't* do and how to stylishly accessorize your PalmPilot without having to call Calvin Klein for wardrobe advice.

Appendixes

Just like the famous (or is that infamous?) Ginzu knife, "that's not all!" In the appendixes, I provide a list of the best PalmPilot resources on the World Wide Web, and I show you how to shoot down trouble when it strikes your

PalmPilot. And did you happen to notice that the back cover of this book is a little stiffer than the front? That's because you also get a CD-ROM; Appendix C tells you all about the cool stuff that you can find on it.

Conventions Used in This Book

You may be a die-hard reader of ...*For Dummies* books, living in a beautiful black-and-yellow home filled with black-and-yellow books. You may be familiar with the approach, and this book works a lot like all the other books in the series.

If you've never read a ...*For Dummies* book, welcome. Buying and reading this book proves that you're one smart cookie who doesn't want to deal with those overgrown paperweights that litter the shelves of your local bookstore's computer section. Instead, you want a clear, no-nonsense explanation of the things that you really need to know, and nothing else. That's what you get here.

How much do you need to know?

I figure that you know how to push a button. This skill will get you far with a PalmPilot, because it's so simple to use. And although you can use a PalmPilot without HotSyncing it with a desktop computer, I assume that you will use your PalmPilot with a desktop machine at some point and that you already know how to use it. If you're still a little iffy on using your desktop computer, I suggest picking up a copy of the ...*For Dummies* book that covers the system you use. A few helpful titles include *Macs For Dummies, PCs For Dummies, Windows 98 For Dummies,* and *Mac OS 8 For Dummies* (all published by IDG Books Worldwide, Inc.).

Some helpful terms

To reduce confusion as you read this book, here are a few tidbits and terms that you need to understand:

- When I refer to a desktop computer, I mean a conventional computer running either Microsoft Windows or Mac OS. If your main computer is a laptop, that's fine. Please forgive me if I always say "desktop"; they all look so big next to a PalmPilot.

- Because the PalmPilot is made to work as an extension of more than one type of computer system, the terms that I use to describe what you should do on your desktop machine cover both the Windows and Macintosh platforms.

- *Tapping* means touching your PalmPilot stylus to a named area on the PalmPilot display.
- *Clicking* means pressing the left mouse button on an item if you're using a Windows computer, or pressing the only mouse button if you're using a Mac.
- *Choosing* means to either tap a menu choice on your PalmPilot or click a given menu choice with your desktop computer's mouse.
- *Right-clicking* means to press the right mouse button if you're using a computer running Windows. There's no right mouse button to click on a Mac.
- *Double-clicking* means quickly clicking the left mouse button (or the only mouse button) twice.
- *Dragging* (on the PalmPilot) means touching an item with your stylus and sliding the point of the stylus from one spot on the display to another.
- *Dragging* (on a Windows PC or a Mac) means holding down the mouse button while moving the mouse.
- *Selecting* or *highlighting* means either tapping a choice on a list or sliding your stylus across a specific area of text, which prepares the PalmPilot for you to do something to that piece of text.

All the tasks that I describe in the preceding list are much easier to do than they sound. You'll catch on in no time. Here are a few items that you'll see me mention from time to time:

- *Dialog boxes* are rectangles that pop up on the screen and can include messages for you to read, buttons for you to tap or click, lists for you to choose from, blanks for you to fill in, and check boxes for you to tap. Don't worry, I'll tell you what to do with each dialog box as you encounter it.
- *Buttons* are real, physical buttons on the front of your PalmPilot case. I normally call each button by the name of the application it runs. Your PalmPilot comes with two types of buttons: hard and soft. The *hard buttons* are those at the bottom of your PalmPilot below the screen. The *soft buttons* are just above the hard buttons but are actually part of the screen. You can find more about all this button stuff in Chapter 1.

I normally simplify menu commands by saying something like Go⇨Cubs, which means "Choose Go from the menu bar and then choose Cubs."

Icons Used in This Book

Sometimes the fastest way to find information in a book is to look at the pictures. In this case, icons draw your attention to specific types of information that are useful to know. Here are the icons that I use in this book:

The Cross-Reference icon alerts you to when you can seek out other ...*For Dummies* books for further in-depth detail on a topic.

This icon clues you in on what you can find on the CD-ROM that accompanies this book. For the full lowdown, see Appendix C.

This Palm III icon indicates information that is specific to only the latest model of the PalmPilot, the Palm III. Those of you who don't own a Palm III or haven't upgraded your older PalmPilot to a Palm III can ignore these sections — unless you're curious about what you're missing, of course.

I use this icon for really important info that you shouldn't forget.

As if the PalmPilot weren't easy enough to use, I've found even shorter ways of doing things. The Shortcut icon points out super-speedy methods for performing a task. But don't confuse this with official PalmPilot ShortCuts — I cover those in a section unto themselves in Chapter 3.

The Tip icon notes a hint or trick for saving time and effort, or highlights text that makes the PalmPilot easier to understand.

The Warning icon alerts you to something that you should be careful about to prevent problems.

Getting Started

Now, seriously, you don't need me to tell you to get started. Just push any PalmPilot button and you're on your way. Enjoy!

Part I
Getting to Know Your PalmPilot

In this part . . .

You can do a lot with the PalmPilot's few tiny buttons and little plastic stylus. You may figure a lot out by just fiddling around, but this part's quick tour gives you a head start. I also show you how to customize your PalmPilot to your specific needs.

Chapter 1
What Can a PalmPilot Do?

In This Chapter
▶ Introducing the PalmPilot
▶ Understanding all the buttons
▶ Making sense of the standard applications
▶ Working with Graffiti
▶ HotSyncing
▶ Replacing batteries

Asking "What can I do with a PalmPilot?" is like asking "Where can I go on a bicycle?" You can go nearly anywhere you want on a bicycle — you can take a ride in the park or cross the Rocky Mountains. Most normal people are better off crossing the Rockies by car or bus, but they can handle the ride in the park quite nicely on a bike. Likewise, your PalmPilot is just the right tool for jotting down a quick note, but you probably wouldn't use it to write the sequel to *Moby Dick*.

Your PalmPilot can do many of the things that a desktop or laptop computer can do, but some things are easier to handle on a larger computer, such as surfing the World Wide Web, while others are perfect for the PalmPilot, such as looking up a phone number. If you ask people what they do most with their PalmPilots, you'll get a wide variety of answers; sometimes they need to find addresses or check their schedules, often they play games or entertain themselves with an electronic book or read their e-mail.

The PalmPilot comes in a small, friendly package but it has plenty of power inside. Even though the unit is barely bigger than a couple of candy bars, it has enough computing power inside to do more than some of the early-1980s Macintosh machines that took up most of your desktop (and may still be taking up your desktop today). Every day, people are finding clever new things to do with their PalmPilots, and you'll probably figure out a few things on your own.

Part I: Getting to Know Your PalmPilot

You can add an endless variety of functions to your PalmPilot by installing programs that don't come in the package with your PalmPilot. For most of this book, I focus on the things that you can do with the stuff that comes in the box with your PalmPilot, and that's plenty. But I do provide a selection of useful applications on the CD-ROM that accompanies this book. See Chapter 12 for more on installing PalmPilot applications and Appendix C for the lowdown on what's on the CD.

What Is This Thing, Anyway?

The PalmPilot is a simple little contraption with almost no moving parts. Sometimes, it's hard to believe that it's a computer at all. After all, computers are supposed to have zillions of buttons and lights and make scary sounds when they start up, right? Well, you don't have to think of your PalmPilot as a computer at all; think of it as your little electronic friend that

Does my PalmPilot do Windows?

Don't make me WinCE! The PalmPilot doesn't run Windows, and for that you should be glad. (The Palm Desktop does connect your PalmPilot to the world of Windows quite nicely, but the PalmPilot itself isn't running the Windows operating system.) Several PalmPilot imitators are out there right now. Most of these imitators use Microsoft's operating system that's specially made for palm-sized computers; it's called Windows CE (usually called "WinCE," a word that sounds like the face you make when you smell something bad). WinCE looks a tiny bit like the version of Windows 95 that you may be running on your desktop, including a Start button and some of the old menus. WinCE also has a feature from the desktop that we could all do without — an hourglass that shows up regularly when the system is too slow to do any work for you. PalmPilots don't make you wait like that; they get right to work.

On the whole, Windows CE isn't any more compatible with your desktop machine than your PalmPilot is. The two types of machines are equally compatible with the version of Windows that you have on your desktop. You can't run your desktop Windows programs, such as Excel, on your WinCE palmtop. As a matter of fact, many WinCE programs won't run on more than one type of WinCE device; for example, some WinCE programs run on a Hewlett Packard handheld but not on a Casio. Virtually all PalmPilot software runs on all PalmPilots. Also, more software is being written for the PalmPilot than is being written for those WinCE devices. As I write this, you can find over 1,500 programs available for the PalmPilot, compared to barely 300 for Windows CE machines. What can I say? Figures don't lie.

One way or another, you'll probably want to synchronize your palm-sized computer to a desktop or laptop computer, and a PalmPilot synchronizes every bit as well as a WinCE palmtop. My recommendation; stick with the PalmPilot. It's the real thing.

Chapter 1: What Can a PalmPilot Do?

helps you keep track of your real friends. If you have imaginary friends, your PalmPilot can help you keep track of them too, along with all those nice people in the white coats. (I can't get my publisher to let me write *Delusions For Dummies,* so you're on your own for the moment.)

The PalmPilot really has only three elements — the buttons, the screen, and the stylus. No mouse, no cables, no disks, none of it. You'll probably want to use your PalmPilot along with a normal computer that has all of those annoying gizmos, but as long as you're just using your PalmPilot, you can keep things simple. Figure 1-1 shows you what the latest version of the PalmPilot — the Palm III — looks like, and the following sections tell you what all those funny little do-dads do.

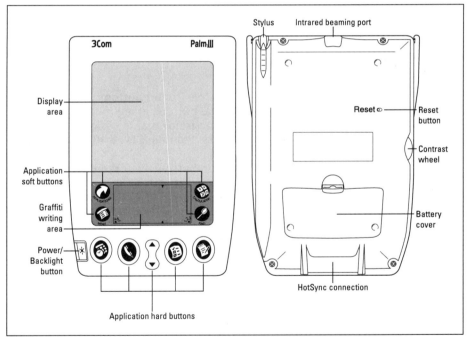

Figure 1-1: The front and back of the Palm III.

What's on the Outside of Your PalmPilot

The case of your PalmPilot has a bunch of little buttons on it that do all sorts of cool stuff. I explain in this section what those buttons do.

Application hard buttons

The application hard buttons are easy. I use the word "hard" to mean real, actual, physical buttons that you can push with your finger to make something happen. Figure 1-2 shows you what those buttons look like.

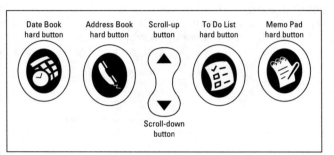

Figure 1-2: The buttons at the bottom of the PalmPilot case are called hard buttons.

The application buttons are the four round buttons at the bottom of the PalmPilot case. Push any of these buttons at any time and the PalmPilot shows you the application (or program) that is assigned to that button. Applications are just jobs that the PalmPilot is ready to do for you.

You can even push an application button when the PalmPilot is turned off. When you do, your PalmPilot automatically turns on and opens the application assigned to that button. A PalmPilot is a little like a microwave oven that way; you don't have to turn on your microwave and then tell it to start cooking; just push the button and you're cooking. Unlike your microwave oven, your PalmPilot needs very little cleaning and it won't make your breakfast eggs explode.

Here's what those buttons do:

- The left-most application button is the Date Book. The Date Book button is easy to identify by the little icon that looks like a clock on top of a bent-out-of-shape calendar. You won't need to get bent out of shape when you use the Date Book, which shows you dates and appointments. See Chapter 8 for more on the Date Book.

- The second button from the left is the Address Book, the one with the little telephone icon. That's the place you go to find names, addresses, and (naturally) phone numbers. See Chapter 5 for more on the Address Book.

PalmPilot — a real computer

Don't be fooled — the PalmPilot is a real computer. It may look like those little electronic organizers that have been around for years, but it contains the same Motorola computer chip that powered the first Macintosh. Yes, you can manage addresses and appointments on a PalmPilot just like you can on those old organizers, but you can also run and load software, just like you can on a conventional computer.

The biggest difference between a PalmPilot and a regular computer is what computer geeks call the *user interface*. The PalmPilot has no keyboard; you write and tap on the PalmPilot's touch-sensitive screen. Many types of programs that people commonly use on conventional computers are being developed for the PalmPilot, including spreadsheets, database managers, and web browsers. The software on the CD accompanying this book gives you a taste of how far you can go with the power of the PalmPilot handheld computer.

  ✔ The next application button is the To Do List. You'll find it second from the right side of the case and decorated with a little checklist. The To Do List button opens the application that tracks your tasks. See Chapter 6 for more on the To Do List. The two applications on the right side of the PalmPilot are separated from the ones on the left by the scroll buttons, which I describe later in this chapter.

  ✔ The right-most button is the Memo Pad, the one with the picture of the tiny pen writing on an itty-bitty notebook. The Memo Pad is the place where you enter and store text. See Chapter 7 for more on the Memo Pad.

You can assign different programs to the four applications buttons than the ones that come installed on your PalmPilot. For example, if you don't use the To Do List or the Memo Pad much, and you want to reassign those buttons to other programs, see Chapter 3 to find out how it's done.

Scroll buttons

In the bottom-center of your PalmPilot case is a button (or a pair of buttons on top of the pre–Palm III models) called scroll buttons. If you own a Palm III or later, the two scroll buttons have been merged into one button that rocks up and down. Scroll buttons work like the power window buttons in a car. If you want to move down through a screen to see what doesn't fit, use the bottom button. If you want to go back to the top of the screen, use the top button. Sometimes the scroll buttons change the way that they act in different applications. Sometimes pressing a scroll button makes the information on the display leap to the next screen instead of crawling gradually. Sometimes the scroll buttons do nothing, especially when there's no next screen to see.

Power button

The green button with the little light bulb on at the left edge of the PalmPilot case is the power button.

The power button has a second job; it turns the PalmPilot backlight on and off. To turn the backlight on, hold the power button down for at least two seconds. (You can also customize your PalmPilot so that the backlight goes on with a certain stroke of your stylus. I discuss that in Chapter 3.) If you own an early PalmPilot (models 1000, 5000, or the PalmPilot Personal), you don't have a backlight. That's too bad. The backlight makes text on the screen of the PalmPilot Professional or the Palm III much easier to read when you're in a dark area and you can't read the screen or when you're in a bright area — outside, maybe — and lots of glare is coming off the screen.

Although the backlight makes reading the PalmPilot screen easier in almost all conditions, the light itself drains the batteries like crazy. The best time to use your backlight is when you can't read text on the screen at all without it.

One nice thing about the way the PalmPilot works is a quality called a *persistent state*. No, that's not the feeling you get after you meet all the salesmen in Utah; it actually means that whatever is happening on the PalmPilot screen when you turn the power off will be happening when you turn the PalmPilot on again. It's like sleep mode on your desktop computer. That's a very handy feature when you get interrupted in the middle of doing something and want to get right back to it, even if you get a call from a long-winded salesman from Utah.

Contrast wheel

The contrast wheel isn't really a button; it's a real moving part that looks like a little volume control on the left edge of the PalmPilot case. If you have a Palm III, the contrast wheel is on the left edge of the back of the case. In certain kinds of light, you can see the text on the PalmPilot screen better if you adjust the contrast a bit.

Reset button

Sometimes you need to tell your PalmPilot to stop what it's doing and start all over again. That's called *resetting* your PalmPilot. Occasionally a program that you've installed on your PalmPilot misbehaves and makes the PalmPilot hang up or act crazy. That's very rare, and usually resetting the PalmPilot fixes the problem.

You can reset your PalmPilot two different ways: the hard way and the kindler, gentler soft way. A soft reset just makes the PalmPilot stop everything and start again. You can perform a soft reset on your PalmPilot by pushing the end of a bent paper clip into the little hole labeled Reset on the back of the PalmPilot.

A hard reset erases all your data as well as your user name. Needless to say, you don't want to do a hard reset without a pretty good reason. If you're selling your PalmPilot to someone else, you could do a hard reset to make the unit act like it did when it was brand new. (I wish I could do that to myself now and then.) To perform a hard reset, hold the power button down and then press the end of a paper clip into the hole marked Reset on the back of your PalmPilot. When you do, a prompt appears on the PalmPilot screen, asking you if you really want to erase all your data. Think hard again whether you want to do this — then either press the scroll-up hard button if you do or the scroll-down button if you don't.

The Screen

You can't miss the most important part of the PalmPilot — the screen, which you can see in Figure 1-3. It shows you the information that you've stored in your applications and lets you know what the applications are ready to do for you next.

But an equally important function of the PalmPilot screen is to take information from you. Two parts of the screen take information from you in different ways — the display and the Graffiti area — and the soft buttons (not to be confused with the hard buttons described earlier in this chapter) let you do all sorts of other neat things.

The display

The largest part of the PalmPilot screen is the main display area, shown in Figure 1-4, which not only shows the text that you're working with, but also contains a number of active areas upon which you can tap your stylus to make something happen, such as display the contents of a memo or mark a task complete. You can also slide your stylus across the surface of the screen to select (or highlight) the text displayed at that point in some applications.

Part I: Getting to Know Your PalmPilot

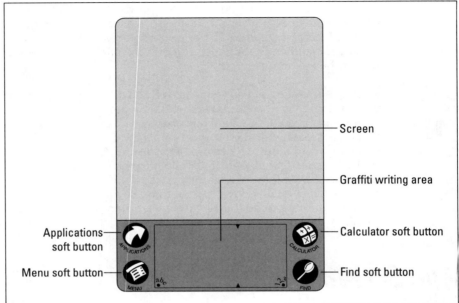

Figure 1-3: Your PalmPilot screen.

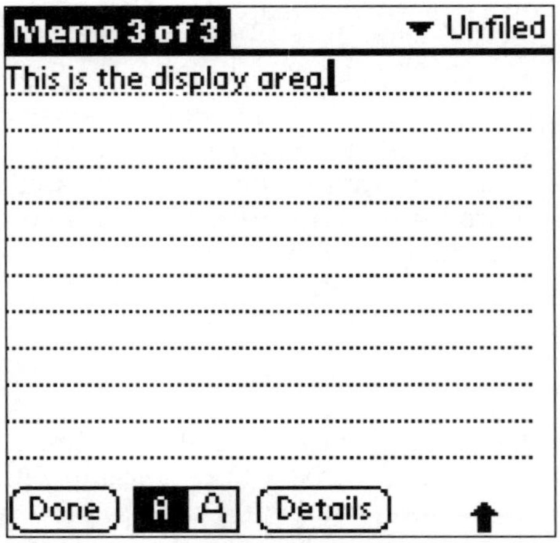

Figure 1-4: The display area.

Chapter 1: What Can a PalmPilot Do? 19

Most standard PalmPilot applications organize the display into areas that do pretty much the same job from one application to the next. The upper-left corner of the screen displays a tab that shows the name of the application that you're using, such as Address List, To Do List, or Memo Pad. The upper-right corner usually tells you the category of the item that you're viewing. The bottom of the display usually contains buttons that you can tap to create, find, or edit items in the application that you're using. The main, central part of the display is the part that shows the bulk of your information. Some applications offer a scroll bar on the right edge of the screen that enables you to scroll the display to show information that's higher or lower on the list of items that you're viewing. This scroll bar does the same thing as the scroll buttons at the bottom of your PalmPilot (see "Scroll buttons" earlier in this chapter).

I used the words *sometimes* and *usually* a lot when describing the display, because every program works a bit differently. So not every element works the same way all the time, but the preceding description is how most well-designed PalmPilot programs tend to work.

Soft buttons

Soft buttons aren't really soft, like a pillow, they're more like pictures of buttons painted onto the PalmPilot screen. Unlike the hard buttons, the soft buttons have no moving parts, and they don't do anything until your PalmPilot is powered on. One advantage to soft buttons is that they're labeled with the name of the thing they do, so you don't have to guess. Figure 1-5 shows what the soft buttons look like.

To use one of the soft buttons, just tap it with your stylus. The four jobs that are assigned to the four soft buttons are Applications, Menu, Calculator, and Find. The following sections outline what each soft button does.

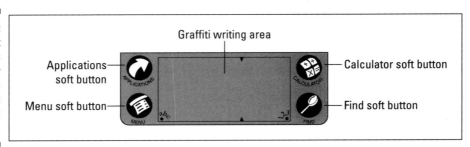

Figure 1-5: The soft buttons work only when the PalmPilot is powered on.

Part I: Getting to Know Your PalmPilot

Applications

The Applications soft button calls up a list of all the applications on your PalmPilot, showing their icons. Figure 1-6 shows you the icons that you should see on your PalmPilot.

Figure 1-6: Every program on your PalmPilot has an icon in the list of applications.

Several applications come already installed on your PalmPilot, including the following:

- **Expense:** You can use this application to keep track of what you spend.

- **HotSync:** The program that makes your PalmPilot communicate with your desktop computer.

- **Mail:** Exchanges messages with the e-mail program on your desktop.

- **Memory:** This shows you how much memory remains on your PalmPilot and how the memory that you have is being used. (The Memory application only appears on models older than the Palm III.)

- **Preferences:** You can use this application to configure your PalmPilot to suit your needs.

- **Security:** With this application, you can set up passwords and hide or show private items.

Any applications that you install on your PalmPilot also show up in this list. I tell you more about the applications that come with your PalmPilot later in this chapter (see "What Do the Standard Applications Do?"), and I show you how to install other applications in Chapter 12. You can start any application that you see in the applications list by tapping the icon for that program. The little battery icon in the applications list tells you how much power is left in your batteries.

Menu

The Menu button activates the menus in any application that you're running. Most PalmPilot programs have a set of menus that enable you to cut, copy, or paste text, as well as create new items or delete old ones (these menus are similar to those you find in the applications for your desktop computer — except they're not as involved). To use the menus in any application, start the application, then tap the Menu button and tap the menu that you want to use. Figure 1-7 shows a sample menu.

Figure 1-7: If you don't like the specials, you can always order from the Menu.

Calculator

The Calculator button contains no mysteries; it starts up the on-screen calculator, as shown in Figure 1-8. Tap the numbers just like you would with a handheld calculator. You can even press the on-screen calculator buttons with your finger. Naturally, it's not a good idea to put your fingers on the screen if you have gooey stuff like chocolate on your hands, because it

22 Part I: Getting to Know Your PalmPilot

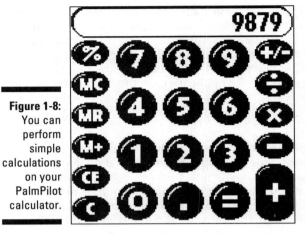

Figure 1-8: You can perform simple calculations on your PalmPilot calculator.

leaves a mess on your screen, which makes your calculations hard to read. I don't know what happens if you try to lick chocolate off your PalmPilot screen (or worse, somebody else's PalmPilot screen). I wouldn't try it.

Find

The Find button starts up a little program that searches your entire PalmPilot for a certain string of text. If you want to find every item on your PalmPilot that contains the word *chocolate,* tap the Find button and enter the word *chocolate* with either the on-screen keyboard or Graffiti (see Chapter 2 for more about entering text), and then tap OK (see Figure 1-9). The Find program then finds all the *chocolate* on your PalmPilot, which is faster and healthier than finding all the chocolate in your grocery store.

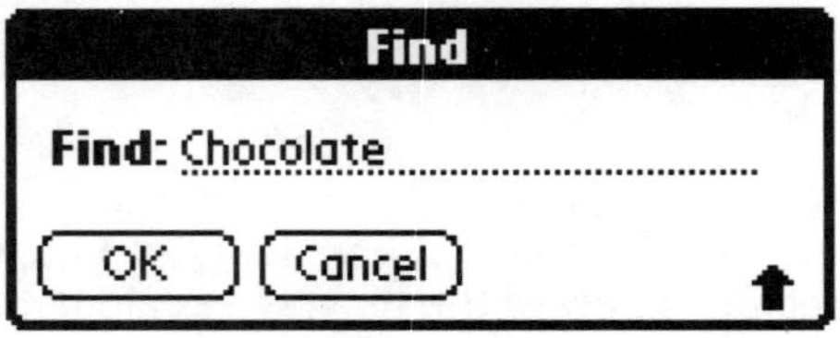

Figure 1-9: You can find a word that occurs in any PalmPilot application by using the Find tool.

TIP

I'll tell you one odd thing about the Find tool; if you enter only the first part of a word, it'll find the word that you're looking for, but if you enter only the last part of the word, your word won't turn up. If you enter *choco,* you'll still find chocolate, but if you enter *late,* you'll come up with *late, later,* and *latest,* but not *chocolate.*

The Graffiti area

Most of the bottom part of the screen is occupied by a large box between the soft buttons called the Graffiti area, as shown in Figure 1-10. A pair of tiny triangles at the top and bottom of the Graffiti area separate the part for entering letters from the part for entering numbers. You can use the PalmPilot stylus to write letters on the left side in PalmPilot's special alphabet, called Graffiti. You can enter Graffiti-style numbers on the right side. Graffiti is a lot like plain block printing that you learned in kindergarten, but a few letters are written a little bit differently. For more about using Graffiti to enter text, see Chapter 2.

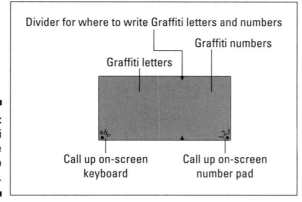

Figure 1-10: The Graffiti area is the place to enter text.

The letters *abc* appear in the lower-left corner, and the numbers *123* appear in the lower-right corner of the Graffiti area. As you may have guessed, abc calls up an on-screen keyboard, and 123 calls up a number pad. For more information on entering text via the on-screen keyboard and number pad, see Chapter 2.

Which PalmPilot Do I Have?

This book covers the latest model of the PalmPilot — the Palm III — but you may be using an earlier version. Users of earlier versions can find plenty of value here, too, not only because you can upgrade any PalmPilot to make it a Palm III, but because the Palm people tend not to make wholesale changes to the basic applications, incorporating only slight changes and improvements with each new release. So newer versions should look pretty familiar to you. See Chapter 14 for more about upgrading your PalmPilot.

Because so many versions of the PalmPilot exist, you may appreciate this quick-and-dirty guide to all the PalmPilots that are out there, somewhere:

- **PalmPilot 1000:** This little guy has only 128K of memory (barely $1/20$ of the memory of a Palm III) and no backlight.
- **PalmPilot 5000:** This version kicks up the memory to 512K, but still doesn't have a backlight.
- **PalmPilot Personal:** You get 512K of memory with this dude, and you finally get a backlight, plus optional use of a modem to HotSync, and better features in all the standard applications.
- **PalmPilot Professional:** This guy comes to you with 1MB of memory, a backlight, and an e-mail application.
- **Palm III:** This version gives you a whopping 2MB of memory and everything any earlier PalmPilot had, plus infrared beaming — which enables you to beam items or whole programs to another Palm III user.
- **IBM WorkPad:** This is a licensed version of the PalmPilot, sold by you-know-who. The WorkPad is identical to the PalmPilot and has been upgraded right along with each new version of the PalmPilot.

If you bought your PalmPilot a while back and you feel that you're missing all the fun that people are having with the new features, don't worry. You can upgrade any PalmPilot to the latest version. I've got more to say about upgrading your PalmPilot in Chapter 14.

What Do the Standard Applications Do?

The PalmPilot wasn't designed just to be a cool little computer, although it's definitely a cool little computer. It was designed to do useful things for you as soon as you take it out of the box. I like nothing better than instant gratification, and that's what you get with the PalmPilot. (I do, anyway.)

The standard PalmPilot applications don't have to be installed, configured, or fussed with in any way; they're ready to use with one press of a button. Of course, you can configure the preferences for the applications to get them exactly the way you want them (for more on preferences, see Chapter 3). To get started, just press the button assigned to that application or tap the Applications soft button for a list of your PalmPilot programs and pick the one you want to use.

Chapter 1: What Can a PalmPilot Do?

The programs that you can use as soon as you take your PalmPilot out of the box include the following:

- **Address Book:** This is your "little black book" of names, addresses, and phone numbers. You can keep a detailed description about everything that you need to know about the people in your list by attaching a note to each record. You can also keep track of everyone's e-mail address and use the Address Book as the Personal Address Book for e-mail that you compose on your PalmPilot. For more about e-mail on the PalmPilot, see Chapter 10, and for more on the Address Book, see Chapter 5.

- **Calculator:** The calculator is a simple tool for punching in numbers and performing arithmetic. The PalmPilot calculator does one trick that a handheld calculator can't handle — it shows a list of recent calculations. After performing a series of calculations, tap Menu and then choose Options⇨Recent Calculations to see a recap of your last few calculations, as shown in Figure 1-11.

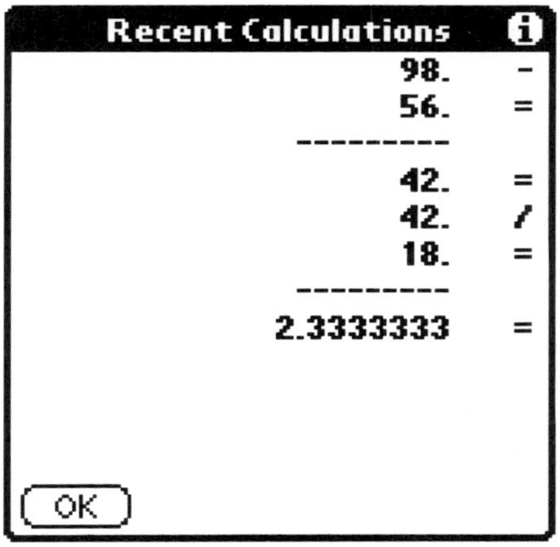

Figure 1-11: You can see a series of calculations on your list of recent calculations.

- **Date Book:** Think of this as your calendar of appointments and events. The Date Book, as shown in Figure 1-12, lets you set appointments and alarms to remind yourself of those appointments. You can also add notes to any appointment to keep details about each appointment handy. For more on the Date Book, see Chapter 8.

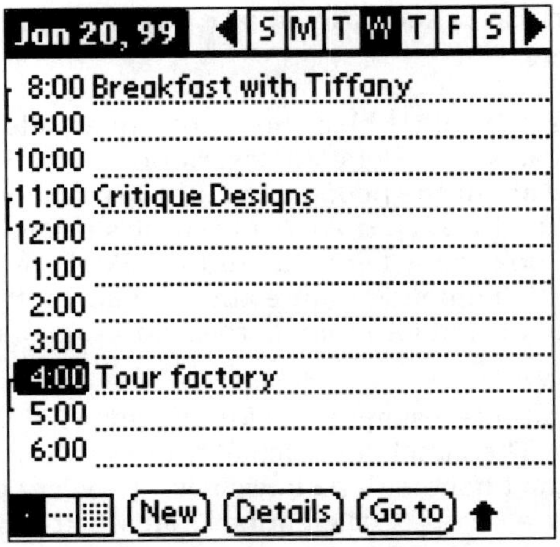

Figure 1-12: Keep up to date with your Date Book.

- ✔ **Expense:** Here's a handy application for keeping track of what you spend. The Expense program, as shown in Figure 1-13, synchronizes to special Microsoft Excel spreadsheets on your desktop to enable you to collect expense figures on the road and then pull them together when you get home. See Chapter 12 for more on Expense.

- ✔ **Giraffe:** Actually, this is a game, but it's also a great way to sharpen your skills at Graffiti, which makes your PalmPilot that much more useful. Figure 1-14 shows a sample screen from the game. The Giraffe game comes pre-installed on the PalmPilot Professional and earlier models, but you have to add it from the CD that comes with the Palm III.

- ✔ **HotSync:** This program links your PalmPilot to your desktop computer. The HotSync program has two parts — the part on the PalmPilot and the part on the desktop. Either a PC or a Mac can synchronize data with the same PalmPilot, but the PC and the Mac need different desktop software. See Chapter 11 for more information on using HotSync.

- ✔ **Mail:** Here's a simple e-mail program that enables you to HotSync your e-mail with your desktop computer so that you can read e-mail, compose replies, and create messages to be sent through your desktop e-mail system. (This is available only on PalmPilot Professional models and later.) For more on the Mail program, see Chapter 10.

Chapter 1: What Can a PalmPilot Do? 27

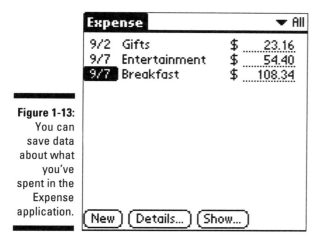

Figure 1-13: You can save data about what you've spent in the Expense application.

Figure 1-14: The Giraffe game makes it fun to learn Graffiti.

- **Memo Pad:** This is your collection of plain old text notes that you can keep around for future reference. Figure 1-15 shows the memos that exist in your PalmPilot when you buy it. You can either create notes on your desktop computer and transfer them to your PalmPilot, to keep critical information handy, or you can create memos on your PalmPilot for later transfer to desktop computer programs, such as your word processor. For more on the Memo Pad, see Chapter 7.

Figure 1-15:
The Memo List shows your memos anytime you want to read them.

```
Memo List                ▼ All
1. Entering text into your PalmPilot
2. PalmPilot Basics




 New
```

- **Preferences:** This program lets you customize your PalmPilot by changing application button assignments, time and number formats, modem setup, and shortcuts. Figure 1-16 shows the General Preferences screen; for other preferences screens, choose from the pull-down menu in the upper-right corner. For more on setting preferences, see Chapter 3.
- **Security:** This program lets you hide or show all the items on your PalmPilot that you've marked private. You can also set, remove, or change a password to protect your information. Figure 1-17 shows you what to expect from the Security screen. For more on using the security features, see Chapter 3.
- **To Do List:** Here's a list of tasks that you need to remember, sorted in order of Priority, Due Date, or by the name of the task. You can also keep track of tasks that you've completed in the To Do List for future reference. For more on the To Do List, see Chapter 6.

Chapter 1: What Can a PalmPilot Do?

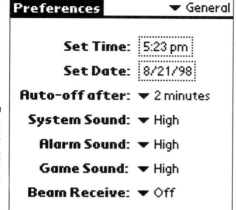

Figure 1-16: Make your PalmPilot your own by setting your Preferences.

Figure 1-17: Protect your sensitive information by setting a password in the Security application.

Of course, the programs that come in the box with your PalmPilot are barely the beginning of what you can do. Thousands of software developers are busily writing new programs that you can add to your PalmPilot to make it do things that you may not even know you want to do yet. Check out the CD-ROM that accompanies this book for a sampling of the best PalmPilot programs out there.

HotSyncing Is Definitely Hot Stuff

HotSyncing, put simply, is when you have your desktop computer and PalmPilot talk to each other — sort of like when you get together with a friend at happy hour. You compare your days, talk about what you did, and maybe exchange notes. HotSyncing does the same thing — only more efficiently.

During a HotSync, the two machines compare data and then match up that data exactly, keeping each other current on who you know, what you've done, when you did it, and what you gotta do tomorrow. HotSyncing also enables you to install additional applications onto your PalmPilot, as well as back up (or archive) all your data on your desktop computer, so that your data is safe (your PalmPilot does this automatically, so you don't even have to think about it).

For more on HotSyncing and using your PalmPilot with your desktop computer, see Chapters 11 and 12.

Batteries Are Included, but . . .

In case you haven't noticed, your PalmPilot doesn't plug into the wall, and though the cradle may look like it could recharge your PalmPilot, it doesn't. Instead, your PalmPilot runs on a pair of plain old AAA batteries, which should last you nearly a month in normal use. If you use the backlight a lot, you'll drain the batteries faster.

When you change batteries, HotSyncing first is a good idea, just in case something goes wrong. When you take out a set of batteries, you have 30 seconds to insert a new set before the PalmPilot starts forgetting things.

If you press the Applications soft button, you can see how much power remains in your batteries on the applications screen. The Palm III battery power is indicated by a silhouette of a battery at the top of the applications screen. When your batteries are at maximum power, the battery is completely black. As the batteries drain, the black part of the battery indicator gets smaller and smaller. Earlier PalmPilots just show a bar graph labeled Battery at the bottom of the screen.

Storing your PalmPilot in the cradle seems to drain the batteries more quickly than usual, so don't leave your PalmPilot in the cradle overnight. Just pop the unit into the cradle when you HotSync, and then take it out when you're done. The manufacturer is trying to fix this little bug. You may be used to leaving rechargeable appliances and laptop computers plugged in to recharge the batteries, but the PalmPilot currently does the opposite. For more on using rechargeable batteries, see the sidebar "Sure, rechargeable batteries are cool, but . . ."

Sure, rechargeable batteries are cool, but . . .

You may like to be environmentally conscious by using rechargeable batteries, but you need to know two things about using rechargeables in your PalmPilot. First, rechargeables don't recharge when you leave the PalmPilot in its cradle. The cradle would have to draw power from the PC that it's connected to, and it doesn't do that.

The second thing is that when rechargeable batteries lose their power, they usually go dead all at once. Nonrechargeable batteries usually drain a little at a time and die slowly. Your PalmPilot pops a warning onto the screen when you need to replace your batteries, but if you use rechargeables, that warning may come too late. I'm not saying that you shouldn't use rechargeable batteries in your PalmPilot, but if you do, you need to watch your battery power more closely than you would if you used regular batteries.

Chapter 2
Going in Stylus

In This Chapter
- Understanding Graffiti letters and numbers
- Moving the Graffiti cursor
- Making capital letters without a shift key
- Graffiti whiz secrets and shortcuts
- Using the on-screen keyboard
- Exploring other text entry options

Getting information out of your PalmPilot is terribly easy, but putting information into your PalmPilot is only sort of easy. If the PalmPilot had a built-in keyboard, I wouldn't need to explain how to enter data at all; you'd know how just by looking. But if the PalmPilot did have a keyboard you'd either be stuck with a set of teeny-weeny keys that you could barely use or you'd have a device the size of a laptop computer, in which case you'd be better off with a laptop computer.

The people who make the PalmPilot recommend that you enter most of your data to the PalmPilot via the PalmPilot desktop program, which I describe how to install in Chapter 11 and how to use in Chapter 12. No doubt, that's the clearest way to deal with data entry. But I think being able to jot down a memo while riding on a train or sitting by a pool is half the fun of having a PalmPilot, so I like to use either Graffiti or the on-screen keyboard that's built into the PalmPilot. Some programmers are creating products that offer interesting new ways to enter text into your PalmPilot, but those products cost extra. I discuss them at the end of the chapter in the section "Other Text Entry Tricks."

Graffiti

Using words to explain Graffiti is like trying to describe a spiral staircase without using your hands. But even though a spiral staircase is tricky to describe, it's easy to use; the same goes for Graffiti. After you've used Graffiti for even a little while, you'll find that it comes naturally.

34   Part I: Getting to Know Your PalmPilot

To write in Graffiti, you need to use a stylus. A *stylus* is a special pen with no ink. You can use the stylus that comes with your PalmPilot, which you'll find stored in a holder on the right side of your PalmPilot (or on the back of your Palm III). You can also go out and buy a fancy, expensive stylus from people who also sell fancy, expensive writing pens, but the cheap plastic stylus that comes with your PalmPilot does the job just as well.

Your PalmPilot will probably work perfectly for a long time with little or no trouble, but if you accidentally scratch the screen, you'll start having problems. Don't use a sharp object as a stylus. Try to use a stylus that was designed to work with a PalmPilot, just to be safe.

You can use the stylus to tap on-screen buttons and select text, but to write text in Graffiti, you need to write in the box at the bottom of the screen, cleverly named the Graffiti area, as shown in Figure 2-1.

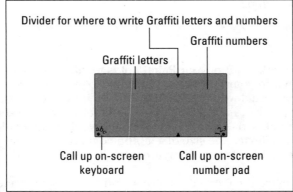

Figure 2-1: The Graffiti writing area.

Graffiti letters and numbers

You need to write letters and numbers in different parts of the Graffiti area. You can see the letters *abc* in the lower-left corner of the Graffiti area. That's to remind you that you need to write letters on the left side of the box. The numbers *123* are printed in the lower-right corner, to remind you that, you guessed it, you can only write numbers on the right side of the screen. Two tiny triangles separate the letter writing area from the number writing area.

Remember that Graffiti is a special alphabet that you have to learn; it's not handwriting recognition software that learns your handwriting style. Most of the letters and numbers in the Graffiti alphabet are the same as the plain block letters that you learned in the first grade, with one important adjustment: *Graffiti letters must be written with a single stroke of the stylus*. If you remember that one rule, Graffiti seems pretty simple.

For example, Figure 2-2 shows the letter A in Graffiti.

The Graffiti letter A looks just like a normal capital A without the crossbar. (That dot on the lower-left end of the A shows where you start the stroke — it's the same place that most people start writing a capital A.) You don't write a crossbar because writing the crossbar requires a second stroke of the stylus. Picking up the stylus is the way you tell Graffiti that you've moved on to the next letter. So for the letter A, just draw the upper, triangular part of the A, and then move on to your next letter. (As I said earlier, it takes a lot less time to do this than to read about doing it.)

Figure 2-2: The letter A.

Your PalmPilot comes with a little sticker that shows you the whole Graffiti alphabet. You can put the sticker on the back of your PalmPilot or on the inside cover of your Palm III so that you'll always have it as a reference.

Nearly all Graffiti charts display the alphabet as little squiggles with a dot at one end. The dot tells you where to begin drawing the Graffiti stroke. Think of it like those connect-the-dot games, except that you only connect one dot.

In case you've lost the little sticker, Figure 2-3 shows the whole Graffiti alphabet.

As you can see, the Graffiti alphabet is easy to understand. The trick is remembering the tiny differences between regular printing and printing Graffiti.

If you need some help with Graffiti while using your PalmPilot, you can bring up a Graffiti cheat sheet right on the screen in most PalmPilot programs, like this:

1. **Tap the Menu soft button.**

    The menu bar appears.

2. **Choose Edit➪Graffiti Help.**

   The Graffiti Help screen appears.

After you've found the Graffiti letter that you want to use, tap the Done button to return to your program and write the letter.

Figure 2-3: The whole Graffiti alphabet.

Remember that the Graffiti Help screen only appears when it's possible for you to enter text. If you're looking at your To Do List, for example, the Graffiti Help screen won't appear, because you need to select a To Do item or create a new To Do before you can enter text.

You may find that it takes a bit of time to get used to writing Graffiti. Don't despair — that's normal. Like most computers, your PalmPilot can be a bit finicky about what it accepts when it comes to individual things like human handwriting. My actual handwriting is pretty awful, so I often need to write a bit more slowly and carefully when I'm entering Graffiti than I do when I'm writing normal text on paper.

If you're a touch typist, you probably won't achieve the kind of speed when you're entering text in Graffiti as you do by typing. The point of Graffiti is not so much speed as convenience; you use Graffiti when it just isn't practical to drag a keyboard around.

Moving the Graffiti cursor

When you're creating text in Graffiti, you always see a little blinking line in the display, called the *insertion point* or the cursor, which shows you where the next letter that you enter will go. Sometimes, you want to make the cursor move without entering a letter, or you just want to enter a space between words or a line between paragraphs.

Chapter 2: Going in Stylus *37*

To create a space, draw the Graffiti space character in the Graffiti area, as shown in Figure 2-4. It's just a horizontal line drawn from left to right.

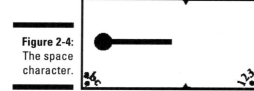

Figure 2-4: The space character.

If you make a mistake, you may want to backspace to erase the last letter that you wrote. The backspace character works just like the backspace key on a regular desktop computer. To backspace, draw the Graffiti backspace character in the Graffiti area, as shown in Figure 2-5. It's just a horizontal line drawn from right to left, the opposite of the space character. Although some characters need to be entered either in the letters or numbers area of the Graffiti box, you can enter spaces and backspaces in either area.

Figure 2-5: The backspace character.

When you want to delete a whole word or a larger block of text, it's quicker to select the text before drawing the backspace character to delete everything that you've selected. To select text, draw an imaginary line through the text that you want to select in the display area (not in the Graffiti area). You can see which text you've selected because the text you select is highlighted. Backspacing after highlighting text erases that text. You can also just start writing again after selecting text; the new text replaces the old.

If you're finished with the line that you're writing and you want to start entering text on a new line, use the Graffiti return character. The return character works a little bit like the Enter key on a regular desktop computer, although you use the return character a lot less on the PalmPilot than you would on a regular computer.

To insert a new line, draw the return character in the Graffiti area, as shown in Figure 2-6. It's a slanted line drawn from the upper-right to the lower-left part of the Graffiti area.

Figure 2-6: The return character.

Making capital letters without a shift key

When you type a capital letter on a regular keyboard, you hold the shift key while typing the letter. You can't hold a key while entering a Graffiti letter, so you have to enter the shift character before entering a letter that you want capitalized.

The shift character is simply an upward, vertical stroke in the Graffiti text area, as shown in Figure 2-7. To enter a capital A, draw a vertical line upwards in the Graffiti text area, followed by the letter A. After you draw the shift character, an upward-pointing arrow appears in the lower-right corner of the screen to show that your next letter will be capitalized.

Figure 2-7: The shift character.

On a regular keyboard, if you want to capitalize a whole string of letters, you press the Caps Lock key and type away. After you finish typing capital letters, you press the shift key to return to regular lowercase text.

Entering two shift characters in a row in Graffiti, as shown in Figure 2-8, is the same as pressing the Caps Lock key. After you enter the shift character twice, you see an arrow with a dotted tail in the lower-right corner of the display, which tells you that all the text you enter will be capitalized. You can cancel the Caps Lock by entering the shift command again.

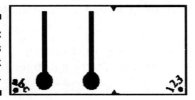

Figure 2-8: The Caps Lock command.

Chapter 2: Going in Stylus 39

 In quite a few cases, PalmPilot applications assume that the first letter of a sentence or proper name should be capitalized, so the shift arrow automatically shows up in the lower-right corner of the screen to indicate that the next letter will be capitalized. If you don't want to capitalize the beginning of a sentence, enter the shift character twice to return to lowercase text.

Graffiti has another type of shift character called the Extended Shift, entered as a downward, diagonal line starting from the top-left, as shown in Figure 2-9. The Extended Shift character offers a way to enter special characters, such as the copyright symbol and the trademark symbol. You can also use the Extended Shift to create certain punctuation characters, such as the upside-down question marks and exclamation points that you need to enter text in Spanish, as well as some mathematical symbols like plus signs. When you enter the Extended Shift stroke, a little diagonal line appears in the lower-right corner of the screen.

Figure 2-9: The Extended Shift stroke.

Another shift character that you may use is the Command Shift, an upward, diagonal line starting in the lower-left part of the Graffiti screen, as shown in Figure 2-10. You can perform quite a few common tasks in many PalmPilot programs by entering the Command Shift followed by a letter. For example, to delete a To Do item, tap the item and then enter the Command Shift stroke followed by the letter *D*. That opens the Delete dialog box, just as if you had chosen Record⇨Delete Item from the menu. You can see what the Command Shift can do in any program by tapping the Menu soft button and looking at the list of commands at the right side of each menu.

Figure 2-10: The Command Shift stroke.

Punctuating your text

Although Graffiti letters and numbers look pretty normal, Graffiti punctuation is pretty strange. You may not want to punctuate at all when you're entering Graffiti text except for the occasional period and dash.

To enter punctuation characters such as periods, dashes, and commas, you need to tap your stylus once in the Graffiti area before entering the character. Many punctuation characters have different meanings if you don't tap first before drawing them. When you tap once, a little dot appears in the lower-right corner of the display to show that you've tapped.

The simplest punctuation character is the period. Tap twice in the Graffiti area to create a period. Figure 2-11 shows a dot where I'm making a period.

Figure 2-11: The Graffiti period.

The second simplest punctuation character is the dash. Tap once in the Graffiti area, and then draw a horizontal line from left to right. After you've used Graffiti for a while, you'll think of this as tapping, then drawing the space character.

If you need to enter e-mail addresses in your Address Book, you'll almost certainly need to be able to enter the @ sign, for e-mail addresses like somebody@something.com. The @ sign is simply a tap followed by the letter O.

Graffiti whiz secrets

I think that most people can get a pretty good handle on Graffiti within a few hours, except for people under 15 years of age, who usually pick it up in about five minutes. I've heard stories of kids in junior high school who write notes to each other in Graffiti. That's pretty clever. I hope they don't write naughty words on walls in Graffiti; that would be redundant.

But even with some experience, certain Graffiti letters tend to stay finicky and hard to enter accurately. One thing to remember is that you need to make your Graffiti characters as large, square, and vertical as possible.

SHORTCUT

Another trick is to learn which letters can actually be entered by writing a number on the letter side of the Graffiti area and a letter on the number side of the Graffiti area. For example, if you write the number 3 on the letter side of the Graffiti area, the letter B turns up more reliably than it does if you draw the actual Graffiti letter B. Table 2-1 shows a list of letters that are often a problem and how to get your PalmPilot to recognize them more reliably.

Table 2-1	Tricks of the Graffiti Trade
To Get This Character . . .	*Perform This Stroke*
B	Draw the number 3 on the letter side of the Graffiti area.
G	Draw the number 6 on the letter side of the Graffiti area.
K	This is the trickiest Graffiti character. Just draw the "legs" on the side of the K, joined by a little loop. Leave out the vertical bar. To me it looks a little bit like a fish swimming from right to left. I describe this in greater detail later in this chapter.
P	Start at the bottom of the P and make the loop at the top pretty small.
Q	Draw an O with a really long tail at the top.
R	Do this just like the P that I describe, but make the tail of the R extra long.
V	Draw the V backwards, that is start from the top right.
Y	Just draw the lower loop of a cursive capital Y. It's just a loop, like the letter K, except the fish is swimming down.
2	Draw the letter Z on the number side of the Graffiti writing area.
4	Draw the letter C on the number side of the Graffiti area.
5	Draw the letter S on the number side of the Graffiti area.
7	Draw a backwards letter C on the number side of the Graffiti area.

Part I: Getting to Know Your PalmPilot

The amazing Graffiti fish loop

One Graffiti character has no counterpart in the normal alphabet, but knowing how to draw this character can help you enormously when you use Graffiti. It doesn't have an official name, so I just call it the *fish loop*.

I know that my fish story is a pretty dopey explanation, but I bring it up for two reasons. First, Graffiti seems to recognize this loop symbol more reliably than most other letters or numbers, so learning to use it will certainly make you a quicker and slicker Graffitist.

The second reason for my fish story is that I find stupid explanations the easiest to remember. By that measure, you'll NEVER forget this explanation.

So, if you draw a little loop that looks like a fish swimming from right to left, as shown in Figure 2-12, Graffiti translates that loop as the letter K.

Figure 2-12: Did you have your Special K today?

If you make the fish look like he's swimming downward, as shown in Figure 2-13, Graffiti translates that loop as the letter Y.

Figure 2-13: No YMCA here; just Y.

If you make the fish look like he's swimming from left to right, as shown in Figure 2-14, Graffiti translates that loop as the letter X.

If you make the fish look like he's swimming upward and you start drawing from the left, as shown in Figure 2-15, Graffiti translates that loop as the shortcut symbol, a very useful tool that I discuss in the next section, "The Graffiti ShortCut Symbol."

By the way, I apologize for referring to the fish as a male in all instances, but because the fish has no eyes, he appears to have no idea where he's going, a

Figure 2-14: X marks the spot, sometimes.

Figure 2-15: Little Red Riding Hood shoulda had a shortcut like this!

situation in which I find myself regularly. That makes me assume that the fish is male, like me. Feel free to draw your own conclusions. About the fish, that is.

The Graffiti ShortCut symbol

Another compelling reason to use Graffiti is that you can create and use ShortCuts. *ShortCuts* are abbreviations that automatically expand themselves into longer blocks of text or automated entries, such as the current date and time.

When you buy your PalmPilot, a few ShortCuts are already built in. Some of the preprogrammed ShortCuts are for useful words such as *meeting, breakfast, lunch,* and *dinner.* You also get some useful time stamp ShortCuts for entering the current date and time.

To add a time stamp to a memo or note, write the Graffiti ShortCut symbol, followed by the letters TS, as shown in Figure 2-16.

Figure 2-16: It's Greek to me, you say? Nope, it's a time stamp!

Part I: Getting to Know Your PalmPilot

As soon as you finish writing the letter S, the 3 characters you entered disappear, and the current time appears.

The three preprogrammed time stamp ShortCuts are

- **TS** for time stamp — enters the current time
- **DS** for date stamp — enters the current date
- **DTS** for date time stamp — enters the current date and time

Other preprogrammed ShortCuts include

- **ME** for the word *meeting*
- **BR** for the word *breakfast*
- **LU** for the word *lunch*
- **DI** for the word *dinner*

In Chapter 4, I show you how to create ShortCuts of your own.

The On-Screen Keyboard

Perhaps you don't want to spend time learning Graffiti. You may just want to get down to business. That's fine. You can call up the on-screen keyboard to enter letters by tapping on a tiny picture of a keyboard, as shown in Figure 2-17.

Figure 2-17: The on-screen keyboard is a handy way to enter text.

Chapter 2: Going in Stylus 45

The on-screen keyboard is too small for touch typing. You'll definitely need the stylus to pick out those tiny little keys. I use the on-screen keyboard as little as possible because I think I type more slowly when I'm trying to find those tiny little keys. But I know plenty of people who stick exclusively with the on-screen keyboard and they do just fine.

To make the on-screen keyboard appear, tap the dot in one of the two lower corners of the Graffiti area. When you tap the dot on the letter side of the Graffiti area, the alphabet keyboard appears. When you tap the dot on the number side, a numeric keypad appears, as shown in Figure 2-18. After you've entered the text that you want, tap Done to make the on-screen keyboard go away.

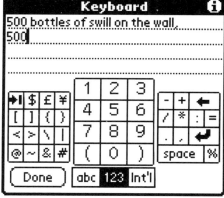

Figure 2-18: Enter numbers with the numeric keypad if you don't like Graffiti.

Remember that the on-screen keyboard only appears when it's possible for you to enter text. If you're looking at your list of memos, for example, the on-screen keyboard won't appear, because you need to open a memo or create a new memo before you can enter text.

On the on-screen keyboard, you can also see a button labeled Int'l that unlocks a special set of keys for entering those festive international characters that English sadly lacks.

Other Text Entry Tricks

I've seen some other promising methods of entering text into your PalmPilot. All of them involve buying a product and adding it to your PalmPilot. If you need to enter text on the run fairly often, one of these can help you.

The T9 system

T9 from Tegic Communications is an on-screen telephone-style keypad that lets you enter text the way you would dial one of those famous alphabetic phone numbers, such as 1-800-FLOWERS. As you press each letter of the word that you want to spell on the nine-key keyboard, a list of possible words appears above the keypad, and the most likely possibility appears in your text. If T9 didn't enter the word you really wanted in your text, tap the word that you had in mind, and that word appears as your text. It works surprisingly well, although I generally find it quicker to use Graffiti. For more information about the T9 keyboard, check out the manufacturer's Web site at `www.tegic.com`.

GoType

Of course, the best keyboard of all is a real, physical keyboard. A company called LandWare makes a special miniature keyboard with a docking port for your PalmPilot, which allows you to enter text the old-fashioned way — by typing. The PalmPilot still isn't the ideal platform for word processing, but if you just want to enter a lot of text quickly without lugging around a laptop with only a few hours of battery life, GoType may be a workable solution. The company's Web site is located at `www.landware.com`.

Chapter 3
Making Your PalmPilot Your Own

● ●

In This Chapter
▶ Setting preferences
▶ Using the Security program
▶ Setting passwords
▶ Hiding and showing private items
▶ Using PalmPilot hacks

● ●

As PalmPilots sell by the million, you can be sure that everyone uses his PalmPilot a little differently. Some people think of their PalmPilots as glorified datebooks, and they're happy with that. Other people install programs that do things you'd never guess, such as track their location by satellite, send e-mail messages by radio, and heaven knows what else.

Because everyone uses a PalmPilot a little differently, many people want to personalize the way theirs work. In this chapter, I show you some of the easier ways to make your PalmPilot work the way that you do, by using the preference and security settings that are standard on the PalmPilot.

Setting General Preferences

When you start up your PalmPilot for the very first time, the General Preferences screen appears automatically as an invitation to set the time and date accurately. You may also want to reset the time, if you travel frequently to different time zones.

Follow these steps to access the General Preferences screen:

1. **Tap the Applications soft button.**

    The list of applications appears on your screen.

2. **Tap the Prefs icon.**

    The Preferences application launches, as shown in Figure 3-1.

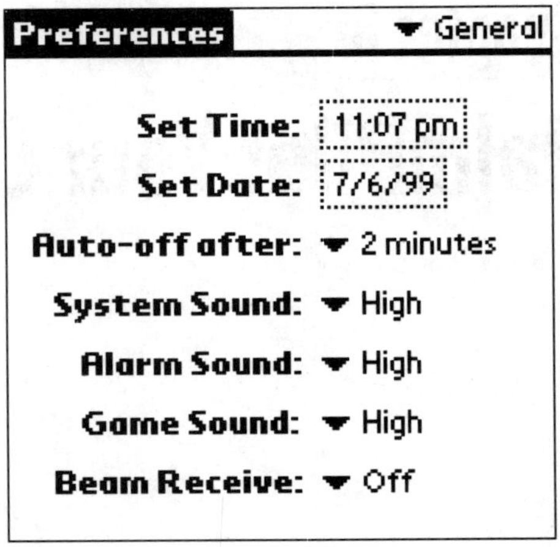

Figure 3-1: The Preferences application enables you to make your PalmPilot your own.

```
Preferences              ▼ General
        Set Time:  11:07 pm
        Set Date:  7/6/'99
   Auto-off after:  ▼ 2 minutes
   System Sound:  ▼ High
    Alarm Sound:  ▼ High
     Game Sound:  ▼ High
   Beam Receive:  ▼ Off
```

3. **Tap the word in the upper-right corner of the screen.**

    The Preferences program has eight options for setting up different types of preferences: Buttons, Digitizer, Formats, General, Modem, Network, Owner, and ShortCuts. The name of the section that you're looking at appears in the upper-right corner of the screen. The triangle next to the name of the section means that you can tap the name of the section to see a pull-down list of the other available sections.

4. **Choose General.**

    The General Preferences screen appears.

To change the individual settings of the General Preferences screen, continue with the following sections.

Setting the time

I like having my PalmPilot remind me of my appointments shortly before they occur, just to avoid missing anything that I've scheduled. But the PalmPilot is a bit like an alarm clock; alarms can't go off at the right time if I don't set the PalmPilot to the right time in the first place.

Here's how to set the time on your PalmPilot:

1. **With the General Preferences screen visible, tap the time shown in the Set Time box.**

    The Set Time dialog box opens, showing the time for which the PalmPilot is currently set, along with a pair of triangles for changing the time. The top triangle sets the time later, and the bottom triangle sets the time earlier, as shown in Figure 3-2.

Figure 3-2:
In the Set Time dialog box, tap the triangles to set the time.

2. **Tap the hour in the Set Time dialog box.**

    The hour is highlighted to show that you've selected it.

3. **Tap the triangles repeatedly until the hour you want appears.**

    The hour changes as you tap the triangles.

4. **Set the minutes by following Steps 2 and 3 for each of the two minutes boxes.**

    The minutes change as you tap the triangles.

5. **Tap the AM or PM box to choose the appropriate setting.**

    The box that you tap is highlighted to show that you've picked it.

6. **Tap OK.**

    The Set Time dialog box closes.

If you like to show the time in a different format than the standard 1:35 PM format, I show you how to change the time format in the section "Setting Format Preferences" later in this chapter.

Setting the date

If you use the calendar frequently or if you enter lots of tasks with due dates assigned, you may want your PalmPilot to know what day it is.

Follow these steps to set the date on your PalmPilot:

1. **With the General Preferences screen visible, tap the date shown in the Set Date box.**

    The Set Date dialog box opens, as shown in Figure 3-3.

Figure 3-3: You can set the date on your PalmPilot by finding the current date on a calendar in the Set Date dialog box.

2. **Tap one of the triangles on either side of the year to set the current year.**

   After you tap the triangle on the left, the year shown moves one year earlier. Tapping the triangle on the right moves the year shown to the next year. Keep tapping until the current year appears.

3. **Tap the month that you want.**

   The name of the month that you tap is highlighted to show that you've selected it, and a calendar for the month that you tap appears.

4. **Tap the day of the month that you want to set.**

   The Set Date dialog box closes, and the date that you chose appears in the Preferences screen.

After you've set the date, your PalmPilot remembers and keeps track of the date automatically, unless you let the batteries go dead for a month or more. If you go around the world for 80 days and come home to a dead PalmPilot, just change the batteries and reset the date and time. For more on batteries, see Chapter 1.

Setting the Auto-off interval

Your PalmPilot goes a long way on a pair of AAA batteries; mine usually runs for the better part of a month before I need to replace the batteries. One method that the PalmPilot uses to stretch battery life is to turn off automatically, if you haven't pressed a button for a few minutes. You don't have many choices about how long the PalmPilot waits before shutting off, but here's how you can choose from what's available:

Chapter 3: Making Your PalmPilot Your Own 51

1. **With the General Preferences screen visible, tap the triangle next to the words Auto-Off After.**

   The pull-down list of Auto-off intervals appears. You can choose either 1-, 2-, or 3-minute Auto-off intervals, as shown in Figure 3-4.

2. **Choose the Auto-off interval that you want.**

   The interval that you tap appears in the Auto-Off After box.

Figure 3-4:
Auto-off saves your batteries by turning your PalmPilot off when you're not using it.

You don't need to worry too much about having the PalmPilot turn off too fast; you only need to press the green power button to switch right back to the program that you were working on when the PalmPilot turned off.

Setting the sound volume

A tiny little speaker that's inside your PalmPilot makes little chirping sounds when you tap the screen and plays a squeaky little fanfare when you run the HotSync program. If you think a PalmPilot should be seen and not heard, you can turn the sound off. If you have a Palm III, you can also change the volume.

You have three volume settings that you can adjust:

   ✔ **System:** System sounds are those that the Palm OS is programmed to make in certain events. For example, when you want to do something specific that your PalmPilot can't do at that moment, you may get an error beep, just like when your desktop PC protests one of your actions.

52 Part I: Getting to Know Your PalmPilot

- **Alarm:** An alarm sounds when you set a reminder for an appointment. You can also get some third-party PalmPilot programs that use the alarm sound.
- **Game:** Game sounds work only with games that are programmed to use them. Most games are more fun with sounds, but those game-like boinks and bleeps are a dead giveaway that you're not using your PalmPilot for serious work. If you plan to secretly play a shoot-'em-up game on your PalmPilot at the weekly staff meeting, a good career move may be to turn off your game sounds.

If your PalmPilot goes off when you're at the movies, you may get some dirty looks, so be a good sport and turn off the sounds when you go to the MegaMultiplex.

Here's how to adjust the volume for all three types of sounds:

1. **With the General Preferences screen visible, tap the triangle next to the type of sound that you want to change.**

   A pull-down list of volume choices appears. On a Palm III, you can choose either Off, Low, Medium, or High, as shown in Figure 3-5. Earlier PalmPilots offer only a check box so that you can turn the sound on or off.

2. **Choose the volume level that you want.**

   The volume level that you tap appears in the System Sound box.

The term *PalmPilot volume* is an oxymoron like *military intelligence* or *jumbo shrimp*. The minuscule speaker inside the PalmPilot case can only make sounds that I'd describe as soft, softer, and softest. You may want to adjust the volume anyway, so it's good that you have a way to do so.

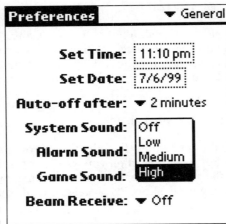

Figure 3-5: The Palm III has adjustable system sound volume. Earlier PalmPilots enable you only to turn sounds on and off.

Turning off beaming

A Palm III can send or receive all sorts of things by *beaming*, which is the rather neat process of sending data between Palm IIIs via an invisible light beam across the air. (Sounds kind of magical, doesn't it? To demystify beaming, see Chapter 9.) The Palm III doesn't distinguish between truly useful information and useless junk when it sends stuff out over the air; it's a little like television that way. If you'd like to avoid having unwanted junk beamed to your Palm III, you can elect not to receive beamed items by following these steps:

1. **With the General Preferences screen visible, tap the triangle next to Beam Receive.**

   The pull-down list of choices appears.

2. **Choose either On or Off.**

   The choice that you tap appears in the Beam Receive box.

Turning off beam receiving doesn't stop you from beaming items to others. If you've turned off beam receiving and you try to beam something, though, a dialog box opens up to ask you if you want to turn beam receiving back on. Switching beam receiving back on, in order to exchange business cards with another PalmPilot user, makes sense. You don't want to be unsociable, do you?

Setting Button Preferences

You may use some programs more than others. As a result, you may want to assign a different program to one of the hard buttons at the bottom of your PalmPilot case. Here's how to switch the programs assigned to the Applications buttons.

1. **Tap the Applications soft button.**

   The list of applications appears, showing icons for all the programs installed on your PalmPilot.

2. **Tap the Prefs icon.**

   The Preferences screen appears.

3. **Tap the word in the upper-right corner of the screen.**

   A pull-down list of preferences options appears.

Part I: Getting to Know Your PalmPilot

4. **Choose Buttons.**

   The Buttons Preferences screen appears and displays five icons, one for each of the buttons at the bottom of your PalmPilot and one for the Calculator soft button (the other soft buttons aren't up for grabs). The name of the assigned program shows up next to each icon.

5. **Tap the triangle next to the button whose program you wish to change.**

   A pull-down list of all the applications installed on your PalmPilot appears in alphabetical order, as shown in Figure 3-6. Your applications list may be long. When the list gets too long to fit on the PalmPilot screen, little arrows appear at the top and bottom of the list to indicate that more programs are available. You can scroll up and down the list by either tapping the arrows at the top and bottom of the list, or by pressing the scroll up and down buttons.

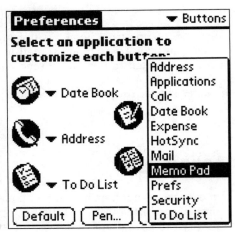

Figure 3-6: You can make your Application buttons start any program you want by changing the settings in the Buttons Preferences screen.

6. **Choose the name of the application that you want to assign to that button.**

   The name of the application that you tap appears in the Buttons Preferences screen next to the button to which it's assigned.

Now when you press that particular button, your PalmPilot runs the newly assigned program. All your programs still appear after you tap the Applications soft button, but only the assigned programs run from the hard buttons.

Setting Format Preferences

People express time and numbers differently in different places, so your PalmPilot has settings to suit a variety of local customs. Here's how to change the way that dates and numbers appear:

1. **Tap the Applications soft button.**

   The list of applications appears, showing icons for all the programs installed on your PalmPilot.

2. **Tap the Prefs icon.**

   The Preferences screen appears.

3. **Tap the word in the upper-right corner of the screen.**

   A pull-down list of Preferences options appears.

4. **Tap Formats.**

   The Format Preferences screen appears.

5. **Tap the triangle next to Preset To.**

   A pull-down list of countries appears, as shown in Figure 3-7. When you choose a certain country, the date, time, and number presets appear for that country.

6. **Choose the country whose presets you want to use.**

   The name of the country that you tap appears in the Preset To box, and all the number formats on the Format Preferences screen change to the formats common to the country that you chose.

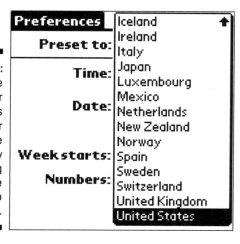

Figure 3-7: Use the number formats of your favorite country by choosing from the Preset To list.

Part I: Getting to Know Your PalmPilot

7. **If you wish to change an individual type of formatting, tap the triangle next to the example of that type.**

    A pull-down list of formatting choices appears. For example, if you choose the United States, the entry in the Time box says HH:MM am/pm, which means that all time entries on your PalmPilot appear the way that people write them in the United States, for example, 11:13 am. If you want the time to appear the way they display time in Italy — for example, 11.13 — choose the entry named HH.MM.

    The format that you tap appears in the Format Preferences screen, as shown in Figure 3-8.

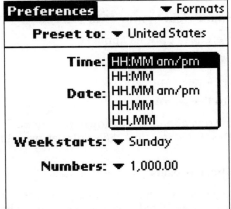

Figure 3-8: You can pick different types of time and number formats in the Format Preferences screen as well.

Changing your format preferences changes the way that numbers appear in all PalmPilot applications. If you want to use one format in one application and another format in a different application, you're out of luck. One format per customer, please.

Using the Security Application

If you keep lots of sensitive business data on your PalmPilot, it's wise to take advantage of the security features that are already built in. You can hide items that you want to protect from unauthorized eyes, and you can even assign a password to lock your PalmPilot from any unauthorized use.

Follow these steps to access the Security screen:

1. **Tap the Applications soft button.**

    The list of applications appears on your screen.

Chapter 3: Making Your PalmPilot Your Own

2. **Tap Security.**

    The Security screen appears, as shown in Figure 3-9.

Figure 3-9: Keep your secrets secret with the Security application.

To change the individual settings in the Security Preferences screen, read the following sections.

Setting your password

Although you can keep confidential information on either a desktop computer or a PalmPilot, very few people misplace their desktop computers in airports or restaurants the way they can misplace their PalmPilots. That makes password-protecting your PalmPilot data all the more important. Follow these steps to set a password:

1. **With the Security Preferences screen visible, tap Unassigned in the Password box.**

    The Password dialog box opens.

    If the word *Assigned* appears, you already have a password. If you want to delete your password, see the section "Deleting a forgotten password," later in this chapter.

2. **Enter the password that you want to set by using Graffiti (see Chapter 2 for more information about entering text).**

    The password that you enter appears in the Password dialog box, as shown in Figure 3-10. And don't forget to remember your password.

3. **Tap OK.**

    The Password dialog box opens again, asking you to verify your password.

Figure 3-10: Enter your password in the Password dialog box.

4. **Re-enter the password that you entered in Step 4.**

   The password that you enter appears again in the Password dialog box. By the way, did I mention that you should remember your password?

5. **Tap OK.**

   The Password dialog box closes, and the word *Assigned* appears in the Password box.

Deleting a forgotten password

It happens. You've been asked to supply 1,001 passwords for various systems, your PalmPilot is the 1,002nd, and you forgot your password. Of course, the easiest way to avoid this problem is simply to remember your password. But if you can't, you can delete the old password, as long as you can turn on the power and get to the Security application.

1. **With the Security screen visible, tap the Forgotten Password button.**

   The Delete Password dialog box opens, bearing a stern warning that all the items you've marked Private are removed until the next HotSync (see Figure 3-11).

2. **If you wish to proceed, tap Yes.**

   After a short pause, the word *Unassigned* appears in the Password box. You can then reassign a new password — just try not to forget it this time, okay? Geesh!

Chapter 3: Making Your PalmPilot Your Own   59

Figure 3-11:
Try not to forget your password; the Security program won't be amused.

If you've locked down your PalmPilot by tapping Turn Off & Lock Device in the Security application and then forgotten your password, you're cooked. You can only get back into your PalmPilot by performing a Hard Reset, which wipes out all the data on your PalmPilot (see Chapter 1 for more information on resetting your PalmPilot). You can recover all the items that you entered before your last HotSync by doing another HotSync. However, whatever you entered after the last HotSync but before you reset is gone for good. So, guess what you better do. . . .

Remember your darn password!

Okay, this is the last time, just in case I haven't said it enough in this section.

Hiding private items

It may not be *Saving Private Ryan,* but *Hiding Private Items* can be heroic stuff, too. The main reason to mark items private is so that you can hide them from the prying eyes of supervisors, paparazzi, and secret agents (or if you want to hide all the phone numbers of your Bond girls from Ms. Moneypenny — but I digress).

Follow these steps to hide private items:

1. **With the Security screen visible, tap the Hide button next to the words Private Records.**

   The Hide Records dialog box opens, telling you what happens when you hide records (see Figure 3-12).

Part I: Getting to Know Your PalmPilot

Figure 3-12:
You can hide your private items by tapping Hide in the Hide Records dialog box.

2. **Tap Hide.**

   The Hide Records dialog box closes, and the Security screen reappears. The word *Hide* is highlighted, and your private items are hidden, as they should be!

After you've hidden your private items, you may want to make them appear again later. Just follow the preceding steps, but tap Show rather than Hide. If you've assigned a password, PalmPilot makes you enter your password before revealing your private items. You can mark any item private by tapping the Details button and then tapping the Private check box.

Setting Up ShortCuts

One very cute feature in the PalmPilot world is the ShortCut. A ShortCut is really an automatic abbreviation. For example, if you write the words *New York* frequently, you may make a ShortCut named NY. Then, when you want to write New York, just enter the ShortCut symbol in Graffiti, which looks like a cursive, lowercase *L*, and enter the letters **NY**. The words *New York* appear automatically. For more about entering Graffiti ShortCuts, see Chapter 2.

ShortCuts can save you lots of tapping and scratching when you want to enter information. Personally, I like to use the time and date stamp ShortCuts to measure how long I've worked on projects, especially when I'm billing those projects by the hour. You can create or edit your own collection of ShortCuts in a jiffy.

To access the ShortCuts screen, follow these steps:

1. **Tap the Applications soft button.**

   The list of applications appears, showing icons for all the programs installed on your PalmPilot.

2. **Tap the Prefs icon.**

   The Preferences screen appears.

3. **Tap the word in the upper-right corner of the screen.**

   A pull-down list of Preferences options appears.

4. **Choose ShortCuts.**

   The ShortCuts screen appears, listing all your current ShortCuts.

Read the following sections to figure out how to add, change, or delete your ShortCuts.

Adding a new ShortCut

A collection of ShortCuts is already set up for your use when you first buy your PalmPilot. But to really get your money's worth out of ShortCuts, create some ShortCuts of your own. Adding a new ShortCut is this simple:

1. **With the ShortCuts screen visible, tap New.**

   The ShortCut Entry dialog box opens, as shown in Figure 3-13.

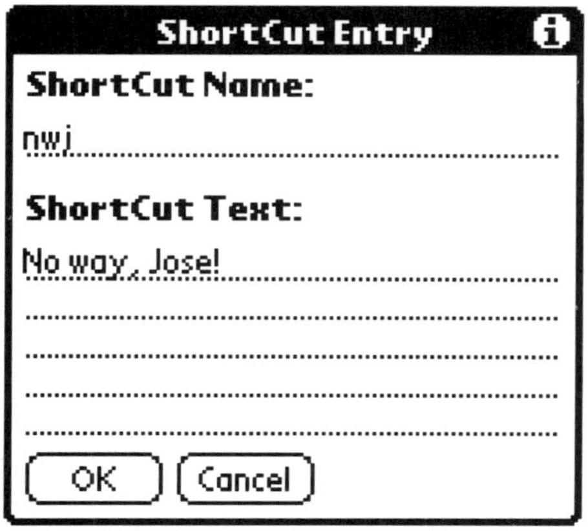

Figure 3-13: Enter the name of your ShortCut in the first line of the ShortCut Entry dialog box, and enter the text in the lower area.

2. **Use Graffiti to enter the ShortCut name that you want (see Chapter 2 for more information about entering text).**

   The text that you enter appears on the ShortCut Name line.

   You can also use the on-screen keyboard to enter your ShortCut name, but be sure that you can enter the characters that you want in Graffiti, because you can't use ShortCuts from the on-screen keyboard, only from Graffiti.

3. **Tap the first line of the ShortCut Text section.**

   An insertion point appears at the point that you tap.

4. **Enter the text of your ShortCut by using either the on-screen keyboard or Graffiti.**

   The text that you enter appears in the ShortCut Text section.

5. **Tap OK.**

   Your new ShortCut appears in the list of ShortCuts.

Don't use a period as the first character of your ShortCut name. For some reason, ShortCuts whose names start with a period (*Dot ShortCuts* to PalmPilot programmers) do nothing useful for you and me, but they can do nasty things, such as erase all your data or drain your batteries. Try to stick to names made up of letters and numbers when creating your ShortCuts. Also, ShortCut names can't contain spaces.

Editing a ShortCut

At some point, you may want to change either the name or the contents of a ShortCut.

Follow these steps to edit a ShortCut:

1. **Tap the name of the ShortCut that you want to edit.**

   The ShortCut that you tap is highlighted to show that you've selected it, as shown in Figure 3-14.

2. **Tap Edit.**

   The ShortCut Entry dialog box opens.

3. **Select the part of the ShortCut that you want to replace.**

   The text that you select is highlighted to show that you've selected it.

Chapter 3: Making Your PalmPilot Your Own 63

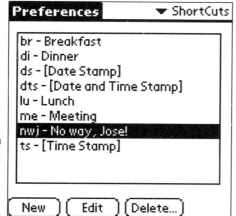

Figure 3-14: Choose a ShortCut to edit.

4. **Enter the new text by using either the on-screen keyboard or Graffiti (see Chapter 2 for more about entering text).**

   The text that you enter replaces the text that you selected.

5. **Tap OK.**

   The ShortCut Entry dialog box closes.

Now your revised ShortCut is ready to use at the drop of a stylus.

Deleting a ShortCut

If you know how to edit a ShortCut, you know how to delete a ShortCut. Just follow the same steps that I describe in the section "Editing a ShortCut," earlier in the chapter, but tap the word Delete rather than Edit. Zap! Your ShortCut is long gone.

Hacking Up Your PalmPilot

No, this isn't the latest sequel to *Halloween*. In the PalmPilot universe, *hacks* are applications that you can install on your PalmPilot to add features or to make your PalmPilot behave differently than a normal PalmPilot. I'm not getting into hacks in any great degree here, but I do want you to know that they exist. PalmPilots are catching on in the corporate world in a big way, and some big outfits customize their PalmPilots to suit the work they expect people to do. That means that you may have a company-issue PalmPilot with hacks installed that make it behave in a totally different way than the way I describe in this book.

You can install hacks that change the functions of your buttons, change the way your screen looks, change the things you can do with cut and paste, and lots more. Programmers are coming up with new PalmPilot hacks all the time. Most hacks are useful, such as AppHack, a program that enables you to assign up to six different programs to each of the four hard buttons. Other hacks are less useful, such as BackHack, which reverses the spelling of all text on your PalmPilot, so the word *Record* comes out *droceR*. I can't begin to explain why someone would want a program to do that, but rest assured, one does.

One of the most important hacks is called HackMaster, the hack that manages other hacks (Geesh, can this get any more complicated?). Many hacks require you to install HackMaster before installing other hacks. If you're adventurous, check out the PalmPilot-related Web sites listed in Appendix A, and download some hacks to install to your PalmPilot. When I say adventurous, I mean that you should be ready to deal with some problems, because some hacks are very experimental. But, fortunately, they're easy to uninstall.

Chapter 4
Saving Time with PalmPilot Timesavers

In This Chapter
▶ Adding several items to a single category
▶ Creating new items by just writing
▶ Reassigning a hard button to launch your favorite program
▶ Beaming your business card with one (long) press of a button
▶ Dragging and dropping to change appointment times

Using your PalmPilot is pretty easy to begin with, and if you know the ropes, you can save steps here and there and really whiz through your work by using the following tips. You may even become a member of the elite ranks of PalmPilot power users. Don't worry — you don't have to buy a uniform or learn a secret handshake, but just be ready for plenty of *esprit de corps*.

I'm going to focus on a handful of features that can make you a speedier PalmPilot user without making you learn anything difficult. I also try to stick to tricks that are part of the PalmPilot operating system and don't require any add-on programs. I deal with accessories and add-on software in Chapters 17 and 18. I've organized all these timesavers into categories so that you can easily find what you need. Enjoy!

General Timesavers

General timesavers are those that you can do at any time or in any application.

Using ShortCuts

The very best timesavers are cleverly named *ShortCuts*. You can expand short abbreviations into words and phrases of up to 45 letters (including spaces) by entering the Graffiti ShortCut symbol, which looks like a cursive letter *L*, and then the abbreviation. For more on the Graffiti ShortCut symbol, see Chapter 2.

When you first buy your PalmPilot, several ShortCuts are already installed. To find out how to create your own ShortCuts, see Chapter 3.

Beaming a business card quickly

If you have a Palm III and you've set up your business card for beaming, just hold down the Address Book button for about two seconds. The Beam dialog box opens and your PalmPilot searches for a nearby PalmPilot ready to receive your card. For more on beaming, see Chapter 9.

Using your finger instead of the stylus

You can't do anything with a stylus that you can't do with your finger. The PalmPilot screen is touch sensitive, so your finger can serve as a perfectly good stylus at times. The only reason for a stylus is that many PalmPilot programs contain buttons that are too small to tap with your finger (unless you have very small fingers). A gentle tap with a fingernail can sometimes do just as well as a stylus tap. Be gentle, though; you don't want to scratch the screen.

Checking the time

If you tap the Date tab at the top of the Date Book display, the current time pops up for a few seconds.

If you use a Palm III, the current time is always displayed at the top of the applications list when you tap the Applications soft button.

If you want to enter the current time into a memo, you can call on the Time Stamp ShortCut. Just enter the Graffiti ShortCut symbol, which looks like a cursive, lowercase *L*, and then enter TS. I like to use the Time Stamp as a primitive way to "punch in" when I'm trying to measure time spent on a job. I create a memo, enter a Time Stamp when I begin, and then enter another Time Stamp into the memo when I'm finished.

Reassigning a hard button to your favorite program

If you use another program more often than one of the standard PalmPilot applications, you can reassign one of the four application hard buttons to start that program. Many people don't use the Memo Pad or To Do List nearly as much as the Date Book or Address Book, so they reassign the Memo Pad button to make it run another program. My girlfriend didn't find the Memo Pad especially useful, so she reassigned the Memo Pad button to make it run the game Boggle. You can also get a hack called AppHack that enables you to launch up to 24 different programs from the hard buttons by pressing two buttons at once (for more on hacks, see Chapter 3). I still just go to the Applications screen to start my programs, but you can take your pick.

Application Timesavers

These timesavers apply directly to the four main applications that come with your PalmPilot. They can save you loads of time.

Pressing hard buttons to change categories

When you first press the Memo hard button, you see all your memos. If you press the Memo button a second time, the memos in the Business category appear. Each time you press the Memo button again, you see a different category until you've cycled back around to the All category. All four standard application hard buttons behave the same way; push the button several times to run through several different categories. The Date Book button is slightly different in that it shows you different views of your Date Book each time — day, then week, then month. Of course, if you don't have any items filed in a particular category, your PalmPilot conveniently skips that category.

Viewing different dates by pressing buttons

When you want to check your schedule in a jiffy, remember that you can get to any date by pressing buttons, so you don't need to dig for your stylus. Just press the Date Book button once to see the daily view, twice for the weekly view, or three times for the monthly view. Once you see the view you want, press the up or down scroll buttons to move to the next day, week, or month. By cleverly combining button clicks, you can see your schedule for any day on the calendar. Granted, you may find it easier sometimes to whip out the stylus and pick the date you want, but when your hands are full, the stylus can be one too many things to hold.

Uncluttering your Date Book

The Date Book shows a blank for every hour of your workday. That can make your schedule look cluttered and hard to read. If you set up your Date Book preferences to have your day start and end at the same time, the display shows only entries for the times at which you've scheduled appointments; the rest of the screen will be blank (see Figure 4-1).

Figure 4-1: If you set the beginning and end of your workday to the same time, your schedule becomes easier to read.

Drag and drop to change appointment times

If you press the Date Book hard button twice, you see the weekly view of your Address Book. The weekly view shows you a collection of bars representing your appointments for the week. If you want to change the scheduled time of an appointment, just drag the bar representing that appointment to the time you prefer (see Figure 4-2). Sad to say, you can't drag an appointment from one week to another.

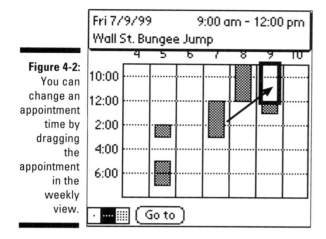

Figure 4-2: You can change an appointment time by dragging the appointment in the weekly view.

Cut, copy, and paste

Windows and Macintosh users have been cutting, copying, and pasting text for years. You can do the same trick with your PalmPilot. Just select some text by drawing an imaginary line through the text with your stylus, and then tap the Menu soft button and choose Edit⇨Cut or Edit⇨Copy. Cutting makes the text you select disappear, but don't worry — it's not gone forever. The text goes to a place called the *clipboard*. The same thing happens when you choose Copy, only the original text stays put and a copy of that text goes to the clipboard. To make the text reappear in another place, just tap where you want to place the text and choose Edit⇨Paste. Even if you turn off your PalmPilot, the last text you put on the clipboard stays on the clipboard, so you may find that you can paste text that you copied weeks or months ago. Be aware, however, that every time you cut or copy text, that text replaces whatever text was previously on the clipboard.

Adding multiple items to a category

If you want to add a series of new items to a single category, simply display that category and start creating items. Whatever category you display before creating new items becomes the category assigned to the new items. For example, if I want to make a list of things I need to do at PC Expo, I press the To Do List hard button several times until my PC Expo category appears (provided that I created a PC Expo category), and then I just start adding items. Every new item I create while in a certain category turns up in that category, so I can see everything in the category as I add items.

Graffiti Timesavers

If you've really taken to Graffiti, then you may appreciate these quick timesavers.

Start writing to create new items

If you want to add a new item to any standard PalmPilot application except for the Address Book, press the hard button for that application and start entering text in the Graffiti area. This is one trick that works only if you use Graffiti. When the PalmPilot senses that you're entering Graffiti, it naturally does the right thing — it opens a new item in which to store the new text.

Opening Graffiti Help with a single stroke

You can open Graffiti Help by drawing a line with your stylus from the Graffiti writing area to the top of the display. If you've already earned your black belt in Graffiti, you can assign that stroke to perform one of four other tasks: turn on the backlight, display the on-screen keyboard, beam the current item to another PalmPilot, or turn off and lock your PalmPilot. To reassign the upstroke command, tap the Applications soft button, tap Prefs, choose Buttons from the pull-down menu in the upper-right corner, and then tap Pen; the Pen dialog box appears (see Figure 4-3). For more about customizing the functions of your PalmPilot, see Chapter 3.

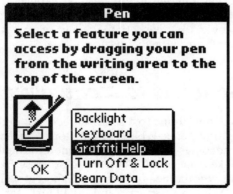

Figure 4-3: Customize what happens when you use the Graffiti upstroke.

Part II
Getting Down to Business

The 5th Wave   By Rich Tennant

"Oh wait – this says, 'Lunch Ed from Marketing', not 'Lynch', 'Lunch'."

In this part . . .

The programs that come with your PalmPilot can do a lot if you know all the options. You can create and manage appointments, addresses, tasks, and memos by following the steps in this part. You also find out how to beam data to other PalmPilots with just the touch of a button.

Chapter 5
Names and Addresses in a ZIP

In This Chapter
- Adding, finding, and deleting new names
- Marking your business card
- Editing an address record
- Attaching and deleting notes
- Setting Address Book preferences
- Setting up custom fields

I find it incredibly handy to have all the names and addresses I need in electronic form rather than on paper. I love being able to find names in a flash, change details, and keep track of bits and pieces of information about everyone in my social and professional life.

You'd get pretty uncomfortable if you had to walk around with a desktop computer stuffed into your pocket or purse — and you'd look pretty funny, too. Just because I want you to be comfortable (and because I *know* you're good-looking), I'm going to show you how to do all your address keeping on the PalmPilot, because your PalmPilot can always be with you.

Accessing Your Address Book

To call up the Address Book on your PalmPilot, just press the Address Book hard button (the second button from the left at the bottom of your PalmPilot; see Figure 5-1), which calls up your Address List. My sample Address List is shown in Figure 5-2. Then read the rest of the chapter.

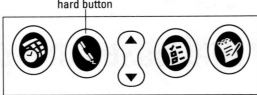

Figure 5-1: The Address Book hard button.

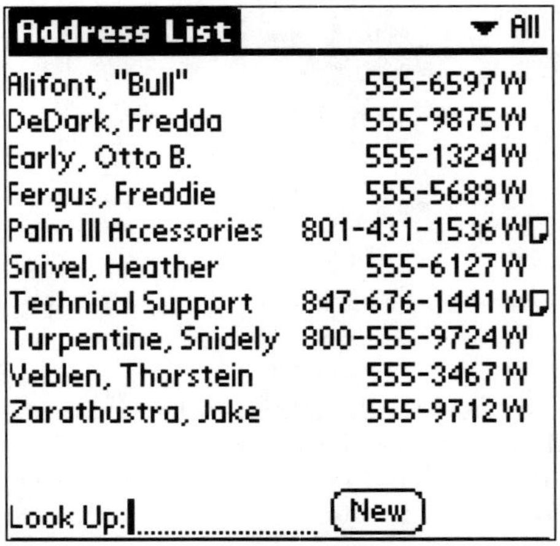

```
Address List              ▼ All
Alifont, "Bull"         555-6597 W
DeDark, Fredda          555-9875 W
Early, Otto B.          555-1324 W
Fergus, Freddie         555-5689 W
Palm III Accessories  801-431-1536 WD
Snivel, Heather         555-6127 W
Technical Support     847-676-1441 WD
Turpentine, Snidely   800-555-9724 W
Veblen, Thorstein       555-3467 W
Zarathustra, Jake       555-9712 W

Look Up:                   ( New )
```

Figure 5-2: Your address list shows all the names that you've collected.

Putting Names into Your PalmPilot

I know more than a few people who enter and make changes to their Address List on a desktop computer, and then transfer the whole shebang to their PalmPilot just to look up names while they're traveling. That's okay. (Actually, most of those folks have employees who enter the information for them; that's the easiest method of all, but most of us don't have that luxury.) See Chapter 12 for more about keeping up your Address List in the PalmPilot desktop program. But the fact is that you can enter all the information you need right on the PalmPilot, no matter where you are.

Adding a new name

Many people have relied on a Little Black Book since even before Casanova. The paper kind served well until the computer came along and enabled you to find one name out of a list of thousands faster than you can say "What's-his-name." Speed isn't the only advantage of electronic address lists; the PalmPilot looks up a name from your list and plugs that name into an item in your To Do List, Memo Pad, or Date Book to save you the trouble of retyping. But before you can look up a name, you need to add the name to your Address Book.

Use these steps to store a name in your Address Book:

1. **With the Address List visible, tap the New button at the bottom of the Address List.**

    The Address Edit screen appears.

2. **Tap anywhere on the Last Name line.**

    The words *Last Name* become highlighted to show that you've selected the Last Name line, as shown in Figure 5-3.

Figure 5-3: The name of the line that you tap is highlighted to show where you're working.

3. **Enter the last name of the person that you're adding by using Graffiti or the on-screen keyboard (see Chapter 2 for more on entering text).**

    The letters that you enter appear on the Last Name line.

4. **Follow Steps 2 and 3 to enter information on the First Name, Title, and Company lines.**

    The text that you enter appears on the lines you choose.

Part II: Getting Down to Business

5. **Tap anywhere on the Work line.**

   The word becomes highlighted to show that you've selected it.

6. **Enter the person's work telephone number.**

7. **Follow Steps 5 and 6 to enter the person's home phone number.**

8. **If you want to enter a type of phone number that isn't shown, tap Other.**

   A list appears, showing the different types of phone numbers that you can enter, including pager and mobile numbers.

9. **Tap the name of the phone number type that you want to enter, such as Mobile.**

   The type you choose replaces the word *Other,* as you see in Figure 5-4.

Figure 5-4: Choose the type of phone number that you want to enter if it's not shown.

10. **Enter the phone number in the Graffiti number area.**

    The text that you enter appears on the new line.

11. **If you want to enter your contact's mailing address, press the scroll-down hard button at the bottom center of the PalmPilot.**

    The lower half of the contact form appears, enabling you to enter mailing address information, as shown in Figure 5-5.

12. **Enter mailing address information on the appropriate lines just as you did in the preceding steps.**

    The information that you enter appears on the appropriate lines.

Chapter 5: Names and Addresses in a ZIP

Figure 5-5:
Wait! You'll find more at the bottom of the form.

13. **When you finish entering the information, click Done at the bottom of the Address Edit screen.**

    The Address Edit screen disappears, and the Address List reappears.

    Now you're ready to find anyone in your personal "Who's Who" faster than you can say "Who?"

You probably noticed the downward-pointing triangle next to each phone number line. Whenever you see that character on a PalmPilot screen, that means that a pull-down list is hiding behind that button where you can choose other options simply by tapping the triangle, and then tapping your choice. Although every address record contains three phone number lines and an e-mail line, you can use any of the phone number lines to store any of seven different types of phone number or an e-mail address. For example, if you want to save one person's work number and pager number, but not his home number, tap the triangle next to Home and pick Pager from the list. Now the number you enter will be shown as a Pager number.

If you have a list of names and addresses in another contact program on a desktop or laptop computer, you can enter them in the desktop program as a list and then HotSync the whole bunch to your PalmPilot. As you can see, entering names and addresses in the PalmPilot is easy, but when you have a large collection of names, you'll save time by letting your computers take care of the job. For more about installing and operating the desktop programs for either Windows or Macintosh, see Chapters 11 and 12.

What's in a name? Editing an address record

It seems that some people change their addresses more often than they change their socks. You can't very well tell them to stop moving, but you can keep up with their latest addresses by editing their address records in your PalmPilot. You may want to say something to them about their socks, though.

These steps help you to change an entry in your Address Book:

1. **With the Address List visible, enter the first few letters of the last name that you want to edit in the Graffiti box.**

    The letters that you enter appear on the Look Up line at the bottom of the display. Of course, if the name you're looking for is visible to start with, you don't have to look it up.

2. **Tap the name of the person whose record you want to edit.**

    The Address View screen (as shown in Figure 5-6) appears, showing details about the contact that you chose.

Figure 5-6: Address View shows you what's already in your Address Book.

```
┌─────────────────────────────────┐
│ Address View           Unfiled  │
│ Magnolia Thunderblossom         │
│ President                       │
│ Clemtexx                        │
│                                 │
│ Work:      555-3200             │
│                                 │
│ Planning to purchase 9000 lbs   │
│ of french fries next month.     │
│                                 │
│ ( Done ) ( Edit ) ( New )       │
└─────────────────────────────────┘
```

3. **Tap Edit at the bottom of the display.**

    The Address Edit screen appears.

4. **Enter new information the same way you did when you first created the address record (see "Adding a new name" earlier in this chapter).**

    New information appears on the appropriate lines of the screen.

5. **If you want to replace existing information, select the text that you want to replace by drawing a horizontal line through it.**

   The text is highlighted.

6. **Enter new text in the Graffiti box at the bottom of the display.**

   As in your favorite word processor, the text that you enter replaces the text that you selected. For more on entering text, see Chapter 2.

7. **When you've made all the changes that you want to make, tap Done.**

   The Address Edit screen disappears and the Address List screen reappears.

PalmPilot saves all your changes as soon as you tap Done. If you want to change the person's address or other details back, you have to go through the whole edit process again. In other words, you don't have an Undo feature to put things back the way they were.

Attaching a note to an address record

You want to know lots of things about a person — where she likes to go, what he said to you the last time you spoke to him, how much she owes you, whatever. You can attach all sorts of information to a person's address record in the form of a note.

To attach a note to an address, follow these steps:

1. **With the Address List visible, tap the name of the person to whose record you want to add a note.**

   The Address View screen appears, showing details about the contact that you chose.

2. **Tap the Menu soft button at the bottom of the display.**

   The menu bar appears at the top of the display, as shown in Figure 5-7.

3. **Choose Record⇨Attach Note.**

   A blank note screen appears.

4. **Enter the note text in the Graffiti box at the bottom of the display, or use the on-screen keyboard.**

   The text that you enter appears, as shown in Figure 5-8.

5. **Tap Done at the bottom of the Note screen.**

   The Note screen disappears, and the Address View screen reappears.

80 Part II: Getting Down to Business

Figure 5-7:
You can order off the Menu to create a note.

Figure 5-8:
Enter plain old text in the Note screen.

6. Tap Done again.

The Address View screen disappears, and the Address List reappears.

If you enter information in a note and want to find it again, you can use the PalmPilot Find tool to search all the data on your PalmPilot. For example, if you added a note to someone's record that says "drives a Studebaker," you can tap the Find soft button at the bottom-right corner of the screen and then enter "Studebaker" to find the person who drives one.

Marking your business card

Now that everybody who's anybody has a PalmPilot (after all, you have one and I have one, and that's all that matters to me), we can take advantage of the PalmPilot infrared port to exchange our business cards. Before you beam your business card to anyone, you need to enter an address record containing your own name and contact information, as I describe in "Adding a new name" earlier in this chapter.

An *infrared (IR) port* is standard equipment on your Palm III and optional on the PalmPilot Professional. Infrared lets you *beam* information from one PalmPilot to another. (*Beaming* is when you point two PalmPilots at each other and send data across the air using an invisible beam of light. See Chapter 9 for more on beaming.) Someday, you'll be able to change the channels on your TV with PalmPilot infrared, but for now, you can beam your business card (as well as other addresses, To Do items, memos, and appointments) to other Palm III users.

When I send my business card to you via PalmPilot, what I'm really doing is beaming a name from my PalmPilot Address Book to the Address Book on your PalmPilot. The name I send you just happens to be my own. Here's how to set up your PalmPilot to send your business card:

 1. **With the Address List visible, enter the first few letters of your last name in the Graffiti box.**

    The letters that you enter appear on the Look Up line at the bottom of the display.

 2. **Tap your name in the Address List.**

    The Address View screen appears, showing details about your contact record.

 3. **Tap the Menu soft button at the bottom of the display.**

    The menu bar appears at the top of the display.

 4. **Choose Record⇨Select Business Card.**

    The Select Business Card dialog box opens, as shown in Figure 5-9.

 5. **Tap Yes at the bottom of the Select Business Card dialog box to close it.**

    A small icon that looks like a file card appears at the top of the Address View screen.

 6. **Tap Done at the bottom of the display.**

    The Address View screen disappears, and the Address List reappears.

Figure 5-9:
Mark your own name to serve as your business card.

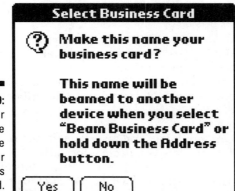

You don't absolutely have to mark a business card if you don't plan to use this feature. If you use the beaming feature a lot, you'll save time if you mark your business card because you won't have to spend time looking up your own name when you want to send a card. As I write this, I have never beamed a business card from my PalmPilot, but I've marked my name anyway. If deep space aliens show up like they do in the movie *Independence Day*, I'll be ready to beam them my friendly greetings (for all the good it'll do — they all use Macs).

Using the Names You've Entered

If you're one of those lucky folks who has an assistant to enter your PalmPilot data so that all you do is use what's been entered, the rest of this chapter is for you. After you know how to find the stuff you've collected, you're in business!

Finding Mr. Right (or whoever)

If you took the time to enter a bunch of names into your PalmPilot, I'd guess that you want to find the names again. Call me crazy, but that's what I thought.

Here's the quickest way to find a name in your Address Book:

1. **With the Address List visible, enter the first few letters of the last name that you want to find in the Graffiti box.**

    The letters that you enter appear on the Look Up line at the bottom of the display, as shown in Figure 5-10.

Chapter 5: Names and Addresses in a ZIP 83

Figure 5-10:
Your PalmPilot figures out who you're looking for when you enter the first few letters of the last name.

If you don't like messing with Graffiti, you can press the hard scroll-down button on the PalmPilot to scroll through your address list. The Address Book can hold thousands of names, so if your list is long, scrolling can be laborious.

 2. **Tap the name of the person whose record you want to view.**

    The Address View screen appears, showing details about the contact you chose.

 3. **When you're finished, tap Done at the bottom of the display.**

    The Address View screen disappears, and the Address List reappears.

If you want to make finding addresses easier, you can assign categories to names on your Address List. Then when you press the Address Book button several times, you cycle through the different address categories until you see the category that you want to use. For example, you can assign the category Business to some names and the category Personal to other names. When you press the Address Book button the first time, you see all the names in your collection. The second time you press it, you see the names assigned to the Business category, and the third time, you see the names assigned to the Personal category, and so on. You may be completely happy keeping all your names uncategorized. That's fine, too.

To assign a category to any name in your list, open the record for editing, as I describe in "What's in a name? Editing an address record" earlier in this chapter, and then pick the category you want to assign to your contact in the upper-right corner of the form. You can manage Address Book categories in exactly the same way you manage categories of To Do items. See Chapter 6 for more about managing To Do item categories.

Part II: Getting Down to Business

The Quicklist category is preset in the Address Book to make room for addresses you use frequently and need to find in a hurry. You can use it for the most important people in your life.

Deleting a name

The main reason to add a name to your Address Book is to help you remember important things about a person. However, sometimes you'd rather forget some people in your list. I won't mention any names.

To delete an unwanted name from your Address Book, follow these steps:

1. **With the Address List visible, enter the first few letters of the last name that you want to delete in the Graffiti box.**

    The letters you enter appear on the Look Up line at the bottom of the display.

2. **Tap the name of the person whose record you want to delete.**

    The Address View screen appears, showing details about the contact you chose.

3. **Tap the Menu soft button at the bottom of the display.**

    The menu bar appears at the top of the display.

4. **Choose Record➪Delete Address.**

    The Delete Address dialog box opens, as shown in Figure 5-11. The dialog box asks if you want to archive the item. For more about archived items, see Chapter 12.

Figure 5-11: Deleting the names of those who no longer interest you is easy.

5. **Tap OK.**

    The Address List reappears, minus one name.

Chapter 5: Names and Addresses in a ZIP 85

If you delete a name in a fit of pique and then wish you could bring it back, all is not entirely lost. If you haven't used HotSync between the time you deleted the name and the time you want it back, you can find the name in the archive on your desktop computer. You can make a slight change in the address information and then resynchronize to make the offending name a part of your list again. Then you can kiss and make up. I discuss synchronization in Chapter 11 and archiving in Chapter 12. Fractured friendships are another issue altogether.

Deleting a note from an address record

Sometimes the note you've attached to someone's address becomes out of date. You can change the contents of the note by using the same steps that you used to create the note, or you can just delete the entire note.

Here's how to delete a note attached to an address:

1. **With the Address List visible, tap the name of the person from whose record you want to delete a note.**

   The Address View screen appears, showing details about the contact you chose.

2. **Tap the Menu soft button at the bottom of the display.**

   The menu bar appears at the top of the display.

3. **Choose Record➪Delete Note, as shown in Figure 5-12.**

   The Delete Note dialog box opens.

Figure 5-12: You can delete a note from a record, too.

Part II: Getting Down to Business

4. **Tap Yes at the bottom of the Delete Note dialog box.**

   The Delete Note dialog box closes, and the Address View screen reappears.

5. **Tap Done at the bottom of the Address View screen.**

   The Address View screen disappears, and the Address List reappears.

Zap! Your note is gone for good. Well, not really for good; see Chapter 12 for details about how to recover an address from your archive.

Setting Address Book preferences

If you don't like the way the Address Book looks when it first opens, you can change its appearance . . . a little. I think the Address Book is just fine as it is, but if you simply must rearrange your list, here's how:

1. **With the Address List visible, tap the Menu soft button at the bottom of the display.**

   The menu bar appears at the top of the display.

2. **Choose Options⇨Preferences.**

   The Address Book Preferences dialog box opens, as shown in Figure 5-13.

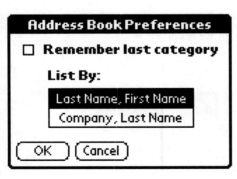

Figure 5-13: You can express your preferences through the Address Book Preferences dialog box.

3. **From the List By box, choose either Last Name, First Name or Company, Last Name.**

   The choice that you make is highlighted.

4. **Tap the Remember Last Category box if you normally want your Address Book to open to the last category you used.**

   If you don't check the Remember Last Category box, your Address Book always opens to show you all names. I think it's better to leave the box unchecked, but that's a matter of personal preference.

Setting up custom fields

Sometimes you need to keep track of something about the people you know that doesn't already have a line (or field) in the Address List. For example, if your job involves selling merchandise to retail stores, your Address Book probably contains the names of all the store buyers to whom you sell. The Address Book includes four lines at the end of the Address Edit screen that you can rename to fit your needs. These four lines are called *custom fields*. You may want to set up one custom field to keep track of which type of merchandise each buyer buys, such as housewares, appliances, shoes, and so on. You can rename one of the custom fields "Specialty" to show each buyer's area of interest.

To set up your custom fields, follow these steps:

1. **With the Address List visible, tap the Menu soft button at the bottom of the display.**

   The menu bar appears at the top of the display.

2. **Choose Options⇨Rename Custom Fields.**

   The Rename Custom Fields dialog box opens, as shown in Figure 5-14.

Figure 5-14: Just replace the name Custom 1 with the field name that you want.

3. **Select the field that you want to rename.**

   The text that you select is highlighted.

4. **Enter the name that you want for the field with either the on-screen keyboard or Graffiti (see Chapter 2 for more about entering text).**

   The text that you enter appears as the new field name.

5. **Rename the other custom fields by following Steps 3 and 4.**

   The text that you enter appears as the new field name.

6. **When you've renamed all the fields that you want to rename, click OK.**

   The Rename Custom Fields dialog box closes, and the Address List reappears.

You don't absolutely have to rename custom fields to use them. You can just enter information in the fields and remember that the field named "Custom 1" contains a certain type of entry. Renaming the custom fields just makes them a little more useful and easier to understand. When you rename a custom field, the field name is changed in all address records.

Chapter 6
To Do's That YOU Do!

In This Chapter
- ▶ Creating To Do's
- ▶ Entering To Do details
- ▶ Attaching and deleting To Do notes
- ▶ Changing and deleting To Do's
- ▶ Marking the To Do's you've done
- ▶ Beaming To Do's
- ▶ Viewing items by category
- ▶ Setting To Do preferences

Who doesn't have a zillion things to do these days? Just keeping track of the tasks you need to take care of is a full-time job. The only thing worse than keeping track of your tasks is actually doing all those things. And even if you use a computer for many of your daily tasks, you probably can't stay chained to the desk all day; you need to move around, while keeping track of all the things you did in all the places you went.

The To Do List on your PalmPilot can help you keep a handle on all those little errands and projects that take up all your time. You can add a task when you think of it, rather than waiting to get back to your computer. By the time I get back to my desk, I usually forget that terribly important detail that I need to take care of.

I assume in this chapter that you're using your PalmPilot exactly the way it comes out of the box. That's what most people do, but that's not your only choice. A couple of other chapters in this book tell you how to find other programs to replace the To Do List and how to install them. If you've replaced your To Do List with some other program, such as To Do Plus, many of the instructions in this chapter won't work for you. I don't want to discourage you from trying other programs — lots of good ones exist — but, unfortunately, I can't cover all the third-party software out there for the PalmPilot.

Part II: Getting Down to Business

Just push the To Do List hard button (it's the second one from the right at the bottom of your PalmPilot — see Figure 6-1) to call up your To Do List. Then do whatever you want to do with your To Do's!

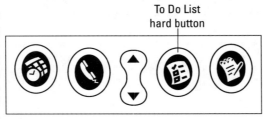

Figure 6-1: Press the To Do List button to bring up your list of To Do's.

Adding New To Do's

Adding items to your To Do List is as easy as you want to make it. If you want to keep track of short lists of simple projects, you can go a long way with the tools that come with the PalmPilot. If your planning process involves long lists of elaborate plans and projects and goes beyond the ability of the PalmPilot To Do List, you may need some extra help in the form of extra software or a daily download from your desktop computer. You can always rely on a desktop program such as ACT! or Goldmine to do all the heavy lifting, and you can just HotSync your PalmPilot to your desktop every day to keep a handy portable copy of your information. For more about using your PalmPilot with third-party software, see Part III.

Creating a To Do item

You can only take advantage of the powers of your To Do List if you've entered the To Do's that you have to do. No voodoo is involved with To Do — just press a button, tap with a stylus, and you're in business.

Here's how to add a new item to your To Do List:

1. **With your To Do List open, tap New at the bottom of the To Do List.**

   A new blank line appears in the To Do List.

2. **Enter the name of your task with either the on-screen keyboard or Graffiti (see Chapter 2 for more about entering text).**

   The name of the task you enter appears on the new line (see Figure 6-2).

Chapter 6: To Do's That YOU Do!

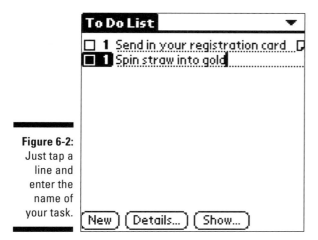

Figure 6-2:
Just tap a line and enter the name of your task.

3. **Tap any blank area of the screen or press the Scroll Down button.**

   The highlighting next to your new item disappears.

   Ta-da! A new task to call your very own.

Of course, you can use an even simpler way to enter a new To Do: Press the To Do List button and enter the name of your task with either the on-screen keyboard or Graffiti (see Chapter 2 for more about entering text). Your PalmPilot automatically creates a new To Do with the name you enter.

Entering details for a To Do item

You may not be satisfied with a To Do List that only keeps track of the names of your tasks. Knowing what a productive, demanding person you are (or could be if you really wanted to be), your To Do List enables you to assign priorities, categories, and due dates to each task.

To add details to your tasks, follow these steps:

1. **With your To Do List open, tap the name of the task to which you want to add details.**

   Highlighting appears next to the name of the task you chose.

2. **Tap Details at the bottom of the display.**

   The To Do Item Details dialog box opens.

3. **To set the priority of your item, tap one of the numbers (1 through 5) next to the word Priority.**

   The number you tap is highlighted.

92   Part II: Getting Down to Business

If the only detail you wanted to change about your task is the priority, you can simply tap the priority number in the To Do List and pick the priority number from the drop-down list.

 4. **To assign a category to your task, tap the triangle next to the word Category.**

    A list of available categories appears. The option of assigning categories helps you organize your To Do list, but you don't have to assign a category to a task. I explain how to use categories in "Viewing Items by Category" later in this chapter.

 5. **Tap the name of the category you want to assign to your task.**

    The list disappears, and the name of the category you chose appears.

 6. **To assign a due date to your task, tap the triangle next to the words Due Date.**

    A list appears, giving you these choices: Today, Tomorrow, One Week Later, No Date, and Choose Date (see Figure 6-3).

Figure 6-3:
Pick the due date for your To Do in the To Do Item Details dialog box.

 7. **Tap the name of the due date that you want for your task.**

    The list disappears, and the date you chose appears, unless you tapped Choose Date. Tapping Choose Date opens the Due Date screen, which looks like a calendar (see Figure 6-4).

 8. **If you tapped Choose Date, tap the desired Due Date for your task on the calendar in the Due Date screen.**

    The Due Date screen disappears, and the date you chose appears in the To Do Item Details dialog box.

 9. **If you wish to mark your entry Private, tap the check box next to the word Private.**

    A check appears in the check box to show that the task is private.

Private entries normally appear with your other entries, but you can also hide your private entries. Just tap the Applications soft button to call up your applications list, choose Security, and tap the word *Hide*. For more about privacy and passwords, see Chapter 3.

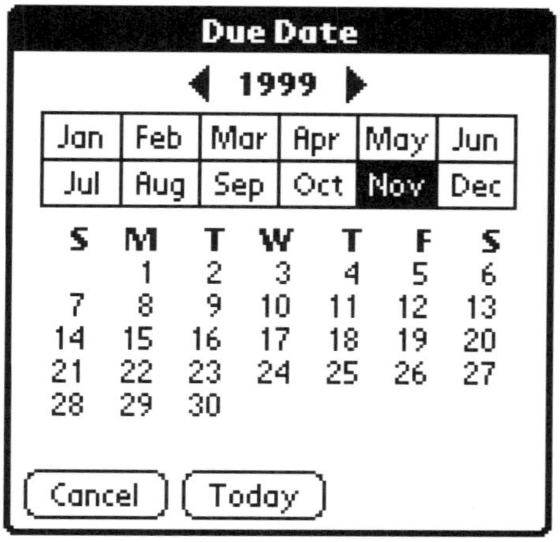

Figure 6-4: You can choose a date from the calendar, if you like.

10. **Tap OK.**

    The To Do Item Details dialog box closes, and your To Do List reappears with the changes you made visible on the screen.

You may have noticed when you were creating a new task that the Details button was available on the screen the whole time. If you want to add all sorts of details while you're adding a new task, nothing can stop you. However, if you're in a hurry and just want to enter the task quickly, you can enter just the name of the task and then add details later.

Attaching notes to items

The popular book by Robert Fulghum tells us that we learn everything we need to know in kindergarten. That's okay, I guess, but if you didn't get past kindergarten, don't mention it in your next job interview.

In the same way, many tasks need a bit more explanation than a quick subject line can describe. So, you may need to add a note to your task if you need to keep track of a detailed explanation along with a task.

Here's how to add a note to a To Do item:

1. **With your To Do List open, tap the name of the task to which you want to add a note.**

    The check box to the left of the item is highlighted to show which task you've selected.

2. **Tap Details at the bottom of the To Do List.**

    The To Do Item Details dialog box opens.

94   Part II: Getting Down to Business

3. **Tap Note at the bottom of the To Do Item Details dialog box.**

   A blank Note screen appears.

4. **Enter text with either the on-screen keyboard or Graffiti (see Chapter 2 for more about entering text).**

   The text you entered appears (see Figure 6-5).

5. **Tap Done at the bottom of the Note screen.**

   The Note screen disappears and your To Do List reappears. A small square icon appears to the right of the item you chose to show that a note is attached. If you want to view a note attached to a To Do, just click the note icon.

Figure 6-5:
If you have more detailed instructions about your task, add a note.

The Note screen also includes a Delete button that lets you delete a note as you read the note. I discuss another way to delete notes attached to To Do items in the section "Deleting a note" later in this chapter, but deleting a note from the Note screen is as good a method as any.

If you have a PalmPilot Professional, the Note screen also features a pair of font adjustment buttons. Each button contains a different size of the letter *A;* tap the type of text you want displayed when you view your note.

If you've created a note in the PalmPilot Memo List, or if you've attached a note to an entry in your Address Book, you'll find the general idea of creating notes stays the same throughout your PalmPilot. Unfortunately, notes attached to different types of PalmPilot items don't have anything to do with each other. For example, you can't move a note from the Memo List to the To Do List, or from the To Do List to the Address Book. Not now, at least; maybe in the future.

Viewing Items by Category

To Do items always belong to a category of one type or another. If you don't assign a category yourself, your PalmPilot automatically assigns the category Unfiled. You can see the name of the category you're viewing in the upper-right corner of the screen. When you first press the To Do List button, the word in the corner is All, which means that you're viewing all your tasks, regardless of category. You can change your view to a different category in two ways — the short way and the even shorter way. (Geesh, they make these things easy to use!) I start with the short way:

1. **With your To Do List open, tap the name of the category in the upper-right corner of the screen.**

   The list of available categories appears. The first time you use your PalmPilot, the list has four categories: All, Business, Personal, and Unfiled. After you have used your PalmPilot the first time, a fifth option, Edit Categories, is available (see Figure 6-6). I talk about that option later in this section.

Figure 6-6:
To switch categories, just pick from the list.

2. **Tap the name of the category that you want to display.**

   The To Do List changes to display only the items assigned to the category you chose. The name of the category that you're viewing appears in the upper-right corner of the screen.

The shorter way to change the category you're viewing is — you guessed it — even shorter. Just press the To Do List button more than once. Each time you press the To Do List button, you see the next category for which you've created entries. The categories appear in alphabetical order, including any categories that you may have added yourself (see "Adding categories"). Neat, huh?

Adding categories

People who use PalmPilots are often busy people with scads of things to do. If you're usually juggling too many tasks to fit on one little PalmPilot screen, you'll find assigning categories to your tasks useful. You can look through them all with a few clicks of the To Do List button. Sooner or later, you'll want to create categories of your own.

Follow these steps to create a new category:

1. **With your To Do List open, tap the name of the category in the upper-right corner of the screen.**

   The list of available categories appears.

2. **Tap the words Edit Categories.**

   The Edit Categories screen appears.

3. **Tap New.**

   The Edit Categories dialog box opens.

4. **Enter the name of the category that you want to add with either the on-screen keyboard or Graffiti (see Chapter 2 for more about entering text).**

5. **Tap OK.**

   The name you entered appears in the Edit Categories dialog box, and the dialog box closes.

6. **Tap OK again.**

   The Edit Categories screen disappears.

Remember that you're best off if you stick to a few well-used categories rather than dozens of categories that you never look at. A To Do list should focus on the things you really plan to do; otherwise you could just call it a Round Tuit list — things you'll do if you ever get around to it.

Deleting categories

If you've gone hog-wild and created categories that you never use, delete some of them. You can also create a category for a special event and then delete the category when the event ends. I do that for trade shows sometimes; I create a category for things I have to do during the show, and then delete the category when the show is over.

Follow these steps to delete a category:

1. **With your To Do List open, tap the name of the category in the upper-right corner of the screen.**

   The list of available categories appears.

2. **Tap Edit Categories.**

   The Edit Categories screen appears.

3. **Tap the name of the category that you want to delete.**

   The category you tap is highlighted to show that you've selected it.

4. **Tap Delete.**

   The Remove Category dialog box opens, warning you that all the items in that category will be reassigned to the Unfiled category. If no items are assigned to the category you picked to delete, the Remove Category dialog box doesn't open.

5. **Tap Yes.**

   The Remove Categories dialog box closes, and your category is deleted.

6. **Tap OK.**

   The Edit Categories screen disappears.

The All and Unfiled categories don't show up in the Edit Categories screen, because they're not really categories. You can't get rid of the view that shows all your tasks (a mistake you probably wouldn't want to make) because finding things that you categorized by mistake would be harder.

Renaming categories

What's in a name? Shakespeare's Romeo thought it didn't matter, but look what happened to him. Sometimes you want your categories to make sense, so you change the names to fit your style.

To rename a category, follow these steps:

1. **With your To Do List open, tap the name of the category in the upper-right corner of the screen.**

   The list of available categories appears.

2. **Tap Edit Categories.**

   The Edit Categories screen appears.

3. **Tap the name of the category that you want to rename.**

   The name of the category is highlighted to show that you've selected it.

4. **Tap Rename.**

   The Edit Categories dialog box opens.

5. **Enter the name of the category that you want to add with either the on-screen keyboard or Graffiti (see Chapter 2 for more about entering text).**

6. **Tap OK.**

   The name you entered replaces the previous name of the category in the Edit Categories dialog box, and the dialog box closes.

7. **Tap OK again.**

   The Edit Categories screen disappears.

Because your categories can be sorted and displayed in alphabetical order, you may want to pick category names that fall in line a certain way. Business tasks come before Personal tasks in more ways than alphabetical order. On the other hand, you can cycle through all your categories with a few clicks of the To Do List button, so you can see all your tasks without much fuss.

What to Do with the To Do's You Do

Even if you don't enter To Do items yourself, you may wind up with a collection of tasks in your list that got sent to you by another person or by a program on your desktop computer. (See "Have I got a job for you? Beaming To Do's!" and Chapters 9 and 12 for more on beaming your To Do's and connecting your PalmPilot to a desktop computer.) After you have To Do's, you need to know what to do. (Anybody else feel a little dizzy?)

Have I got a job for you? Beaming To Do's!

You don't have to keep your To Do's to yourself. If you have a Palm III, you can beam tasks to other people if they're similarly equipped. Although beaming To Do's is reasonably safe and totally sanitary, beaming too many tasks at people can make them sick — that is, sick of all the tasks you're sending. You can read more about beaming in Chapter 9.

To beam a To Do item to another Palm III, follow these steps:

Chapter 6: To Do's That YOU Do! 99

1. **With your To Do List open, tap the name of the task that you want to beam to another Palm III.**

   The check box to the left of the item is highlighted to show which task you've selected.

2. **Tap the Menu soft button at the bottom of the display.**

   The menu bar appears at the top of the display.

3. **Choose Record⇨Beam Item, as shown in Figure 6-7.**

   The Beam dialog box opens.

4. **Tap OK.**

   The Beam dialog box closes, and your To Do List reappears.

Remember that the beaming feature of a Palm III works just like the remote control for your TV. The two PalmPilots have to be pointed at each other and reasonably close together, within 3 feet. If you want to beam a task to someone in the office building across the street, or to the driver of an oncoming car, you're out of luck.

Figure 6-7: With a Palm III, you can beam your tasks away.

Changing To Do's

The French have a saying, *"Plus ça change, plus c'est le même chose,"* which means "The more things change, the more they're the same." Even if you don't speak French, you know that makes no sense, but it sounds terribly charming in French.

The charming thing about changing To Do items is that you do pretty much the same things to change an item that you did to enter it in the first place.

To change the priority of a To Do item, follow these steps:

1. **With your To Do List open, tap the name of the task that you want to change.**

   The check box to the left of the item is highlighted to show which task you've selected.

2. **To change the priority of your task, tap the number next to the name of the task.**

   A list of numbers 1 through 5 appears (see Figure 6-8).

3. **Tap the number for the new priority that you want to give your task.**

   The highest priority is 1; the lowest is 5. When you tap a number, the list disappears, and the new priority number appears next to your task.

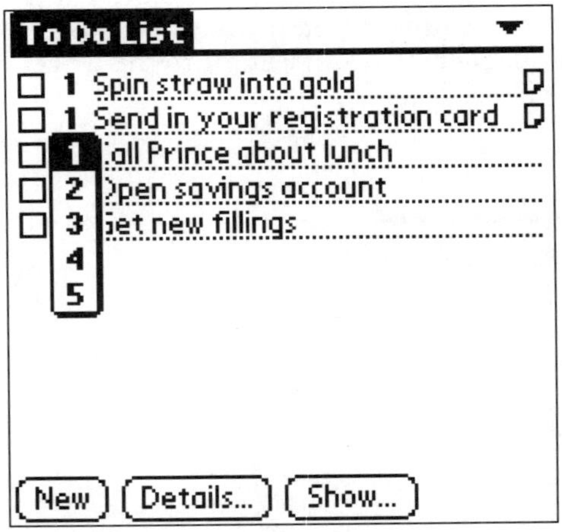

Figure 6-8: Set priorities to sort out what's REALLY important.

If you want to change the name of a To Do item, follow these steps:

1. **With your To Do List open, tap the name of the task that you want to change.**

   The check box to the left of the item is highlighted to show which task you've selected.

2. **Select the text you that want to change by drawing a horizontal line through it with your stylus.**

   The text is highlighted to show that you've selected it.

3. **Enter new text with either the on-screen keyboard or Graffiti (see Chapter 2 for more about entering text).**

   The selected text is replaced by the text you enter.

If you want to make further changes to a To Do item, follow these steps:

1. **With your To Do List open, tap the name of the task that you want to change.**

   The check box to the left of the item is highlighted to show which task you've selected.

2. **Tap Details at the bottom of the To Do List.**

   The To Do Item Details dialog box opens.

3. **Make whatever changes you want in the To Do Item Details dialog box.**

   You can use the same methods for changing the details of your task that you did to enter the details in the first place (see "Entering details for a To Do item" earlier in this chapter).

4. **Tap OK.**

   The To Do Item Details dialog box closes, and the To Do List reappears.

The one trick about changing To Do items is that the To Do List almost never displays all the things that you can change about a task. That means that you may change something that's not displayed, so at first you may think that your changes didn't take. See "Setting preferences for your To Do List" later in this chapter to find out how to show everything you want to see.

Undoing a mistake

If you make a mistake when changing the text in a To Do item, you can fix it in a jiffy by doing this:

1. **With your To Do List open, tap the Menu soft button.**

   The menu bar appears at the top of the display.

2. **Choose Edit➪Undo.**

   Your text returns to the way it was before you changed it.

Undo only works when you change or replace text. You can't use the Undo command to recover a To Do item that you accidentally delete. If you have archived deleted items, you can go to the archive on the Palm Desktop to recover the item. See Chapter 12 for details on recovering items from the archive.

Marking the To Do's that you've done

As you finish the tasks that you've assigned to yourself, mark them as completed. Marking To Do items as completed does more than give you a feeling of satisfaction; it can also shorten that depressing list of things left to do. I say "can," because you can either set up your PalmPilot to display all tasks, completed or not, or you can choose to hide completed tasks. See "Setting preferences for your To Do List" later in this chapter for information on hiding tasks.

To mark a task as completed, tap the check box next to the name of the task that you want to mark. A check mark appears in the check box to show that you've completed the item (see Figure 6-9). If you told your PalmPilot in the To Do Preferences not to show completed items, the item disappears from the To Do List.

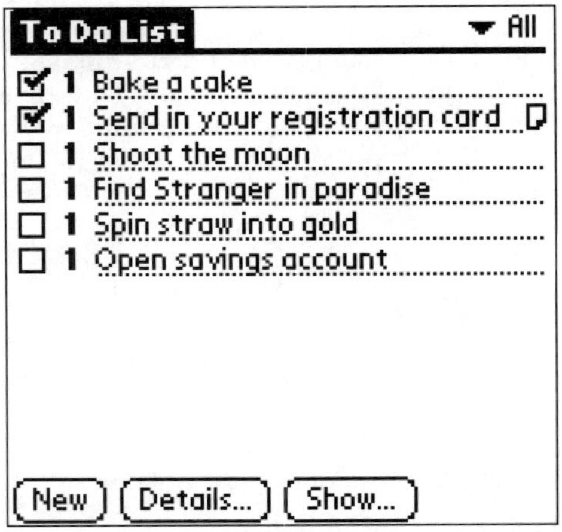

Figure 6-9: When you finish a task, check it off.

Deleting a To Do

Perhaps you added a task to your To Do List and then lost your nerve and decided to erase any trace of it. If you've made it your task to tell what's-his-name that he's a dirty, rotten so-and-so, you may be wiser to delete the thing. If you end up telling him anyway, don't forget that I told you so.

To delete a To Do List item, follow these steps:

1. **With your To Do List open, tap the name of the task that you want to delete.**

    The check box to the left of the item is highlighted to show which task you've selected.

Chapter 6: To Do's That YOU Do! 103

2. **Tap the Menu soft button.**

   The menu bar appears at the top of the display.

3. **Choose Record➪Delete Item.**

   The Delete To Do dialog box opens (see Figure 6-10).

4. **Tap OK.**

   The Delete To Do dialog box closes, and your To Do List reappears.

Figure 6-10: If you don't want to complete it, delete it.

 Some people like to delete tasks rather than marking them as completed because it keeps their list of tasks short. The reason not to delete completed tasks is so that you can brag about all the things you've accomplished. That's a particularly useful approach if you have a job that gives performance reviews. It's up to you: complete or delete.

The Delete Items dialog box offers to save an archive copy of each item you delete to your PC. By doing so, you'll be able to dig up old deleted items through the Palm Desktop on your PC if you need them in the future. If you leave the box checked, each item is archived automatically. If you click the archive check box once, it stays unchecked for every item you delete until you check it again. For more about archived items, see Chapter 12.

Deleting a note

After you've done a task a few times, you may not need a note telling you how to do the task anymore. You can delete a note attached to a To Do item without deleting the item.

To delete a note, follow these steps:

1. **With your To Do List open, tap the name of the task from which you want to delete a note.**

   The check box to the left of the item is highlighted to show which task you've selected.

2. **Tap the Menu soft button.**

   The menu bar appears at the top of the display.

3. **Choose Record➪Delete Note.**

   The Delete Note dialog box opens, asking if you're sure that you want to do this.

4. **Tap Yes.**

   The note is deleted, but the task remains.

When you delete a note, it's gone for good; notes are not archived separately, and the Undo command doesn't bring them back. So, be sure that you *really* want the note that you pick to be deleted.

Setting preferences for your To Do List

If you never change a thing about your To Do List, you'll still get plenty of mileage out of your PalmPilot. But everybody works a little differently, so you may want to slice and dice the items in your To Do List in a way that works better for you.

To change your To Do List preferences, follow these steps:

1. **With your To Do List open, tap Show.**

   The To Do Preferences screen appears.

2. **Tap the triangle next to the words Sort By to set up your sort order.**

   Your choices, as shown in Figure 6-11, are

   - Priority, Due Date
   - Due Date, Priority
   - Category, Priority
   - Category, Due Date

3. **Tap the check boxes that correspond to the elements that you want displayed in the To Do List.**

   The To Do Preferences screen has a half-dozen check boxes that set your display to show Completed Items, Due Dates, Priorities, Categories, and other items. If you display everything, your screen can get a bit crowded, but that's your choice.

Figure 6-11: You can sort your tasks four different ways.

[To Do Preferences dialog showing Sort by dropdown with options: Priority, Due Date / Due Date, Priority / Category, Priority / Category, Due Date. Checkboxes for Show Completed Items, Show Only Due Items, Record Completion Date, Show Due Dates, Show Priorities (checked), Show Categories. OK and Cancel buttons.]

If you check any of the following boxes, here's what happens:

- **Show Completed Items:** Tasks that you complete stay on the list until you delete them. This is for people who'd rather not forget what they did yesterday.

- **Show Only Due Items:** Tasks with Due Dates set in the future don't show; only tasks with no Due Date or with a Due Date set for today or earlier appear. This is for people who like to wait until the last minute.

- **Record Completion Date:** The Due Date of a task changes to the date on which you mark the task as completed. For example, if I set the Due Date of a task for Friday, but I mark the task complete on Wednesday, the Due Date is automatically changed to Wednesday. This one's for people who like to remember when things were really completed instead of when things should have been completed.

- **Show Due Dates:** This option makes a Due Date appear on the screen along with the name of each task. It's for people who like to put first things first.

- **Show Priorities:** This option makes the Priority number appear next to each task. It's for people who put the most important things first.

- **Show Categories:** Use this option to make the category of each task appear next to the name of the task. This one's for people who like to put everything in its place.

4. **Click OK.**

   The To Do Preferences screen disappears, and your To Do List reappears.

Part II: Getting Down to Business

TIP

If you choose to sort by category or priority, displaying the category or priority is also a good idea. Otherwise, your screen looks confusing.

Looking up an address and phone number

Creating To Do items that involve other people is fairly common, even if the task is something as simple as calling someone on the phone. You can get your PalmPilot to look up a name from your Address List and plug that person's name and phone number into the To Do item. Phone Number Lookup can save you the trouble of looking up the person's number when it's time to make the call.

Here's how to look up a name and phone number from your Address Book:

1. **With the To Do List open, create or begin to edit a To Do List item.**

   See "Creating a To Do item" or "Changing To Do's" earlier in this chapter.

2. **Tap the Menu soft button.**

   The menu bar appears.

3. **Choose Options➪Phone Lookup.**

   The Phone Number Lookup screen appears. If this screen looks like your address book, don't be surprised — that's where the phone numbers come from (see Figure 6-12).

4. **Tap the name of the person whose phone number you want to add to your To Do item.**

   The name is highlighted to show that you've selected it.

Figure 6-12: Use the Phone Number Lookup feature to find important numbers.

```
Phone Number Lookup:
Alifont, "Bull"              555-6597 W
DeDark, Fredda               555-9875 W
Dogg, Pat D.                 555-5474 W
Early, Otto B.               555-1324 W
Fergus, Freddie              555-5689 W
Palm III Accessories         801-431-1536 W
Rumplestiltskin              555-6666 W
Short, Peg                   555-1213 W
Snivel, Heather              555-6127 W
Technical Support            847-676-1441 W
Thunderblossom, Magnoli      555-3200 W

Look Up:           (Add) (Cancel)
```

5. **Tap Add.**

   The name and phone number of the person whose name you chose appear as part of your To Do item. Bear in mind that only the first phone number of the address record you pick appears in the To Do item, no matter how many phone numbers the address record contains.

   Unfortunately, you can't get from the To Do List to the person's Address List entry to see other details about the person, such as his street address or other details. You have to press the Address List button and find the name.

Purging To Do's that you've done

The reason for keeping a To Do list is to help you get things done. After you've done the things on your list, you have no reason to leave them hanging around. The Purge function automatically deletes items that you've marked as completed. You could delete all your completed items one by one, but the purge function deletes them *en masse*.

To purge completed To Do items, follow these steps:

1. **With your To Do List open, tap the Menu soft button.**

   The menu bar appears at the top of the display.

2. **Choose Record⇨Purge.**

   The Purge dialog box appears. Make sure that a check mark appears in the box that says "Save archive copy on PC." Otherwise, you won't have a record of all the things you've done.

3. **Tap OK.**

   The Purge dialog box closes, and the items you marked as completed disappear.

If you need to dig up a list of the things you've done to show your boss at review time or as dramatic courtroom testimony ("Just where were you the night of . . . ?"), you can go back to the archives of your To Do items, provided that you checked the archive box in the Purge dialog box. For more on retrieving To Do items from the archive, see Chapter 12.

Chapter 7
Memo Mania

In This Chapter
- Creating memos
- Reading memos
- Changing and categorizing items
- Making a memo private
- Deleting memos
- Setting preferences
- Beaming memos

The Memo Pad isn't the flashiest feature of the PalmPilot, but I must confess that it's my favorite. Like many writers, my best ideas always hit me when I'm farthest from my desk and least able to record them. Now I keep my PalmPilot nearby 24 hours a day, 7 days a week, so that every Brilliant Flash of Insight gets recorded to my Memo Pad, along with every Foolish Whim. At this point, the Foolish Whims outnumber the Brilliant Flashes by a long shot, but because I can change and delete a memo anytime, I can make myself look foolish less often. As you've probably noticed, I haven't yet figured out how to look brilliant.

When you synchronize your PalmPilot with a desktop computer, you can copy and paste the text from your memos to regular word-processing programs. That's the best way to format, print, or e-mail the precious prose you've collected in your PalmPilot Memo Pad.

To access your Memo List, just press the Memo Pad button (it's the far-right button at the bottom of your PalmPilot — see Figure 7-1) and continue with adding, deleting, or whatever you want to do with your memos.

Figure 7-1: Press the To Do List button to bring up your list of To Do's.

Take a Memo

If you plan to use the Memo Pad to write down large amounts of information while you're away from your desk, it really pays to learn Graffiti. You can get by in all the other PalmPilot programs by using the little on-screen keyboard to tap out short pieces of text, but that gets tiresome quickly. (I discuss the keyboard and Graffiti in Chapter 2.) Even Graffiti can get a little tiring if you're used to the speed of a standard computer keyboard, but that little keyboard is worse.

Adding items

Many people don't enter memos into their PalmPilot Memo Pad at all; they either enter data from the PalmPilot desktop program (see Chapter 12), or they ignore memos altogether. Take your pick. As I've said, I'm a big fan of the Memo Pad, so I add stuff constantly.

To create a new memo, follow these steps:

1. **With your Memo List open, tap New.**

   A blank note screen appears.

2. **Enter the text that you want with either the on-screen keyboard or Graffiti (see Chapter 2 for more about entering text).**

   The text you enter appears on the memo screen (see Figure 7-2).

3. **Tap Done.**

   The memo screen disappears, and your Memo List reappears.

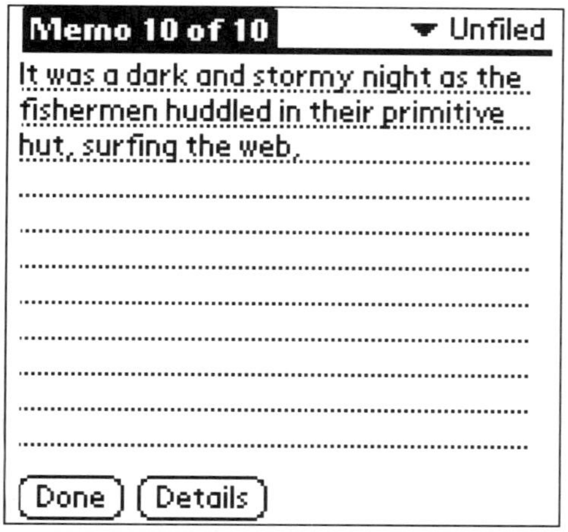

Figure 7-2: Create memos using the Memo Pad.

What I've just described is the prescribed way of entering a memo. An even easier way is to press the Memo Pad button and just start writing stuff in the Graffiti box. The Memo Pad just assumes that you want to create a new memo and opens a new memo screen. You still have to tap Done to close the new memo.

Reading memos

The word *memo* looks like someone started to write the word *memory,* but forgot to finish. You won't have to worry about forgetting how to read your memos, though; it's just a matter of press and tap. Here's how:

1. **With your Memo List open, tap the name of the memo that you want to read (see Figure 7-3).**

   The memo that you selected opens.

2. **Read your memo to your heart's content.**

3. **Tap Done.**

   Your memo closes.

The other sneaky thing I like about memos is that you can read them in the dark. The PalmPilot Pro and later models have a backlight, so you can read (or write) memos after the lights go out. It's just like being back in the days when you used to read comic books under the covers with a flashlight. Don't get caught, though.

Bear in mind that the backlight can drain your batteries rather quickly, so use the backlight sparingly.

Figure 7-3: Pick the memo you want to read from the list.

Changing items

What's the difference between a Foolish Whim and a Brilliant Insight? Editing! (My editors certainly agree with me about that.) Editing your memos is just as easy as reading and creating them.

The simplest change you can make to a memo is adding new text. I have certain memos to which I add one or two lines every day. Adding more text to a memo only takes a second.

To add new text to a memo that you've already created, follow these steps:

 1. **With your Memo List open, tap the name of the memo that you want to change.**

    The memo opens on your screen.

 2. **Tap the spot in the memo where you want to add new text.**

    A blinking line, called the *insertion point,* appears at the spot where you tapped.

 3. **Enter the text that you want with either the on-screen keyboard or Graffiti (see Chapter 2 for more about entering text).**

    The text you enter appears in the spot you tapped.

 4. **Tap Done.**

    Your memo closes.

Another common way to edit a memo is to change the text that's already there. When you select any text you've entered in your PalmPilot and then enter new text, the text you select is automatically replaced by the text you enter. Most Windows and Macintosh programs work pretty much the same way, so you should be ready to edit PalmPilot memos in a flash.

To replace existing text in a memo, follow these steps:

1. **With your Memo List open, tap the name of the memo that you want to change.**

   The memo opens on your screen.

2. **Select any text that you want to replace.**

   The text that you select is highlighted to show that you've selected it (see Figure 7-4). For more about selecting text, see Chapter 2.

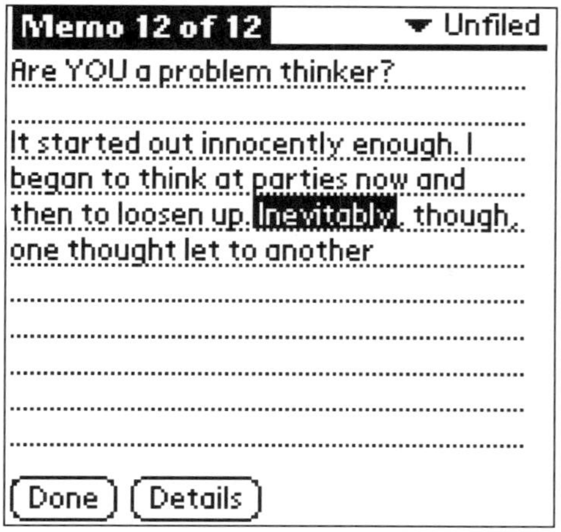

Figure 7-4:
Get rid of pesky typos by highlighting text to change it.

3. **Enter replacement text with either the on-screen keyboard or Graffiti (see Chapter 2 for more about entering text).**

   The text you enter replaces the selected text.

4. **Tap Done.**

   Your memo closes.

If you want to select the whole memo and replace everything in it, you can open the memo, tap the Menu icon, and choose Edit➪Select All. If you're going to go that far, though, you may as well just delete the memo and start over.

You may have noticed that the first line of the memo is what shows up on your Memo List. If you let your PalmPilot sort alphabetically, the first word of the first line determines where the memo turns up on your memo list. You can make sure that a certain memo always ends up at the top of your memo list by making the first character in the memo 0 (zero).

Part II: Getting Down to Business

Categorizing items

After you've created a large enough collection of memos, you may want to start organizing them so that you can find the information you want quickly. You can assign a category to each memo so that it shows up along with other memos with similar content. Here's how:

1. **With your Memo List open, tap the name of the memo that you want to categorize.**

   The memo opens.

2. **Tap the name of the category in the upper-right corner of the display.**

   If your memo is uncategorized, the word Unfiled appears in the upper-right corner of the screen. When you tap the down-pointing arrow next to the category name or the name itself, a list of categories drops down (see Figure 7-5). Categories work pretty much the same way in the Memo Pad as they do in the To Do List, so see Chapter 6 for more about dealing with categories.

Figure 7-5: Tap the name of the memo category and pick a new category.

3. **Tap the name of the category to which you want to assign your memo.**

   The list disappears, and the category you chose appears in the upper-right corner.

4. **Tap Done.**

   Your memo closes, and the Memo List reappears.

Making a memo private

If you want to be wise about recording your Foolish Whims, you can mark them all private so that only you know what you've entered. It's a good way to keep from looking foolish if anybody else gets hold of your PalmPilot. I've thought about marking my sillier memos private, but I suspect everybody already knows I'm foolish, so it's probably too late.

Follow these steps to keep private memos to yourself:

1. **With your Memo List open, tap the name of the memo that you want to make private.**

    Your memo opens.

2. **Tap Details.**

    The Memo Details dialog box opens (see Figure 7-6).

Figure 7-6: The Memo Details dialog box lets you keep your secrets safe.

3. **Tap the check box marked Private.**

    A check mark appears in the check box.

4. **Tap OK.**

    The Private Records dialog box appears if you haven't elected to hide private records. The Private Records dialog box warns you that marking this item Private won't matter until you choose to hide private records. I discuss hiding and showing private records in Chapter 4. If you have elected to hide private records, the Memo Details dialog box simply closes at this point.

5. **Tap OK in the Private Records dialog box.**

    The Private Records dialog box closes.

6. **Tap Done.**

    Your memo closes, and the Memo List reappears. If you have chosen to hide private records, the memo that you marked Private is no longer listed.

You can choose whether to show or hide all private items on your PalmPilot by going to the Security application and picking either Show or Hide. If you pick Show, all your items can be seen, private or not. If you pick Hide, the items marked Private seem to disappear. If you mark an item Private while hiding items marked Private, the item seems to vanish, only to reappear when you go back to the Security application and pick Show Private Items again. For more on hiding private items, see Chapter 4.

You can also set up a password to protect your private items. That's one more way of keeping your private items private. Check out Chapter 4 for more about passwords.

The tricky thing about items marked Private is that nothing appears on the screen to tell you whether you're seeing the private items. One way to remind yourself is to create a memo whose first line starts with a zero and says "0 PRIVATE ITEMS SHOWING." That way, you're reminded to check for items that you previously marked as Private.

Using What You Have

Even if you don't enter memos directly into your PalmPilot, you still want to read the memos you've collected and organize your memo collection in a useful way. The PalmPilot Memo Pad offers you a collection of organizing tools that are simple but useful. You can sort your memos in different ways, view different categories, and change the font that the PalmPilot displays to make your memos easier to read.

Deleting items

An old axiom says "When in doubt, throw it out." Deleting a memo takes a few more steps than I wish it did, but not much mystery is involved.

To delete a memo, follow these steps:

1. **With your Memo List open, tap the name of the memo that you want to delete.**

   Your memo opens.

2. **Tap the Menu icon.**

   The menu bar appears.

Figure 7-7:
You can delete a memo when you don't want it anymore.

   3. **Choose Record➪Delete Memo, as shown in Figure 7-7.**

      The Delete Memo dialog box opens and asks if you want to delete the current memo.

   4. **Tap OK.**

      The Delete Memo dialog box closes, and your memo is deleted. If you've changed your mind about deleting this memo, you can tap the Cancel button in the Delete Memo dialog box to call off the deletion. Be sure that a check mark appears in the box marked Save Archive Copy on PC. That's the only way that your deleted memos can be recovered at a future date. For more about archiving, see Chapter 12.

Boom! It's gone.

Viewing memos by category

My, how memos multiply! In no time at all, you'll probably gather up dozens and dozens of memos, full of stuff that you're sure you want to keep handy at all times. Of course, the catch is this: The more memos you try to keep handy on your PalmPilot, the less handy they get, because you have so doggone many of 'em.

Earlier in this chapter, I show you how to assign categories to your memos (see "Categorizing items" for more information), but to really use categories, you need to be able to see which memos are in each category.

To view your memos by category, follow these steps:

   1. **With your Memo List open, tap the name of the category in the upper-right corner of the screen.**

      The list of available categories appears. When you first use your PalmPilot, the list has four categories: All, Business, Personal, and Unfiled.

118 Part II: Getting Down to Business

2. **Tap the name of the category that you want to display.**

   The Memo List changes to display only the items assigned to the category you chose. The name of the category you're viewing appears in the upper-right corner of the screen.

If you really want to impress your friends with your PalmPilot prowess, you can whip through your memo categories even faster by clicking the Memo Pad button more than once. Each time you press the Memo Pad button, you see a different category.

Changing fonts

Changing the font on your PalmPilot means to change the size and style of lettering that you see in the display. The itty-bitty letters that the PalmPilot usually displays allow you to show a lot of information on that tiny little screen, but if your eyes aren't so sharp or if the light isn't just right, your PalmPilot can be tough to read. Each model of PalmPilot has offered a few more choices in the type of font you can choose to display your text.

The PalmPilot Professional shows a couple of little buttons with the letter A at the bottom of every memo. One button contains a small letter A, and the other contains a slightly larger letter A. If you want to see slightly larger text, tap the larger A, and the text of all memos will appear in the larger font. When you want to go back to smaller text, tap the smaller A. The size of text in the Memo List can't be changed.

The Palm III lets you change the font in both the Memo List and in the text of your memos, but you choose the font from the menu bar. Tap the Menu icon, choose Options➪Font, pick the font that you want to display from the Select Font dialog box, and tap OK. The Palm III lets you choose from among three fonts. You have to choose the font for your memo text and your Memo List separately. If you change the font for the Memo List, you haven't changed the font you'll see for the text of your memos. You need to open a memo to change the font for the body of memos. When you change the font for the body of one memo, all memos appear in that font until you pick another font.

Setting preferences to organize your memos

When it comes to organizing memos, I believe in freedom of choice: alphabetical or manual. You can either let your PalmPilot organize your memos by the first letter of the first word contained in each memo, or you can set up the PalmPilot to let you drag the titles of memos around the Memo List and drop them off in the order you like. I prefer the alphabetical arrangement.

Follow these steps to let PalmPilot know your preferences:

1. **With your Memo List open, tap the Menu icon.**

    The menu bar appears.

2. **Choose Options➪Preferences.**

    The Memo Preferences dialog box opens, as shown in Figure 7-8.

3. **Tap the triangle next to Sort By.**

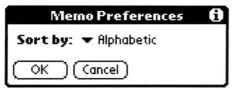

Figure 7-8: You have preferences; your memos do, too.

A list appears offering you two choices: Manual and Alphabetic.

4. **Tap the choice that you prefer.**

    The list disappears, and your choice appears.

5. **Tap OK.**

    The Memo Preferences dialog box closes, and your Memo List appears in the sort order of your choice.

If you choose to sort your memos Alphabetically, you get the result you'd expect; all your memos line up in alphabetical order according to the first word in the memo. If you choose Manual sorting, memos appear in the order in which you created them so that the last memo that you created appears at the bottom of the list. But when you sort your memos in Manual order, you can also drag them to the point in your memo list where you want them to appear. It doesn't matter what category you're looking at when you set the preferences; the setting you choose applies to all categories.

If you've sorted your memos manually and then switch to alphabetical sorting, your manually sorted arrangement is lost for good. The memos are still there, but you have to re-sort everything.

Beaming your memos

Yes, Virginia, there is a Santa Claus, and if he has a Palm III next Christmas, you can write your gift list on your Palm III memo pad and beam it to Santa. Of course, that way you don't get to sit on his lap.

You can beam nearly anything on one Palm III to another Palm III, not just memos. For more about beaming, see Chapter 9.

To beam a memo, follow these steps:

1. **With your Memo List open, tap the name of the memo that you want to beam.**

   Your memo opens.

2. **Tap the Menu icon.**

   The menu bar appears.

3. **Choose Record⇨Beam Memo, as shown in Figure 7-9.**

   The Beam dialog box opens.

4. **Tap OK.**

   Your memo is magically sent to the other Palm III.

Figure 7-9: Beam your memos to another Palm III at warp speed.

Of course, you have to set the Palm IIIs within about three feet of each other for the beaming process to work, which means that you can't beam your list to Santa as he flies over. The Palm IIIs must also be within line of sight of each other, so you can't beam through walls; that's definitely a job for Superman.

Chapter 8
The Date Game

In This Chapter
▶ Adding and deleting appointments
▶ Setting alarms
▶ Repeating appointments
▶ Marking items private
▶ Setting preferences
▶ Purging your Date Book

The Date Book may soon become your favorite PalmPilot feature. Everybody knows how powerful a computer can be at keeping track of your schedule — you may use one at work to keep track of your appointments. The PalmPilot lets you carry that power around in your pocket and keep your schedule up-to-date while you're carrying it out. Then, when you return to your office or your home, just HotSync to your desktop computer to keep your Date Book current. For more on performing a HotSync, see Chapter 11.

To access your Date Book, just press the Date Book hard button (it's the far-left button at the bottom of your PalmPilot case; see Figure 8-1) and then arrange your appointments as you like.

Figure 8-1: The Date Book hard button.

Date Book Views

I think that you'll find the Date Book pretty easy to use after you've tried it a bit. The only tricky part about understanding the PalmPilot Date Book comes from the size of the screen. You can't really show a whole calendar on that little bitty display and still be able to show what's going on each day, so the PalmPilot breaks the calendar up into different views that show a day, a week, or a month.

Each view of your calendar includes three icons at the bottom of the screen representing the three calendar views: day, week, and month. The icon for the view you're seeing appears darkened; if you want to switch to another view, tap a different icon. For example, when you look at the day view, the leftmost icon is darkened. When you tap the middle icon, the week view appears.

Another way to switch between Date Book views is to press the Date Book button more than once. Each time you press the Date Book button, you see a different view of your Date Book, either the day, week, or month view. If you don't like the view you see, keep pressing the Date Book button until the view you want appears.

The Daily view

The first time that you press the Date Book button, you see a daily schedule, as shown in Figure 8-2. It shows a line for each hour of the day, and any appointments on your schedule are listed in order of starting time.

Figure 8-2: The Daily view displays a list of your appointments for a particular day.

Your PalmPilot usually shows today's appointments first. If you want to see appointments for a date earlier or later in the week, tap the letter for the day of the week at the top of the screen. You can also move from day to day by pressing the scroll buttons on the PalmPilot case.

The Week view

The Week view (see Figure 8-3) just shows you a diagram of your schedule for the week. It shows a grid of days and times, and shaded bars represent blocks of time when you have appointments scheduled, but the bars don't tell you specifically what's scheduled. If you want to find out what you've scheduled at a certain time, tap the bar representing that scheduled item, and the information regarding the appointment appears at the top of the screen.

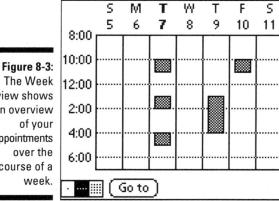

Figure 8-3: The Week view shows an overview of your appointments over the course of a week.

 You can look at your weekly schedule for the future or the past by pressing the scroll buttons on the PalmPilot case, just like you can in the Daily view. You can also change the week you're looking at by tapping one of the triangles at the top of the screen.

 The Week view has one important feature that the other two views don't have: You can change an appointment to a different time in the week by dragging the bar representing the appointment time and dropping it off at another time in the week. Figure 8-4 shows an appointment (represented by the box with the heavy border) being dropped in at 2:00 p.m. on September 10.

Part II: Getting Down to Business

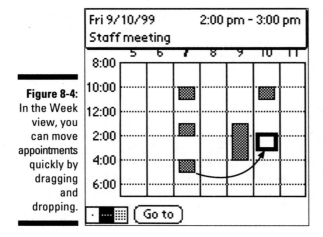

Figure 8-4: In the Week view, you can move appointments quickly by dragging and dropping.

As you're dragging and dropping, the name and time of your appointment appear at the top of the display to let you know exactly when you've set the new appointment time. You need to be pretty steady with the stylus if you drag and drop this way, but it's the fastest way to change an appointment time.

If you've never done the drag and drop (no, it's not a dance step from the 1960s; that was the Watusi), don't fret. It's very simple; here's how:

1. **Put the tip of your stylus on the bar representing an appointment.**
2. **Slide the stylus tip along the screen to where you want the appointment to end up.**

   As you slide the stylus tip along the screen, a little box representing the appointment slides right along with your stylus, as if you were dragging the box along the screen. As you drag, the appointment listed in the banner at the top of the screen changes to show you what the new appointment time will be if you "drop" the appointment at the current position by lifting your stylus.

3. **Lift up the stylus when the appointment is where you want it.**

Now you're a drag-and-drop champ!

The Month view

The Month view (see Figure 8-5) is the most familiar-looking view in your Date Book because it resembles a regular wall calendar. Unfortunately, the Month view offers very little information about your schedule; only dots represent your appointments. The main advantage of the Month view is the ability to navigate through your schedule easily. If you tap any date in the Month view, you see the Daily view for that date.

Again, the scroll buttons change the Month view from one month to the next. If you need to take a quick look at a date in the distant future (a year or more from now), tap Go To at the bottom of the Date Book screen and pick the date that you want to see.

The Go To icon shows you a calendar that enables you to tap the date you want to see. If you want to view a date later this month, tap Go To and tap the date you want to see. If you want to see a date in a different month of this year, tap the month you want from the list of months at the top of the screen, and then tap the day you want. If you want to look at a day in a different year, tap Go To, tap one of the triangles next to the year at the top of the screen (depending whether you want to time warp into the past or the future), and tap the month you want to see.

Figure 8-5: The Month view shows a very general diagram of your appointments for a month.

Making Dates

You can keep track of a surprising amount of detailed information in your Date Book. Thousands of appointments fit comfortably in your Date Book along with reminders, notes, and other details. You don't have to enter your appointments directly into your PalmPilot if you don't want to; you can do most of the keyboard work on your desktop computer and then HotSync everything to your PalmPilot. But in some situations, you may be better off entering appointments right in your PalmPilot.

Adding appointments the simple way

Some folks are into dates; some aren't. You don't have to go crazy entering lots of details when you add an appointment to your Date Book. You can enter many types of appointments with very little effort.

Follow these steps to add a new appointment the simple way:

1. **With the Date Book visible, tap the line next to the hour when your appointment begins.**

    A blinking line, called the *insertion point,* appears on the line that you tapped.

2. **Enter the name of your appointment by using either the on-screen keyboard or Graffiti (see Chapter 2 for more about entering text).**

    The name of your appointment appears on the line that you tapped. (See Figure 8-6.)

Figure 8-6:
Just write the name of your appointment in the appropriate time slot.

3. **Tap the blank spot on the bottom of the screen to the right of Go To.**

    The insertion point disappears, and your appointment is set. (If you don't complete this step, nothing terrible happens; your PalmPilot just waits for you to do something else.)

The simple way to enter appointments is to enter the name of the appointment at the time when the appointment starts. What could be easier?

Chapter 8: The Date Game

Adding appointments the complete way

If all your appointments start right on the hour and last exactly an hour, the simple way to enter appointments (see the previous section) will suit you just fine. When you have appointments that start at odd times or don't last exactly an hour, you need to resort to the more complete method for entering appointments. Follow these steps to enter detailed information about an appointment:

1. **With the Date Book visible, tap Go To.**

   The Go To Date dialog box opens.

2. **Tap the date for your appointment.**

   The Date Book appears in Daily view, showing you the appointments that you've scheduled for that date.

3. **Tap the hour closest to the starting time of your appointment.**

   The Set Time dialog box opens, as shown in Figure 8-7.

Figure 8-7: The Set Time dialog box accommodates appointments with details.

4. **Tap the hour and minute for the starting time of your appointment.**

   The hour and minute that you tap appear in the Start Time box.

5. **Tap the End Time box.**

   The End Time box is highlighted to show that you've selected it.

6. **Tap the hour and minute for the ending time of your appointment.**

   The hour and minute that you tap appear in the End Time box.

Part II: Getting Down to Business

 7. **Tap OK.**

    The Set Time dialog box closes, and your Date Book screen reappears.

 8. **Enter the name of your appointment by using either the on-screen keyboard or Graffiti (see Chapter 2 for more about entering text).**

    The name of your appointment appears on the line next to your starting time.

 9. **Tap Details.**

    The Event Details dialog box opens.

 10. **If you need to make any changes to the details of your appointment, tap the appropriate box and enter that information.**

    Because you've already entered the date and time, you probably don't need to change those details. I explain more about setting alarms, setting private appointments, and repeating appointments later in this chapter.

 11. **Tap OK.**

    The Event Details dialog box closes, and your Date Book screen reappears.

There! You've done it! Isn't that satisfying? Okay, maybe not, but you've done all that you can do, so take heart. If you didn't find this method helpful or efficient, you can enter your next appointment the simple way by following the steps in the preceding section.

No Time Events

Not everything on your schedule happens at a particular hour of the day. Birthdays and holidays, for example, just happen, all day long, even if it rains. If you want to enter an event without a time attached, just open the Date Book to the Daily view, and then enter the name of the event in the Graffiti box. For more about using Graffiti, see Chapter 2. Your new event appears at the top of the screen. You can also use the complete method of entering an appointment in the preceding section and tap No Time in the Set Time screen in Step 6.

Alarms

I'm the first to admit that I need a lot of reminding. Fortunately, my PalmPilot is always around to gently pester me into doing what needs to be done when it needs to be done. It's sort of a like an electronic mother-in-law.

Chapter 8: The Date Game **129**

Even if your PalmPilot is turned off, the alarm wakes up your PalmPilot and makes a series of tiny beeps. You need to turn off the alarm by tapping OK on the PalmPilot screen.

Follow these steps to set an alarm:

1. **With the Date Book visible, tap the name of the appointment for which you want to set an alarm.**

    The insertion point appears on the line with your appointment's name.

2. **Tap Details.**

    The Event Details dialog box opens.

3. **Tap the Alarm check box.**

    A check mark appears in the check box, and the alarm setting appears to the right of the check box, as shown in Figure 8-8. Normally, the alarm setting is 5 minutes. That means that the alarm will go off 5 minutes before the scheduled appointment time.

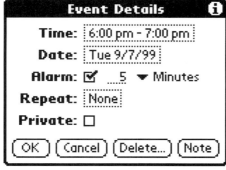

Figure 8-8: In the Event Details dialog box, set your PalmPilot to remind you of an important appointment.

4. **If you want to change the alarm time, tap the word Minutes.**

    A list appears with the choices Minutes, Hours, or Days.

5. **Tap your choice of Minutes, Hours, or Days.**

    The list disappears, and the choice that you tapped appears.

6. **Enter the number of minutes, hours, or days before the appointment that you want the alarm to sound with either the on-screen keyboard or Graffiti (see Chapter 2 for more about entering text).**

    The number that you enter appears next to the Alarm check box.

7. **Tap OK.**

    The Event Details dialog box closes.

TIP I usually check the Alarm check box while creating an appointment rather than after creating it.

Adding notes to appointments

Every Date Book item can also contain a note explaining details about the appointment. Date Book notes work exactly the same way as the notes you can attach to To Do items. See Chapter 6 for more about attaching notes.

Address Book Lookup

Another feature shared by the Date Book and the To Do List is the ability to look up a name in your Address Book and automatically copy that person's name and phone number into the appointment. To look up a name, tap the Menu soft button and choose Options⇨Phone Lookup. When the Address Book appears, tap the name you want to include in the appointment and then tap the Add button.

Repeating appointments

You certainly don't want to forget that important weekly meeting of Electronics Shoppers Anonymous. Rather than input each of those meetings individually, you can set up a repeating appointment.

To mark an appointment as a repeating appointment:

1. **With the Date Book visible, tap the name of the appointment that you want to set up as a repeating appointment.**

   The insertion point appears on the line with your appointment's name.

2. **Tap Details.**

   The Event Details dialog box opens.

3. **Tap the Repeat box.**

   The Change Repeat dialog box opens, as shown in Figure 8-9.

4. **Tap one of the interval pattern buttons to set the frequency that you want.**

   Your choices are None, Day, Week, Month, and Year. When you tap one, the screen changes to show intervals that are suitable to your choice. If you choose nothing, PalmPilot assumes that you mean None.

Chapter 8: The Date Game 131

Figure 8-9:
Come again? Set up your recurring appointments in the Change Repeat dialog box.

5. **Enter a number to indicate how often you want the appointment to repeat.**

   If you enter nothing, the PalmPilot assumes that the number is 1, meaning the appointment occurs every day, week, month, or year, depending on which frequency you chose. If you change that number to the number 2, your appointment occurs every 2 days, 2 weeks, 2 months, or 2 years, and so on.

6. **If your appointment repeats until a certain date, tap the End On box.**

   Some appointments repeat for a certain period of time. If you go to night school, for example, your class may occur once a week for 10 weeks. When you tap the End On box, a menu appears giving you two choices: No End Date and Choose Date.

7. **Tap Choose Date from the End On box.**

   The Ending On screen appears.

8. **Tap your desired end date on the calendar in the Ending On screen.**

   The Ending On screen disappears, and the date that you chose appears in the End On box.

9. **Tap the appropriate box to indicate other information about your repeating appointment.**

   You have one other choice to make if your appointment repeats on either a weekly or monthly basis. You can set weekly appointments to recur on several days of the week, such as Monday, Wednesday, and Friday, by simply tapping the various days. Notice that the days are set on a *toggle,* meaning that you must tap them again to deselect them. If you're setting up a monthly appointment, tap either Day (for example, the 3rd Monday of every month) or Date (for example, the 15th of every month).

132 Part II: Getting Down to Business

When you make any of these choices, text describing your recurrence pattern appears in the box at the bottom of the Change Repeat dialog box, such as "The 3rd Monday of every month." Keep an eye on this text to be sure that you've set up your appointment correctly.

10. **Tap OK.**

    The Change Repeat dialog box closes, and the Event Details dialog box opens.

11. **Tap OK.**

    The Event Details dialog box closes.

When you create a repeating appointment, each instance of the appointment looks like a separate item, but the occurrences are all connected in the mind of your PalmPilot. So if you change or delete one occurrence of the appointment, your PalmPilot wants to know if you're changing every occurrence or just that one. When your PalmPilot asks, just tell it what you want.

Private items

You can enjoy the thrill of a secret rendezvous with your PalmPilot. I suppose that you can enjoy the rendezvous without your PalmPilot, too, but your PalmPilot helps you remember the rendezvous while keeping it a secret to anyone else who looks at your PalmPilot.

1. **With the Date Book visible, tap the name of the appointment that you want to make private.**

    The insertion point appears on the line with your appointment's name.

2. **Tap Details.**

    The Event Details dialog box opens.

3. **Tap the check box next to Private.**

    A check mark appears in the check box to show you that you've marked the appointment private.

4. **Tap OK.**

    The Event Details dialog box closes. If you haven't chosen to hide all private records, you see a dialog box telling you how to hide all private records. In case you forgot, see Chapter 3 for more about hiding private items.

Of course, there is such a thing as too much secrecy. If you mark an appointment Private and then tell your PalmPilot to hide all Private Records, the appointment doesn't show on your PalmPilot. So you can't even see your private records yourself. That's a problem. To prevent keeping your secrets secret from yourself, tap the Applications icon, choose the Security icon, and then pick Show Private Records.

Putting Appointments in the Past

You may be the type of person who rarely enters anything directly into your PalmPilot. If you enter everything via a HotSync from your desktop computer, you'll still want to be able to delete existing appointments and set up your PalmPilot to suit your fancy.

Deleting appointments

Sooner or later, all your appointments become history. Perhaps you want to save all your appointment records for posterity. Perhaps you think posterity is baloney, and you want to get rid of the stuff once it's over. I go for the second choice.

Here's how to delete an appointment:

1. **With the Date Book visible, tap the name of the appointment that you want to delete.**

    The insertion point appears on the line with your appointment's name.

2. **Tap Menu.**

    The menu bar appears at the top of the display, as shown in Figure 8-10.

Figure 8-10: Want to delete an appointment? Choose Delete Event from this menu.

3. **Choose Record➪Delete Event.**

    The Delete Event dialog box opens.

4. Tap OK.

The Delete Event dialog box closes, and your appointment disappears. Simple as that. If you check the box that says "Save archive copy on PC," a wonderful thing happens: The next time you HotSync, the HotSync Manager saves a copy of the deleted item on your desktop computer. Who'd have thunk it? For more about archived items, see Chapter 12, and for more on HotSyncing, see Chapter 11.

 Another way to delete an appointment is to tap the appointment name, then tap Details, and then tap Delete. You get the same result either way: no more appointment.

Setting preferences

You can change your Date Book two ways: the number of hours it displays for each day and the type of alarm. If you feel compelled to customize your Date Book, here's how to do it.

To set Date Book preferences:

1. With the Date Book visible, tap Menu.

The menu bar appears at the top of the display.

2. Choose Options⇨Preferences.

The Preferences screen appears, as shown in Figure 8-11.

3. To change the start time, tap one of the triangles next to the Start Time box.

Tapping the top triangle makes the start time later. Tapping the bottom triangle makes the start time earlier.

Figure 8-11: Express your preferences in the Preferences screen. Otherwise, keep them to yourself, thank you.

4. **To change the end time, tap one of the triangles next to the End Time box.**

    The End Time box works just like the Start Time box (see the previous step).

5. **To change the default alarm preset, tap the Alarm Preset check box.**

    A check mark appears in the check box, and the alarm setting appears to the right of the check box. Normally, the alarm setting is 5 minutes.

6. **If you want to change the Alarm preset time, tap the word Minutes.**

    A list appears with the choices Minutes, Hours, or Days.

7. **Tap your choice of Minutes, Hours, or Days.**

    The list disappears, and the choice that you tapped appears.

8. **Enter the number of minutes, hours, or days before the appointment you want the alarm to sound with either the on-screen keyboard or Graffiti (see Chapter 2 for more about entering text).**

    The number that you enter appears next to the words Alarm Preset.

9. **To change the type of alarm sound that you hear when the alarm goes off, tap the triangle next to the words Alarm Sound.**

    A list of all the possible alarm sounds appears.

10. **Tap the type of the alarm sound that you want.**

    You have several squeaks and squawks to choose from. The sound that you tap plays, and its name appears in the Alarm Sound box.

11. **Tap the Remind Me box to choose the number of times that you want to be reminded of your appointment.**

    A list appears, offering choices ranging from Once to 10 Times.

12. **Tap the number of times that you want to be reminded.**

    The choice you tap appears in the Remind Me box.

13. **Tap the Play Every box to choose how often to replay the Alarm.**

    A list appears, offering choices ranging from 1 to 30 minutes.

14. **Tap the choice that you want in the Play Every box.**

    The choice that you tap appears in the Play Every box.

15. **Tap OK.**

Maybe I'm boring, but I've never changed my Date Book preferences. Maybe you're different. If I could get the alarm to play "Tea for Two," I might change my mind.

Purging your Date Book

Your PalmPilot can hold up to 10,000 appointments. That sounds like a lot, but sooner or later, you'll want to clear out some space and make room for more items. The fastest way to make room is to purge old Date Book items. Purging your Date Book is quick and easy, and it doesn't hurt a bit.

To purge your Date Book, follow these steps:

1. **With the Date Book visible, tap Menu.**

   The menu bar appears at the top of the display.

2. **Choose Record➪Purge.**

   The Purge dialog box opens, as shown in Figure 8-12. By default, your PalmPilot is set to purge appointments older than one week. If you want to change the age of purged appointments, tap the words 1 Week and choose from the list that appears.

3. **Tap OK.**

   The Purge dialog box closes.

Now you're rid of all the great things that you've done, and you can move on to the great things you're going to do. Isn't that inspiring?

Figure 8-12: Is your schedule too full? Purge it to make room for more appointments.

Chapter 9
Beaming PalmPilot Data through the Air with Infrared

In This Chapter
▶ Sending and receiving items
▶ Sending and receiving categories
▶ Sending and receiving applications

*P*eople often will pay more for something cool than they'll pay for something useful. At the moment, the ability to *beam* (or send) information between two Palm IIIs is more cool than useful; in fact, I would call this feature ultracool, and fortunately, it doesn't cost you anything extra. However, you may not find yourself in many situations in which you can use it — at least not until more people upgrade to the Palm III or later models. In this chapter, I give you the skinny on beaming so that you'll be ready when that first momentous beaming occasion presents itself.

The Beaming Thing

Beaming is a new feature on the Palm III that enables you to send information from one Palm III to another by directly pointing the two units at one another. As long as the units are within about 3 feet of one another, the process is quick and simple. My very subjective tests show that two Palm IIIs lose sight of each other when they're 4 feet apart, and they also have some trouble communicating at less then 3 inches or so. At a typical meeting table, you should have no trouble beaming information to a Palm III across from you.

The Palm III is currently the only model with the ability to beam information, but you can easily upgrade whatever PalmPilot you have by adding a $129 Palm 2MB memory card that turns any earlier PalmPilot model into a Palm III. For more about upgrading your PalmPilot, see Chapter 14.

The Palm III beaming feature uses *infrared* (or IR) light, which is what the remote control for your TV uses. Computer manufacturers have begun to include IR communications on laptops and printers. You also can find IR capability on certain advanced pagers and cellular telephones. But until more people own more devices that use IR, you won't get much mileage out of the technology.

Beaming is new enough to the PalmPilot world that few applications other than the standard PalmPilot applications have been built to use it. Even the PalmPilot Mail and Expense programs can't beam items at this point. I think that forwarding e-mail by beaming would be useful. Maybe next year.

In the following sections, I show you how to beam individual items, categories, and even applications.

Sending an item

When you beam information between a pair of Palm IIIs, you're copying information from one Palm III to the other. The data that you send remains on your unit and is duplicated on the second unit. Think of the process like sending a fax: Before you send a fax, only you have a copy of the information; after you're done, you and the receiver both have a copy of the information — only without the annoyingly poor quality of faxing!

Here's how to send an item:

1. **Make sure that both Palm IIIs are turned on and pointed at one another.**

   Keep the two Palm IIIs within 3 feet of one another.

2. **Select the item that you want to beam.**

   The item appears on your PalmPilot screen. You can send a memo, an address, a To Do item, or an appointment.

3. **Tap Menu.**

   The menu bar appears.

4. **Choose Record⇔Beam.**

   The menu indicates Beam Event for a Date Book appointment (as shown in Figure 9-1), Beam Address for an Address Book entry, and so on.

   The Beam dialog box opens for a short time, first telling you that it's preparing to beam and then that it's searching for another Palm III. After your Palm III finishes beaming the item, the dialog box closes.

Figure 9-1: This event will be on the air.

If all goes well, both Palm IIIs beep to let you know that the item reached its destination. Recipients actually know more about the transfer than you do because dialog boxes pop up on their Palm IIIs to say what's been received. If your transfer fails, your PalmPilot displays a message saying that something's wrong and that you should try again.

If you enter your own address in your PalmPilot Address Book and mark it as your business card, all you need to do when you want to beam your business card is hold down the Address Book button for about two seconds until the beaming process starts.

Receiving an item

Just because you're receiving an item rather than sending one doesn't mean that you can just stand there and do nothing. You can stand there and do *almost* nothing. Just watch the screen and tap Yes when the time comes, like this:

1. **Make sure that both Palm IIIs are turned on and pointed at one another.**

   The two Palm IIIs should be within 3 feet of one another.

2. **When your buddy sends an item to you, wait for the Beam dialog box to open.**

   The Beam dialog box tells you what's being beamed to you and asks whether you want to accept the item.

3. **Tap Yes or No.**

    If you tap No, the Beam dialog box closes, and that's the end of the process. If you tap Yes, the application to which the beamed item belongs opens, and shows you details of the item. For example, if the beamed item is someone's business card, your Address Book screen appears, showing the new address record that you're about to add to your Address List.

4. **Make any changes that you want to the beamed item.**

    You may want to change the category of the item, or just make a note about when or where the beamed item originated. For example, if someone beams you her business card at a trade show, you may want to make a note of the trade show at which you met.

5. **Tap Done.**

    The item closes, and you see the main screen of the application to which the beamed item belongs.

People can beam unsolicited items to you, but you can always refuse them by tapping No. My only gripe about how the routine works is that once you say Yes, your PalmPilot buries the item in the list of items in the unfiled category. If I want to go through the items that I received today, I have to guess which item came in when. If you assign categories to everything promptly, you won't have trouble figuring out what's new. For more about using categories, see Chapter 6.

Sending a category

You don't have to beam items one at a time, you can send an entire category at once. Of course, you're limited to sending bunches of items that can handle categories; for example, the Date Book has no categories, so you can only beam one appointment at a time. For more about using categories, see Chapter 6.

To beam an entire category, follow these steps:

1. **Make sure that both Palm IIIs are turned on and pointed at one another.**

    Keep the two Palm IIIs within about 3 feet of one another.

2. **Display the category that you want to beam.**

    The category appears on your PalmPilot screen.

3. **Tap Menu.**

   The menu bar appears.

4. **Choose Record➪Beam Category, as shown in Figure 9-2.**

   The Beam dialog box opens for a moment and then closes.

Figure 9-2:
Beam a whole category of tasks for someone else to do. That's how I spell relief.

Before the Beam dialog box closes, it tells you very briefly the name of the category that you're sending. A little Cancel button in the dialog box enables you to cancel the transfer if you've sent the wrong thing, but the dialog box closes so quickly that you really can't stop the transfer. Therefore, be sure that you really want to send the items that you're beaming.

Receiving a category

The process of receiving a whole category of items works just like receiving a single item (see "Receiving an item" earlier in this chapter). But receiving a category of items is a problem for two reasons:

✓ The first reason is that when you tap Yes to accept incoming items, the Palm III opens only one of the items that you received. If you want to edit or categorize the incoming items, you can only do so to the first item; all the others get mixed up with your unfiled items, so you have to dig them out one by one. Because you have no way of knowing exactly which items the other person sent, you may have trouble figuring out which items were sent by whom.

✔ The second reason is that the category markings are removed from incoming items; they're all marked "unfiled." There's a good reason for that: The Palm III can handle only 15 categories. If you were able to accept categorized items from lots of different people, you'd end up with a messy collection of categories. On the other hand, if someone sends you a category, you logically expect to get that category. I figure that the Palm people will address this issue in a future upgrade.

Sending an application

Believe it or not, you can beam an entire application from one Palm III to another. Frankly, beaming programs between Palm IIIs is much easier than installing programs from your desktop computer. Of course, you have to install the program first on your Palm III before you can share it with anyone else.

Some PalmPilot applications refuse to be beamed. The standard PalmPilot applications, for example, appear in the Beam list with a little padlock next to them, which means that you can't beam those programs because they're locked. In the future, many other PalmPilot programs will be locked the same way to prevent software piracy. At the moment, though, you can beam most PalmPilot software between Palm IIIs, by following these steps:

 1. **Make sure that both Palm IIIs are turned on and pointed at one another.**

    Keep the two Palm IIIs within about 3 feet of one another.

 2. **Tap the Applications soft button.**

    The Applications screen appears.

 3. **Tap Menu.**

    The menu bar appears.

 4. **Choose App⇨Beam.**

    The Beam screen appears, as shown in Figure 9-3, listing all your applications. The applications with little padlocks next to them are locked and can't be beamed.

 5. **Tap the name of the application that you want to beam.**

    The application that you tap is highlighted to indicate that you selected it.

 6. **Tap Beam.**

    The Beam dialog box opens, indicating which program you're sending. If you change your mind, tap Cancel.

Figure 9-3:
The locks show the programs that can't be beamed.

[Beam screen showing:
Address   2K
AirCalc   45K
BrainForest   80K
Date Book   1K
DietLog   87K
DigiPet   21K
EEToolkit   30K
Flash!   61K
Mail   2K
Memo Pad   2K]

Programs normally take longer to beam than individual items, so keep the Palm IIIs pointed at each other until the Beam dialog box closes, indicating that the process is complete. Programs take longer to beam because they're bigger, and bigger programs take longer to beam than smaller ones. You can see how big a program is by checking the number next to the name of the program in the Beam screen. I've never seen it take more than a few minutes to beam a program between Palm IIIs.

Receiving an application

The process of receiving a beamed application is just like receiving anything else (see "Receiving an item" earlier in this chapter, for details). After you agree to receive the application by clicking Yes in the Beam dialog box, your display switches to the Applications screen, showing the new program.

Here's the big catch to beaming applications: Only the actual program is copied to the receiving Palm III. Files created or used by the program don't come over with the program. For example, if you beam AportisDoc — the document-reading program — from a Palm III that has several text files in AportisDoc, those files aren't copied, only the program itself is. You can't beam AportisDoc files; you have to install the documents through the regular Palm Install Tool from a desktop. The problem is even worse if you want to beam a program that requires an additional file, such as a dictionary, in order to run. If you beam Bogglet (the PalmPilot version of the word game Boggle), the dictionary file that Bogglet relies on to create puzzles doesn't transfer along with the program, so the program doesn't work unless you use Palm Desktop to install the dictionary.

Beaming into the Future

Naturally, plenty of people want to write PalmPilot programs that take advantage of the ability to sling data through the air, but only a few programs are finished so far. A couple of products that I've heard of (but not tested myself) sound pretty interesting.

PalmPrint from Stevens Creek Software (www.stevenscreek.com) is working on a program that enables you to print via infrared to any suitably equipped printer. At this point, HP, Canon, and other companies have printers with IR capability. With the PalmPrint IR program, you'll be able to point your Palm III at a printer and print a memo, task, or appointment on the spot.

Several software vendors are talking about creating IR HotSync products, which would enable you to point your Palm III at a desktop or laptop computer and perform a HotSync without placing your Palm III in a cradle.

I've even heard rumors about products that enable you to use your Palm III as a remote control for your TV or VCR. The IR capabilities of the Palm III would be useful that way, but some folks say that the tiny IR transmitter in the Palm III is too weak to get all the way from your couch to your TV. If you have to get off the couch to move within 3 feet of your TV, I guess that you may as well make the rest of the journey, right? But I like the idea anyway.

Chapter 10
Special Delivery: Using PalmPilot Mail

In This Chapter
- Understanding the PalmPilot Postal System
- Creating, reading, and replying to messages
- Deleting and purging messages
- Saving drafts
- Setting HotSync options
- Filtering messages
- Using signatures

Romantic movies always have a scene where a character moons over a letter from his Special Someone. Romantic Reader ambles down the streets of Paris reading the letter and hearing Special Someone's voice as the movie soundtrack swells.

That scene would be difficult to imagine if Special Someone had sent Romantic Reader an e-mail. Imagine poor Romantic Reader trying to drag a desktop computer through the Left Bank with an endless extension cord, or trying to balance a laptop on his knee while overlooking the Seine, hoping that the laptop batteries don't go dead in ten minutes.

Although e-mail is convenient, the business of sitting in front of a computer to read and write e-mail isn't so convenient. Your PalmPilot includes a rather basic e-mail program that enables you to carry a little bucket of messages wherever you go. You can read messages and compose replies while you're sitting on the Seine or riding the subway. I have to admit that the program has its limits, but I often find it handy to deal with my e-mail on my PalmPilot; plugging in my desktop computer on the crosstown bus can be a bit difficult.

Making Sense of the PalmPilot Postal System

The PalmPilot Mail program doesn't exchange messages like a desktop e-mail package does. Like the PalmPilot itself, the Mail program acts as an accessory to the programs on your desktop, in this case your e-mail program. When you perform a HotSync, the PalmPilot Mail program copies the messages in your desktop e-mail program's Inbox and stores those copies on your PalmPilot. You can read or reply to those messages or compose new messages on your PalmPilot when you're away from your desktop computer. When you get back to your desktop computer, you need to perform another HotSync to move your outgoing messages to your desktop e-mail program, which does the work of actually delivering the messages.

The PalmPilot Mail program can't send messages directly to their recipients without a desktop e-mail program acting as a middleman (or middleperson for all you politically correct readers out there). That's not what it's designed to do.

You can overcome this limitation by taking a few extra steps. If you want to send e-mail directly from your PalmPilot, you need something that connects your PalmPilot to the Internet: either the PalmPilot Modem or one of those very cool wireless modems like the Minstrel Modem that I mention in Chapter 17. You also need to buy an independent e-mail program for your PalmPilot, such as HandMail, which I mention in Chapter 14.

In the following sections, I focus on showing you how to use what comes out of the box with your PalmPilot.

Working with Your Messages

You can use the built-in PalmPilot Mail program only if you have a desktop mail program with which to synchronize it. You can do many of the same tasks with PalmPilot Mail that you can with your desktop e-mail program, such as read and write messages, reply to messages, and forward messages. However, some popular e-mail features aren't available in PalmPilot Mail, especially the ability to attach files or read files that are attached to incoming messages. You may be willing to trade those features for the ability to read your e-mail on a bicycle built for two (preferably on the backseat), but the choice is up to you.

To access your PalmPilot e-mail program, tap the Applications soft button and then choose the Mail application. The Mail program's Inbox opens.

Creating a message

Creating a new e-mail message is a lot like writing a regular paper letter. All that you need is an address and a message. Actually, all that you really need is an address; but sending a message as well is a sign of good manners.

Follow these steps to create a new message:

1. **With the Mail program open, tap New.**

    The New Message screen appears. If you know your recipient's e-mail address by heart, then enter that address by using Graffiti or the on-screen keyboard. If you do this, skip ahead to Step 7.

    If you don't know your recipient's address, you can look it up in your Address Book. Continue with Step 2 if you're in this particular boat.

2. **Tap the word To.**

    The To screen appears.

3. **Tap Lookup.**

    The To Lookup screen appears (see Figure 10-1), showing the e-mail addresses of the people that you entered in your Address List. It doesn't show everyone in your Address Book, just those who have e-mail addresses. Convenient, eh?

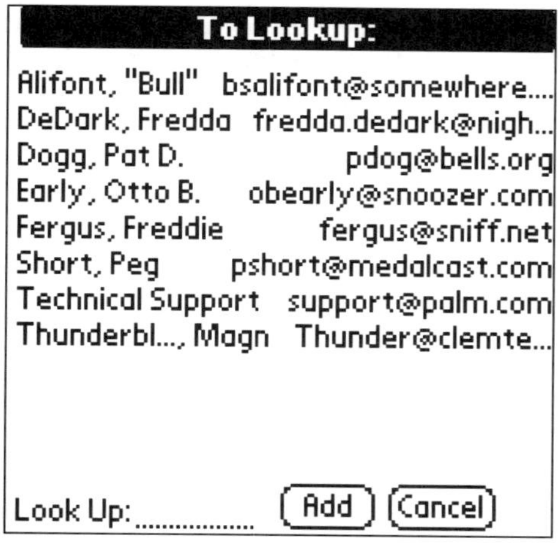

Figure 10-1:
If you don't know your recipient's e-mail address, you can pick a name from your Address Book in the To Lookup screen.

```
        To Lookup:
Alifont, "Bull"   bsalifont@somewhere....
DeDark, Fredda    fredda.dedark@nigh...
Dogg, Pat D.              pdog@bells.org
Early, Otto B.       obearly@snoozer.com
Fergus, Freddie        fergus@sniff.net
Short, Peg          pshort@medalcast.com
Technical Support    support@palm.com
Thunderbl..., Magn   Thunder@clemte...




Look Up: .............  (Add) (Cancel)
```

4. **Tap the name of the person to whom you're sending your message.**

    The name that you tap is highlighted to show that you selected it.

5. **Tap Add.**

   The e-mail address of the person that you selected appears in the To screen. You can repeat Steps 3 through 5 for each person to whom you want to send copies of the message.

6. **Tap Done.**

   The New Message screen reappears showing the names of the people that you've chosen to send your message to.

7. **If you want to send copies of your message to additional people, tap the line to the right of CC.**

   CC is highlighted to show that you selected it. If you know your recipient's e-mail address, just write it in by using Graffiti or the on-screen keyboard. If you don't know the e-mail address and want to check your Address Book, repeat Step 2 (tapping CC instead of To) through Step 6 for each CC addressee that you want to add.

8. **Tap the line to the right of Subj.**

   A blinking line, called the *insertion point,* appears, and Subj is highlighted, as shown in Figure 10-2.

   If you tap Subj itself, the Subject screen appears. Opening the Subject screen is an extra step that you don't really need to take because you can enter your subject in the New Message screen. But if you prefer to use the Subject screen, tap Done when you finish entering your text, and continue to Step 10.

9. **Enter the subject of your message by using either the on-screen keyboard or Graffiti (see Chapter 2 for more on entering text).**

   The text that you enter appears on the Subject line.

Figure 10-2: In the New Message screen, enter the subject of your message as you would any other text.

Chapter 10: Special Delivery: Using PalmPilot Mail

10. **Tap to the right of Body.**

    The insertion point appears, and Body is highlighted.

    If you tap Body itself, the Body screen appears. Just like with the Subject line, this is an extra step that you don't really need to take. But if you prefer using this screen to enter your message, just tap Done when you finish, and continue to Step 12.

11. **Enter the text of your message by using either the on-screen keyboard or Graffiti.**

    The text that you enter appears on the screen.

12. **Tap Send.**

    Your message closes and moves to the Outbox.

Even though you tapped Send, your message isn't on its way to your recipient. Tapping Send simply moves your message to the Outbox. The next time that you HotSync your PalmPilot, everything in the Outbox moves to your desktop e-mail program, which then sends your message off.

Reading a message

A true boon to humanity, the PalmPilot now enables me to read my e-mail while waiting for the bus, so I can waste time two ways at once. While I'm at it, I can also do some deep knee bends to make myself look foolish in public. (I don't need a PalmPilot to make me look foolish; I do that quite nicely on my own, thank you very much.)

To read your messages:

1. **With the Mail program open, tap the pull-down list in the upper-right corner of the Mail screen to see the list of available folders.**

    The list includes Inbox, Outbox, Deleted, Filed, and Draft. You can expect to find new messages in the Inbox.

2. **Tap the name of the folder that you want to view.**

    The folder that you tap appears on the screen, showing a list of messages.

3. **Tap the message that you want to read.**

    The text of the message that you tap appears.

4. **After you finish reading the message, tap Done.**

    Your message closes, and the list of messages reappears. A check mark appears next to the message that you just read.

If you want to cycle through your messages but don't want to return to the message list, just use the two left- and right-pointing triangles at the bottom of each message screen. Tapping one of those triangles enables you to see the next message or the previous message. That feature is useful, but for some reason I think of the next message as being *below* the current message, rather than to the right. Anyway, that's what those triangles do, in case you were wondering.

While you're reading a message, you may also notice a pair of icons in the upper-right corner of the message screen. One looks like a tiny message containing a lot of text, and the other looks like a tiny message with only a little bit of text. If you tap the icon that looks like it holds a lot of text, you'll reveal the message *headers,* the information that comes before the body of the message, including who the message is to and from, the subject of the message, and the date the message was sent. The other icon conceals everything except the name of the person who sent the message and the subject of the message. You can tap either icon any time to see as much or little header information as you want. I prefer to see less header information.

Replying to a message

The simplest way to address a message to somebody is to reply to a message that they've sent you. Here's what to do:

1. **With the Mail program open, tap the message that you want to reply to.**

    The text of the message that you tap appears.

2. **Tap Reply.**

    The Reply Options dialog box opens, as shown in Figure 10-3.

Figure 10-3: You can reply just to the person who sent you the message or to everyone that it was addressed to.

3. **Tap either Sender or All.**

   If you choose Sender, your reply goes only to the person(s) listed on the To line of the message. If you choose All, your reply goes to the person(s) on the CC line as well. To see what happens when you tap Forward, see the next section of this chapter.

   You probably notice two additional options: Include Original Text and Comment Original Text. If you check the first option, the text of the message that you're replying to is included with the message that you're sending. Checking the second box puts a caret symbol (>) in front of every line of the original text so that the person getting your reply can quickly see which text they wrote and which text you added. You can check the first box, neither box, or both boxes, but if you just check the second box, nothing happens. You can't add comment marks to the original text unless you include the original text. Normally, I leave both boxes checked.

4. **Tap OK.**

   The New Message screen appears. Your recipient's e-mail address appears on the To line, and the Subject line shows Re: followed by the subject of the original message. If you chose in Step 3 to include the original message text in your reply, that text appears in the body of your new message.

   You can change any of this text by deleting and adding text as you normally would.

5. **If you want to add new addresses to either the To or CC line of the message, enter the new addresses on those lines.**

   You can add an address to a message that you're replying to the same way that you do when you create a new message. See "Creating a message," earlier in this chapter, for details.

6. **If you want to add text to your message, tap to the right of Body.**

   The insertion point appears. If you chose to include the original message's text, your PalmPilot conveniently leaves you a blank line to start writing your reply text.

   If you tap the word Body itself, the Body screen appears with the subject of your message at the top. If you enter your text in the Body screen rather than the New Message screen, just tap Done when you finish entering your text, and continue to Step 8.

7. **Enter the text that you wish to add by using either the on-screen keyboard or Graffiti (see Chapter 2 for more about entering text).**

   The text that you enter appears with the original message's text.

8. **Tap Send.**

   Your message closes and moves to the Outbox to await delivery.

Forwarding a message

Forwarding a message is just like replying to a message (see the previous section), except that instead of sending a message back to the person who sent you the original message, you send a message to a third person.

To forward a message:

1. **With the Mail program open, tap the message that you want to forward.**

   The text of the message that you tap appears.

2. **Tap Reply.**

   The Reply Options dialog box opens.

3. **Tap Forward.**

   When you forward a message, the text of a message that you received from one person is sent to another person.

4. **Tap OK.**

   The New Message screen appears, containing the text of the message that you're forwarding. In the Subject line, you see Fwd:, followed by the subject of the original message.

5. **On the To line, enter the e-mail address of the person to whom you're forwarding the message.**

   You address a message that you're forwarding the same way that you do when you create a new message. See "Creating a message," earlier in this chapter, for the lowdown.

6. **If you want to add text to your message, tap to the right of Body.**

   The insertion point appears. If you tap the word Body itself, a new screen appears for the body text, with the subject of the message at the top. You can enter text in either this screen or the New Message screen, your choice. If you choose to enter text in the Body screen, just tap Done when you're finished, and continue to Step 8.

7. **Enter the text that you wish to add by using either the on-screen keyboard or Graffiti (see Chapter 2 for more on entering text).**

   The text that you enter appears with the message text.

8. **Tap Send.**

   Your message closes and moves to the Outbox to await delivery.

Chapter 10: Special Delivery: Using PalmPilot Mail   153

People seem to enjoy forwarding jokes by e-mail. I guess forwarding a joke to 25 people is faster than standing around the water cooler, waiting for them to show up so you can repeat the joke to each of them, one by one. Also, using your PalmPilot to forward jokes by e-mail makes you look like you're working (except to those who know better).

Deleting a message

Your PalmPilot seems to have plenty of space until you start loading it with e-mail. You'd be surprised how easy you can collect enough e-mail to fill 1 or 2MB of memory. Fortunately, deleting a message is just as easy. Here's how:

1. **With the Mail program open, tap the message that you want to delete.**

   The text of the message that you tap appears.

2. **Tap Delete.**

   Your message disappears. If you have Confirm Deleted Message checked in the Preferences dialog box (tap the Menu soft button, and then choose Options➪Preferences), the Delete Message dialog box opens, as shown in Figure 10-4. Just tap Yes to get rid of that pesky message.

Figure 10-4: Tap Yes to delete.

Presto! Your message has magically disappeared — sort of. Actually, when you choose to delete messages, they move to the Deleted folder and wait for you to purge them.

If you change your mind after deleting a message, you can undelete a message from the Deleted Items folder. Open the Deleted Items folder by tapping the list of folder names in the upper-right corner of the Mail screen, and then choose Deleted. Tap the message that you want to undelete to open it, and then tap the Undelete button at the bottom of the message screen. When you tap Undelete, your message returns to the Inbox.

Part II: Getting Down to Business

When you HotSync, your PalmPilot Inbox is forced to match the Inbox on your desktop e-mail program. Therefore, if you delete a message from your desktop e-mail program, the next HotSync removes that message from your PalmPilot Inbox as well. You may find it easier to delete messages from your desktop and then HotSync. Most desktop e-mail programs enable you to delete batches of messages all at once, which is faster and easier than deleting messages one by one on your PalmPilot.

If you want to take a message out of the Inbox but leave it on your PalmPilot, you can move the message to the Filed folder. Just tap the Menu soft button and then tap Message➪File. That way, when all the messages in your Inbox are replaced by a new set during the next HotSync, the ones that you sent to the Filed folder stay put. To see the contents of your Filed folder, tap the folder list at the upper-right corner of the Inbox screen and then tap Filed.

Purging deleted messages

Deleting a message doesn't totally eliminate that message from your collection. A deleted message moves to the Deleted folder until you purge your deleted items, like this:

1. **With the Mail program open, tap Menu.**

   The menu bar appears.

2. **Choose Purge➪Deleted.**

   The Purge Deleted Message dialog box opens, as shown in Figure 10-5.

3. **Tap Yes.**

   The Purge Deleted Message dialog box closes, and your messages are gone forever.

Figure 10-5: The Purge Deleted Message dialog box warns you about wiping out your deleted messages.

Chapter 10: Special Delivery: Using PalmPilot Mail

The Deleted folder exists to save you if you accidentally delete an item and then change your mind and want to undelete it. But the best way to save space on your PalmPilot is to purge deleted messages frequently.

One big difference between deleting e-mail messages and deleting other items on your PalmPilot is that no archive for deleted messages exists on the Palm Desktop. Your desktop e-mail program serves as the archive. So make sure that you really want those message to disappear forever before you delete them.

Saving drafts

If you tap Cancel while composing a new message, the Save Draft dialog box asks you if you want to save a draft of the message. If you tap Yes, your incomplete message moves to the Drafts folder where you can return to it later. Isn't that thoughtful?

Tapping No deletes your incomplete message forever, and Cancel simply returns you to the message itself.

Sending a blind copy

Sending blind copies of your messages is a sneaky way to inform someone about your communications with a third person without that third person knowing. For example, if you need more cooperation from someone in another department of your company, you can send that person an e-mail asking for the help that you need, and at the same time, send a blind copy to the person who supervises both of you. The person that you're addressing the message to doesn't know that you've clued in the boss.

Blind copies, or BCCs, are so sneaky that the line for them is hidden unless you know how to find and use it. Here, I let you in on the secret:

1. **With the Mail program open, tap New.**

   The New Message screen appears.

2. **Tap Details.**

   The Message Details dialog box opens.

3. **Tap the check box labeled BCC.**

   A check appears in the box, as shown in Figure 10-6.

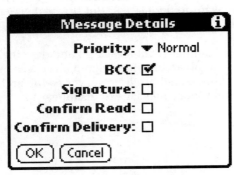

Figure 10-6: To send a secret blind copy of a message, find the secret check box in the Message Details dialog box.

4. **Tap OK.**

   The Message Details dialog box closes, and the BCC line appears in the New Message screen.

5. **Tap BCC in the New Message screen.**

   The BCC screen appears. If you know the e-mail address of your BCC addressee by heart, enter the address by using Graffiti or the on-screen keyboard, tap Done, and continue creating your message. If you need to look up the address of the BCC addressee, continue on to Step 6.

6. **Tap Lookup.**

   The BCC Lookup screen appears, showing all the names and e-mail addresses in your Address Book. Not everyone in your Address Book shows up on this list, only the ones with e-mail addresses.

7. **Tap the name of the person to whom you want to send a blind copy.**

   The name that you tap is highlighted to show that you selected it.

8. **Tap Add.**

   The name that you chose appears in the BCC screen.

9. **Tap Done.**

   The name that you chose appears on the BCC line of your message.

10. **Continue creating your message.**

Well, now the secret is out. Don't forget; you saw it here first.

Sorting messages

Usually I like to read messages in the order in which I receive them, but sometimes I like to see all the messages from a certain person lined up in a row. Other times I want to read all the messages about a certain subject all at once. You can sort your messages three different ways, depending on what you need.

To change the sort order of your messages:

1. **With the Mail program open, tap Show.**

    The Show Options dialog box opens.

2. **Tap the triangle next to Sort By.**

    A list of ways to sort your messages appears, including Date, Sender, and Subject (see Figure 10-7).

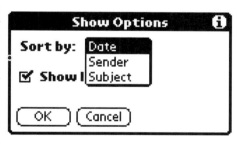

Figure 10-7: In the Show Options dialog box, you can sort your messages by date, sender, or subject.

3. **Tap your choice.**

    The sort type appears next to Sort By.

4. **If you want to display the date that you received each message, tap the check box next to Show Date.**

5. **Tap OK.**

    Your messages appear sorted the way that you chose.

This sort order remains in effect until you choose a different sort order.

Customizing Your PalmPilot E-Mail

After you develop a serious PalmPilot e-mail habit, you'll need to know some techniques for managing the messages that you get, customizing the messages that you send, and speeding up the process of synchronizing your messages with your desktop. You many never use these tricks, but I want you to know they're available.

Setting HotSync options

After you gather a healthy-sized collection of items on your PalmPilot, the HotSync process may slow down quite a bit. At first a HotSync should take only a few seconds, but after a couple of months, a HotSync may take several minutes, which is a big deal for people as busy as you and me. You may want to shorten your HotSync time by telling your PalmPilot to limit e-mail activity to just sending or just receiving messages that you haven't read yet. You can ignore the HotSync options if you want, with no ill effect.

To set HotSync e-mail options:

1. **With the Mail program open, tap Menu.**

    The menu bar appears.

2. **Choose Options⇨HotSync Options.**

    The HotSync Options screen appears, as shown in Figure 10-8.

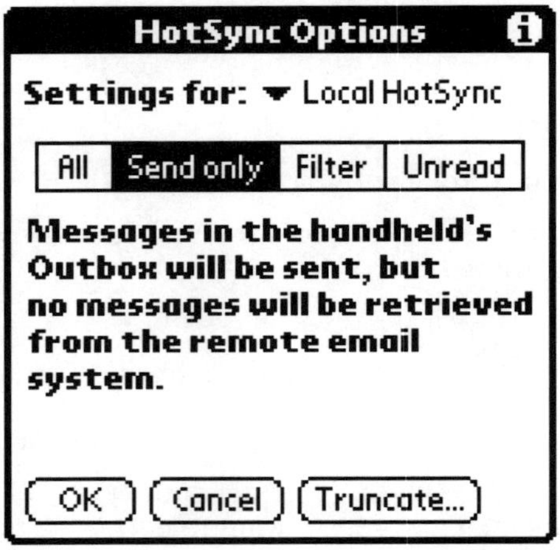

Figure 10-8: In the HotSync Options screen, you can take your pick of HotSync e-mail options.

3. **Tap the triangle next to Settings For.**

   A list appears that enables you to choose either Local HotSync or Remote HotSync. You may want to make different things happen when you perform a modem HotSync than when you do a local HotSync. Modem HotSyncs are slower than local HotSyncs, so if you only download unread messages, for example, you save time and money when you do a long-distance modem HotSync. On the other hand, you may want to get all your messages when you do a local HotSync, so you need to be able to create different settings for the two types of HotSyncs. If you never attach your PalmPilot to a modem, you don't need to think about modem HotSync options.

4. **Tap either Local HotSync or Remote HotSync.**

   Your choice appears next to Settings For. You're not limited to setting only Local or only Remote HotSync options; you just have to set the options for each type of HotSync one at a time.

5. **Tap one of the boxes below Settings For.**

   A definition for each setting appears in the space below. Here's the skinny on each setting:

   - **All** means that all messages in your desktop Inbox are copied to your PalmPilot and all outgoing messages are transferred to your desktop when you HotSync.

   - **Send only** means that only outgoing messages are transferred to your PalmPilot when you HotSync. Incoming messages stay on your desktop computer.

   - **Filter** means that you can tell your PalmPilot to accept certain kinds of messages and reject others. For example, you can set up a filter to accept only messages marked high priority. I discuss message filtering in greater detail in "Filtering messages," later in this chapter.

   - **Unread** means that your PalmPilot accepts only those messages that you haven't read yet. The ones that you've read stay on your desktop.

6. **Tap OK.**

   The HotSync Options screen disappears, and your message list reappears.

If you frequently perform remote HotSyncs via a modem, you can set remote HotSync options separately from your local HotSync options. Your PalmPilot automatically picks the options that you want depending on which type of HotSync you're doing. For example, you may want to exchange all messages when you're doing a local HotSync, but send messages only when you do a remote HotSync.

Filtering messages

Filtering is a fairly sophisticated HotSync option. Filtering enables you to set up rules to limit the messages that the system copies to your PalmPilot, based on the priority of the message, the name of the person whose address appears in the To or From line, or the text in the Subject line.

I know people who get hundreds of e-mail messages every day. If performing a HotSync copied all their messages to their PalmPilots, no room would be left for anything but e-mail. Filtering is a good idea for those who get more e-mail than they want on their PalmPilots, but still want to take some messages with them. Here's how to filter your messages:

1. **With the Mail program open, tap Menu.**

    The menu bar appears.

2. **Choose Options⇨HotSync Options.**

    The HotSync Options screen appears.

3. **Choose either Local or Modem HotSync.**

4. **Tap Filter.**

    Options for filtering messages appear, as shown in Figure 10-9.

5. **If you want to copy only High Priority messages to your PalmPilot, tap the check box next to Retrieve All High Priority.**

6. **If you want to create a rule for selecting a type of message to retrieve, tap the triangle at the left edge of the screen.**

    A list appears with two choices: Ignore Messages Containing and Retrieve Only Messages Containing.

Figure 10-9: You filter the junk out of your water, so why not filter the junk out of your e-mail messages, too!

7. Choose the type of rule that you want to create.
8. **If you want to ignore or receive messages according to the address of the person they're sent to, enter that e-mail address on the To line.**

    "Wait a minute," you say. "I'm the recipient of my own e-mail, so if I choose to ignore my own e-mail address, then I won't get any messages, right?" Well, technically, yes. It may seem silly to filter messages addressed to yourself, but you may discover reasons to exclude certain messages. First, you may get e-mail addressed to a mailing list. People on mailing lists often get dozens of messages every day, and you may not want to clutter up your PalmPilot with that kind of stuff. Besides, you can still look at the excluded messages on your desktop computer. Another reason is that your desktop e-mail program may collect messages from two e-mail addresses. If you have one address for business and another for personal, you can filter out one or the other type of message by putting that e-mail address on the To line.

9. **To ignore or receive messages from a particular sender, enter that sender's address on the From line.**

    You can enter multiple addresses on this line; just separate them with a comma.

10. **To ignore or receive messages in which the subject line contains a certain word or phrase, enter that text on the Subj line.**
11. **Tap OK.**

    The HotSync Options screen disappears, and your message list reappears.

If you're used to the more elaborate rules and filters in your desktop e-mail program, you can have your desktop computer do all the filtering for you before you HotSync your PalmPilot. Remember, only the items in the Inbox of your desktop program are copied to your PalmPilot, so if you sort your desktop Inbox before running HotSync, only the messages that make the cut on the desktop find their way to your PalmPilot.

Most people that I know are perfectly happy without ever using any kind of e-mail rule or filter. So if you ignore filtering entirely, you're probably just as well off.

Using signatures

Lots of people like to personalize their e-mail with a standard bunch of text at the end of each message. Most popular e-mail programs enable you to set up a signature, so why not use signatures on the messages that you create with your PalmPilot? Why, indeed, when the process is this simple:

1. **With the Mail program open, tap Menu.**

   The menu bar appears.

2. **Choose Options➪Preferences.**

   The Preferences screen appears, as shown in Figure 10-10.

Figure 10-10: Individualize your e-mail with a flashy signature.

3. **Enter your signature text by using the on-screen keyboard or Graffiti (see Chapter 2 for more on entering text).**

   The text that you enter appears on the Preferences screen.

4. **Tap OK.**

   The Preferences screen disappears, and your message list reappears. Your signature will automatically be added to all your outgoing messages from now on.

One little detail about signatures: You can't see them yourself when you create your messages. The Mail program adds the signature when you send a message, so don't worry if you don't see your signature.

Setting truncating options

One of the limitations of using a tiny device like a PalmPilot for reading e-mail is severe space limitations. You may not care much about megabytes or RAM until you run out of them. That's why the PalmPilot Mail program automatically truncates, or chops off, messages at a certain length. You can determine the length, but you're still limited to 8,000 characters. Because the full text of your messages is stored on your desktop computer, you can always look in your desktop e-mail program to see what got lopped off of the messages on your PalmPilot.

Chapter 10: Special Delivery: Using PalmPilot Mail

Here's how to set the length at which messages are truncated:

1. **With the Mail program open, tap Menu.**

   The menu bar appears.

2. **Choose Options➪HotSync Options.**

   The HotSync Options screen appears.

3. **Tap Truncate.**

   The Truncate Options dialog box opens, as shown in Figure 10-11.

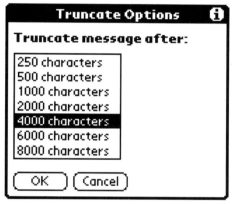

Figure 10-11: You can include anything you want in a message, as long as the message is less than 8,000 characters.

4. **Tap the maximum message length that you want.**

   The choice that you tap is highlighted to show that you selected it.

5. **Tap OK.**

   The Truncate Options dialog box closes, and the HotSync Options screen appears.

6. **Tap OK.**

   The HotSync Options screen disappears, and your message list reappears.

The other thing that your PalmPilot Mail program chops off is attachments. If someone sends you a file — such as a word-processing document or a spreadsheet — that's attached to a message, you won't see the extra file on your PalmPilot. You can still see the file on your desktop computer, but the PalmPilot just doesn't have space for the extra file. Instead, it simply tells you that a file was attached.

Part III
PalmPilot and the Outside World

The 5th Wave — By Rich Tennant

"Well, here's what happened—I forgot to put it on my To Do List."

In this part . . .

Your PalmPilot isn't meant to be left all alone. You need to hook it up to a regular desktop or laptop computer to take full advantage of the PalmPilot's features. In this part, you find out how to help your PalmPilot and your regular computer carry out a meaningful relationship.

Chapter 11

Installing and HotSyncing to the Desktop Programs for Windows and Mac

In This Chapter
- Installing the Palm Desktop for Windows
- Installing the Pilot Desktop for Macintosh
- HotSyncing between your PalmPilot and your PC or Mac

*I*n theory, you could use your PalmPilot all by itself, with no other computer involved. But if you're only interested in doing things the easiest way possible (my favorite way), then the PalmPilot desktop programs (pick your flavor: Windows or Macintosh) may be the best way to put things into your PalmPilot. You can carry your PalmPilot around to read your saved data and fiddle with it a little bit, as you see fit. I still prefer to enter most of my PalmPilot data by using Graffiti (see Chapter 2), but most people that I know don't. You can put information into your PalmPilot in many clever ways, but the desktop program is the simplest and most understandable method for anyone who has used a computer before. In this chapter, I show you how to install the Palm Desktop for Windows and the Pilot Desktop for the Macintosh, and I tell you all that you need to know about HotSyncing your PalmPilot to your desktop computer. In Chapter 12, I show you how to do all that cool PalmPilot-type stuff on your desktop computer.

Installing Palm Desktop for Windows

Hold up! Stop! (Did I get your attention?)

Before you install your desktop software, you need to hook up the PalmPilot cradle to your desktop computer.

> ### Different names for the same program? What gives?
>
> Palm Desktop 3.0 is the latest name for the program that manages your PalmPilot from your desktop, Windows-based computer. For those of you who have PalmPilot models prior to Palm III, Palm Desktop was once called PalmPilot Desktop. The two programs look a little bit different, but in action they're mostly similar.
>
> You can run Palm Desktop 3.0 under Windows 95, 98, or NT. The program is on the CD that comes with your PalmPilot, so you need a CD-ROM drive to install the program onto your desktop computer. If you don't have a CD-ROM drive, contact 3Com, the manufacturer of the PalmPilot, and the folks there will send you the program on floppy disks.
>
> You can still get a copy of the Palm Desktop for Windows 3.x if you contact 3Com and ask for the old program on floppy disks. Frankly, Windows 3.1 is a perfectly good host for a PalmPilot. The desktop program works like a champ, and there's absolutely no difference in what you do to make the PalmPilot do its thing.
>
> The Pilot Desktop 1.01 for the Macintosh is pretty much like the Palm Desktop for Windows. Don't ask me why the Palm people changed the name — I just work here. The Pilot Desktop works on any Mac running System 7.5 or higher, but it doesn't come in the box with your PalmPilot. You have to go out and buy something called a MacPac, which costs about $20 and has the program on four installation floppy disks. The MacPac also includes a serial port adapter for your PalmPilot cradle.
>
> By the time you read this, the Palm people should have straightened out this name game thing (at least that's the plan). They intend to give their Mac desktop program the name *Palm Desktop for Macintosh* to make it similar — only in name — to the Windows version. The Palm Desktop for Mac, however, will be based on Claris Organizer, which is the feature-rich personal information manager (PIM) that Palm recently bought from Apple Computer. This new desktop program wasn't available for review at the time of this writing, but it promises to make users of the Windows desktop program salivate with envy. To keep up on the latest news about this update, check out the Mac area of the 3Com Web site at www.palmpilot.3com.com/macintosh/index.html.

Connecting the cradle to your PC

Normally, you can simply plug your PalmPilot cradle into the only plug — or serial port — on the back of the PC in which it fits. If you can plug the cradle into the back of your PC easily, you've got it made. Just shout "Hooray!," pass Go, and collect $200 (or just jump ahead to the next section). If you can't plug the cradle right in, you have to do some fiddling around (see the sidebar "Cradle connection woes and how to fix 'em").

Cradle connection woes and how to fix 'em

If your desktop computer is fairly new, chances are that the serial port is unoccupied and working. The serial port is usually a small plug with 9 small pins. However, some serial ports are slightly larger and have 25 small holes instead of 9 small pins. The PalmPilot cradle comes with an extra adapter that you can put on the end of your cradle cable so that it plugs into the port with 25 small holes. But don't mistake the larger serial port plug for your printer port, which has 25 small pins. That port won't work with your PalmPilot. Is that clear? Of course not. The collection of ports on the back of a PC often confuse the most experienced technician, so don't be too concerned if they seem to make no sense.

Another common problem with PC serial ports is that sometimes they're occupied. You may have a mouse plugged into your serial port or an external modem or who knows what else. Most PCs have two serial ports, named COM1 and COM2; if you've filled up both serial ports, you may need to have your friendly local computer technician install a couple of extra serial ports to accommodate your PalmPilot. Technicians often own PalmPilots themselves, so they know what to do.

Now, you get to install Palm Desktop

Palm Desktop 3.0 for Windows enables your computer to talk to and work with your PalmPilot through a process called HotSyncing. You need to install the desktop software only once, and then you're through. All that you need to do after that is place your PalmPilot in the cradle and press the HotSync button on the cradle every day or so. More on HotSyncing later in the chapter.

After you connect the cradle to your computer, you can install Palm Desktop by following these steps:

1. **Put the CD that came with your PalmPilot in your CD-ROM drive.**

   The Palm Desktop Installer Menu appears.

2. **Click Install.**

   The Welcome screen appears to tell you what's about to happen.

3. **Click Next.**

   The preinstall screen appears, telling you to connect your HotSync cradle, leave the PalmPilot out of the cradle for the moment, and install the batteries in your PalmPilot.

4. **Click Next.**

   The Select Components dialog box opens, as shown in Figure 11-1. If you don't want to install something listed in the Select Components dialog box, uncheck the item by clicking the box with your mouse. I recommend leaving everything checked.

Part III: PalmPilot and the Outside World

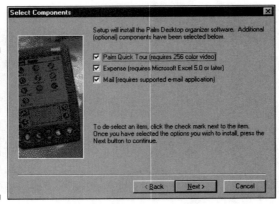

Figure 11-1: You can pick and choose which Palm Desktop components you want to install.

5. **Click Next.**

   The Choose Destination Location dialog box opens. Normally, the destination is C:/Palm, which is fine, so you can leave this default alone, too. If you want to change the location, click the Browse button and choose a different location for your PalmPilot files.

6. **Click Next.**

   The Select Program Folder dialog box appears. Palm Desktop is the folder that comes up if you don't make any changes. I'd leave it alone.

7. **Click Next.**

   The Create User Account dialog box opens, as shown in Figure 11-2. This dialog box is where you assign a user name to your PalmPilot.

8. **Type in your name.**

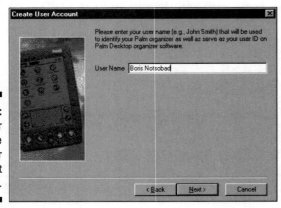

Figure 11-2: Type your name in the Create User Account dialog box.

Chapter 11: Installing and HotSyncing to the Desktop Programs

9. Click Next.

   The Serial Port Setup dialog box opens. The only reason for this dialog box is to remind you to put your PalmPilot in the cradle so that the Install program can test the connections between your PalmPilot and your desktop computer.

10. **Place your PalmPilot in the cradle and click OK.**

    The Install program copies files for a few moments, and then the Perform Mail Setup dialog box opens.

11. **If you want to set up the PalmPilot Mail application, click Yes.**

    The Palm Mail Setup dialog box opens. If you choose No, you can set up mail later through the HotSync Manager. For more on the PalmPilot Mail program, see Chapter 10.

12. **Pick the type of e-mail system that you currently use from the Synchronize With list.**

    You can choose from a variety of e-mail systems, including Microsoft Exchange, Microsoft Outlook, Lotus Notes, and Eudora (see Figure 11-3).

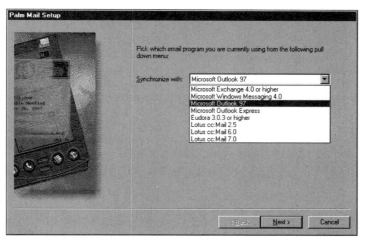

Figure 11-3: Most of the popular e-mail systems work with your PalmPilot.

13. Click Next.

    The Setup Complete dialog box opens.

14. **Click Finish.**

    The Palm Desktop Installer closes.

Installing the Pilot Desktop for Macintosh

Pilot Desktop 1.01 for the Macintosh is the main part of the MacPac, which you have to buy separately; the CD-ROM that comes with your PalmPilot doesn't include this software. You have to install Pilot Desktop from four floppy disks, which harkens back to the old days before everybody had CD-ROM drives. So crack your knuckles and be ready to switch disks when your Mac asks for them.

If you just bought your MacPac, then you have the latest version. If you bought it some time ago and haven't installed it yet, check the version number on the disks. If you have 1.01, you're set. If you have 1.0, then you need to download the Conduit Manager 1.01 Updater from the 3Com Web site at www.palmpilot.3com.com/custsupp/downloads/indexdl.html. Trust me, take the time to download this update — it makes the HotSync process much easier.

But before you do anything, you have to hook the PalmPilot cradle to your Macintosh.

Connecting the cradle to your Mac

The MacPac comes with a serial port adapter for your PalmPilot cradle. Don't ask me why PCs and Macs can't have the same type of serial ports — *c'est la vie,* as they say. Just hook whichever end of the adapter fits on the end of your cradle's plug. The other end of the adapter plugs into the back of your Mac.

Most Macs have two serial ports — a printer port and a modem port — that enable you to add peripherals (other pieces of hardware) to your machine. You can plug your cradle into either one. If you have an internal modem, then you have a free port. Rejoice and be happy. However, you may have both a printer and an external modem already using those two ports. Unfortunately, you don't have many options if that's the case. You can discuss other options with your local Mac guru, or you can tough it out like many other users and unplug one of your peripherals, plug in the cradle, unplug the cradle when you're done, and then plug in the other peripheral again. But that routine can get pretty tedious after a while.

If you use the oh-so-not-fun method of continually unplugging and plugging back in, here's a bit of advice that may make life a bit easier: Decide which peripheral you use least and alternate with that one. For example, you may live on the Internet, so you constantly use your modem and may not use your printer very often. The printer port would be the perfect choice for you. If you're, say, a graphic designer, though, and you're constantly printing out pages of your latest design masterpiece, then maybe the modem port would be a better choice.

Macs, just like PCs, come in all shapes, sizes, and ages. It's impossible for me to know what type of Mac you're using — whether you just bought a brand new iMac or you use an old Powerbook 190. Do a little research to make sure that your Mac's configuration can handle the requirements.

Now, on to installing Pilot Desktop

Installing Pilot Desktop for the Macintosh is easy; you essentially just put in the disks and follow the prompts, though you do have to tinker a bit when setting up your Mac to HotSync (more on that in the next section).

Here's how to install the Pilot Desktop onto your Macintosh; I recommend that you reboot with extensions turned off beforehand (restart your computer and hold down the Shift key until you see your desktop again).

1. **Insert Disk 1.**

   The Disk 1 icon appears on your desktop.

2. **Double-click the Disk 1 icon to see the contents of the disk.**

3. **Double-click Install Pilot Desktop.**

   The Pilot Desktop install screen appears.

4. **Click Continue.**

   The Pilot Desktop Installer screen appears, as shown in Figure 11-4.

   The pull-down menu gives you three options: Easy Install, Custom Install, and Custom Remove. Easy Install is (you guessed it) the easiest; it installs everything on the disks onto your hard drive. Custom Install enables you to choose which components to install; for example, if you don't want to install the Pilot Tutorial, don't put an *X* in that box. Custom Remove acts just like Custom Install, only in reverse; if you want to uninstall certain components after you install them, you choose this option.

   For now, just do an Easy Install.

5. **Choose a Destination Folder.**

   The default setting puts all the files in one folder on your hard drive. If you want to install the files in a specific folder on your hard drive or onto another hard disk, click Select Folder and browse until you find the place where you want the files to go.

Part III: PalmPilot and the Outside World

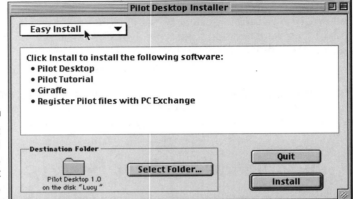

Figure 11-4: Easy Install is the well, easiest option.

Most of the time, I just install programs to the default placement and then move them to wherever I want them later, such as to the folder that has all my applications in it.

 6. **Click Install.**

    A dialog box opens, telling you that you must quit all applications before the program can be installed.

 7. **Click Continue.**

    Your computer automatically quits all running applications, and the install progress dialog box opens. The bar at the bottom of the dialog box shows you the progress of the installation.

 8. **When your computer asks for them, insert Disks 2, 3, 4, and then Disk 1 again.**

    When the installation finishes, another dialog box opens (see Figure 11-5), asking you to select the serial port that you hooked up your PalmPilot cradle to.

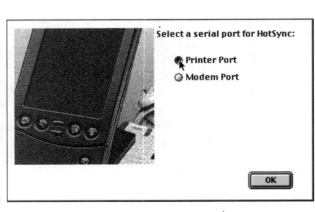

Figure 11-5: Select which serial port you hooked up your PalmPilot cradle to.

Chapter 11: Installing and HotSyncing to the Desktop Programs 175

9. **Choose either Printer Port or Modem Port and click OK.**

   A dialog box in which you enter your user name opens, as shown in Figure 11-6.

10. **Enter the user name that you plan to assign to your PalmPilot.**

    Your name is the best bet. Spell it with normal capitalization and spacing.

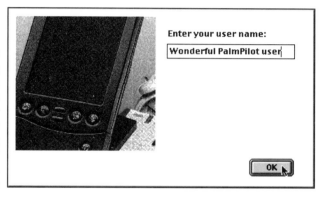

Figure 11-6: Introduce your Mac to your PalmPilot by entering your user name.

11. **Click OK.**

    A dialog box telling you what to do after the installation finishes opens, as shown in Figure 11-7. Don't worry about remembering this techno-jargon; I tell you in the next section how to do all that.

12. **Click OK.**

    The last screen of the Installer appears, telling you to restart your Mac.

13. **Click Restart.**

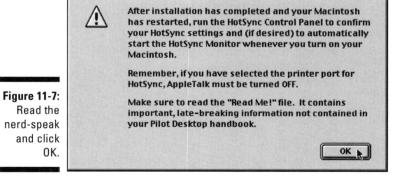

Figure 11-7: Read the nerd-speak and click OK.

14. **Wait, wait, wait for your computer to reboot.**

    Ha! You thought you were finished. Just hang on — now, you have to install the Conduit Manager Update.

15. **When you see your desktop again, reinsert Disk 1 and double-click its icon.**

    You see the contents of the disk again. You can skip this step if you downloaded the Conduit Manager Updater from the Web. Just go and find it.

16. **Double-click the Conduit Manager Updater icon.**

    The Conduit Manager Updater dialog box opens, showing you eligible files that you can update (see Figure 11-8).

    If you've installed the program only once, you should see only one Conduit Manager listed. Make sure that it's highlighted.

17. **Click Update.**

    The Updating dialog box shows you the progress of the update. This process takes only a minute or two.

    If all goes well, a dialog box telling you that the update was successful opens.

18. **Click OK.**

19. **Click Quit to exit the Updater.**

    You don't have to restart your Mac after the update.

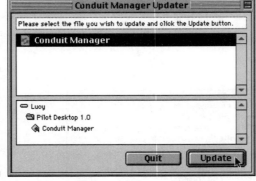

Figure 11-8: The Conduit Manager Updater's main screen.

Setting up your Mac to HotSync

I wish that simply installing Pilot Desktop was all that you needed to do to set up your Mac to HotSync with your PalmPilot. But, alas, 'twas not meant to be (at least not yet). The elegance of the PalmPilot is partly the result of how well it deals with the complexity of PC hardware. Unfortunately, this design doesn't work quite as seamlessly on the Mac. You have to tinker a bit with your Mac's settings.

If you hooked your PalmPilot cradle up to your modem port, you're pretty much set; you can skip right to Step 5 and configure your HotSync control panel. But if you plugged the cradle into your printer port because you have an external modem that you use all the time, you have to turn off AppleTalk before you can HotSync. Here's the process:

1. **Choose Apple Menu➪Chooser.**

    The Chooser dialog box opens.

2. **Turn off AppleTalk by clicking the Inactive button in the bottom-right corner of the box.**

    A dialog box telling you to disconnect from your network opens. Don't worry about this message.

3. **Click OK.**

4. **Close the Chooser by clicking the box in the upper-left corner.**

5. **Choose Apple Menu➪Control Panels➪HotSync.**

    The HotSync control panel opens, as shown in Figure 11-9.

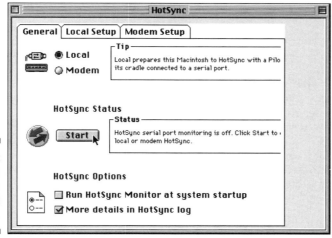

Figure 11-9: The HotSync control panel.

6. **Make sure that Local is selected at the top of the panel (it's the default setting).**
7. **Click Start underneath HotSync Status.**

   The button then changes to show the word *Stop*. You just told the control panel to watch the serial port that your PalmPilot cradle is plugged into for any request for a HotSync.

8. **Close the HotSync control panel by clicking the box in the upper-left corner.**

Now, you can simply place your PalmPilot in its cradle and press the HotSync button to kick off the HotSync process.

Remember that you may have unplugged your printer or external modem so that you could plug in the PalmPilot cradle. In order to use either of those peripherals, you have to plug them back in and repeat the preceding steps, pressing Stop in the HotSync control panel first, and then turning AppleTalk back on.

To HotSync or Not to HotSync . . . Just Do It

When you install the Palm Desktop for Windows or the Pilot Desktop for Macintosh, you end up with a pretty good tool for tracking all your To Do's, addresses, memos, and appointments. That's fine if you're always at your desk. But if you divide your time between sitting at your desk and being on the go (and who doesn't nowadays?), then keeping track of the data on two different machines can be a real pain. That's where HotSyncing comes in.

HotSyncing your PalmPilot with your desktop computer is blindingly simple. All that you do is make sure that your desktop computer is running, put the PalmPilot in the cradle, and push the HotSync button. That's it. The HotSync button, shown in Figure 11-10, is the only button on the cradle and has two arrows pointing at each other, so you can't go wrong. You don't even have to launch the desktop program. Pressing the HotSync button calls the HotSync Manager into action, which coordinates the whole process of swapping data. The HotSync Manager automatically turns on your PalmPilot, compares the data on your PalmPilot and your desktop computer, and updates each machine with the most current info. After a few minutes, you end up with the same data on two different machines.

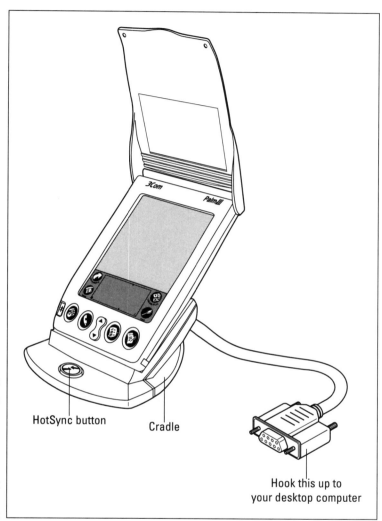

Figure 11-10: The HotSync button is the only button on the PalmPilot cradle.

Most of the time, you don't need to know how the HotSync process works. However, every once in a while, you have to deal with HotSync problems, which happen most often when you synchronize your PalmPilot with other personal information managers, such as Microsoft Outlook, Goldmine, or Act! Then you need to mess around with something called a *conduit,* which moves data between your PalmPilot and non-PalmPilot programs. I say more about conduits in Chapter 18.

Chapter 12
Operating the PalmPilot Desktop Program for Windows and Mac

In This Chapter
- Working with memos
- Arranging your appointments
- Setting up your Address Book
- Tracking To Do's
- Managing archived items

In this chapter, I focus on using the PalmPilot desktop program for both Windows and Macintosh. If you still need to install the desktop program, go back to Chapter 11, where I give you the skinny on installing both the Palm Desktop for Windows and the Pilot Desktop for Macintosh. These two programs work almost exactly the same way— I explain any differences as they arise. However, because Windows is the predominant computing platform (sorry, Macophiles), I refer to the program throughout the chapter as the Palm Desktop and use figures from the Windows platform. Mac users, your Pilot Desktop looks a little different from the figures, but not so much that you'll get lost.

Even for the folks who take to Graffiti like a fish to water, entering data through the Palm Desktop now and then has some advantages. Typing is normally faster than using Graffiti, even for experienced users, and you can do things — such as copy multiple items and perform tricks with drag and drop — that the PalmPilot can't handle just yet. The biggest benefit of the Palm Desktop is that you can manage archived items that you've purged or deleted from the PalmPilot itself. At the end of this chapter, I tell you how to manage archived items.

Of course, the Palm Desktop isn't your only choice if you'd rather feed data to your PalmPilot from your desktop. You can set up many popular personal information managers (PIMs) — such as Microsoft Outlook, Lotus Organizer, and ACT! — to send data back and forth to your PalmPilot. Because you may have spent years entering names and dates into another PIM, you may not want to change now. However, you will need a special something called a *conduit* to be able to HotSync your PIM to your PalmPilot. I talk a bit about conduits in Chapter 18; for more about operating your PIM, check out your local bookstore for a *...For Dummies* book on the subject. Odds are, you'll find one!

Palm Desktop Basics

The PalmPilot does an amazing amount of work for a little gizmo with a tiny screen and barely a half-dozen buttons. But there's nothing like a big old computer with an old-fashioned keyboard and mouse for whipping off appointments, memos, To Do's, and addresses in a flash. But don't be prejudiced; you can use both the Palm Desktop and your PalmPilot to enter your data — whatever suits your fancy. In this section, I give you an overview of the Palm Desktop interface and take you on a tour of the basic applications of the Palm Desktop.

Understanding the Palm Desktop interface

Interface is a techie term that computer geeks use to describe what you see on your computer screen after you launch a program. The interface of the Palm Desktop is made up of the same elements as the screens of most computer programs, combined with elements of the PalmPilot screens. You can see the name of the program in the upper-left corner of the screen in the area called the *title bar* (see Figure 12-1). Below that you find the *menu bar,* which works just like the menu bar in other programs that you use on your computer. Below the menu bar sits the *toolbar,* containing a row of icons that you can click to perform tasks that you need to do most often.

On the left edge of the Palm Desktop screen is a column of buttons called the Launch Bar. The names of the buttons correspond to those of the standard PalmPilot applications: Date, Address, To Do, and Memo. Clicking any of these buttons launches the corresponding application.

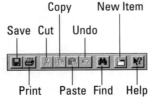

Figure 12-1: The Palm Desktop toolbar.

Chapter 12: Operating the PalmPilot Desktop Program for Windows and Mac

Below the four application buttons are two more icons labeled Expense and Install (Mac users don't have these buttons). The Expense icon starts up the special Microsoft Excel spreadsheet that's filled with data from your PalmPilot Expense application (if you use it). If you don't have Excel on your computer, the Palm Desktop Expense button does nothing, although you can still see it.

The Install icon, which is new to Palm Desktop 3.0, launches the Palm Install Tool for installing programs to your PalmPilot. Users of earlier versions of the Palm Desktop had to search for the Install Tool in the Windows Start menu. Now, just one click launches it for you. For more about installing applications from either a Windows PC or a Macintosh to your PalmPilot, see "Installing applications" later in this chapter.

The main part of the screen looks a bit different depending on which application button you click. Normally, it's divided into two big sections, two panes of the window, if you wish. The left pane, or the List Pane (yes, it has a name), displays information in a format that's nearly identical to the way your PalmPilot displays information. The right pane, called the Record Pane, shows you more detailed information. I go into more detail in the following sections about what you see for each application.

Arranging your Date Book

The Date Book in the Palm Desktop has many of the same parts as the PalmPilot Date Book screens, but the Palm Desktop organizes things a bit differently because your computer screen has more room to display items than your PalmPilot screen does. Also, your computer monitor probably has a color screen, which is something you can't get on a PalmPilot (yet).

Along the right edge of the Date Book, you can see three tabs labeled Day, Week, and Month. When you click any of those tabs, the view on the screen changes to the view that you clicked. Here's the lowdown on what you see in each view:

- **The Day view:** You may end up using the Day view more than the other views (at least I do). As shown in Figure 12-2, the left side of the Day view shows a list of appointments for a single day. The right side of the screen shows a miniature monthly calendar. When you click a date on that calendar, the list of appointments for that date appears. A list of the months of the year appears above the monthly calendar. Tap the month, and the calendar for that month appears. Above the list of months is a block showing the current year. If you want to see a date in a past or future year, click the triangle on either side of the year display.

184 Part III: PalmPilot and the Outside World

Below the calendar, Palm Desktop conveniently displays your To Do List and your Address Book, so that you don't have to keep clicking the buttons on the left to switch between them. To toggle between your To Do List and Address Book, just click the name of whichever one you want to see.

- **The Week view:** When you want to see how your week is shaping up, the Week view shows a grid representing the whole work week. The Week view works just like it does on your PalmPilot, although Palm Desktop shows you the names of your appointments, whereas your PalmPilot shows you only bars representing the appointments.

- **The Month view:** If you really like to think ahead, the Month view shows you what you're doing for the whole month. Palm Desktop gives you more detail, however, than the Month view on your PalmPilot, because your computer screen is larger.

For more on using the Date Book on your PalmPilot, see Chapter 8. To bring up your Date Book in Palm Desktop, just click the Date button on the left side of the screen or choose View➪Date Book, and then continue on to the following sections.

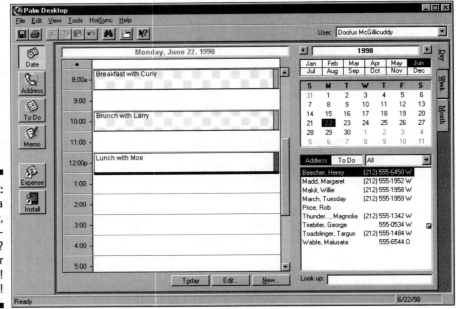

Figure 12-2: Whaddya doin' today, knucklehead? Check your Date Book! Nyah!

Chapter 12: Operating the PalmPilot Desktop Program for Windows and Mac

Adding appointments

Entering appointments in your Palm Desktop is undoubtedly faster than entering them on your PalmPilot itself, as long as you're sitting at the big computer. If you're out in the field or at a meeting, it's a different story. But while you're sitting at the keyboard, here's how to add an appointment to the Palm Desktop:

1. **With the Date Book visible, click the Day tab on the right edge of the screen (or press Alt+D for Windows or ⌘+D for Mac).**

   The Day view of your Date Book appears.

2. **Click the date of your appointment on the calendar on the right side of the screen.**

   The Date Book shows the appointments currently scheduled for that date.

3. **Click the line next to the hour when you want your appointment to begin.**

   A box opens where you clicked, and a blinking bar (called an *insertion point*) appears. The very first line of the Day view, next to the black diamond, has no time assigned to it; you can click there to enter events that last all day or that have no specific time assigned.

4. **Type a subject for your appointment.**

   The subject appears on the schedule.

5. **Click any other part of the screen (or press Tab).**

   Your appointment appears yellow to show that you entered it.

I describe the method of adding appointments to the Day view of your calendar on the Palm Desktop because it is most similar to the way that you add appointments on the PalmPilot itself. You have more flexibility in how you enter appointments on the desktop, though. For example, Palm Desktop enables you to add appointments in the Week view as well as the Month view, something that you can't do on the PalmPilot. Figure 12-3 shows you what the Week view looks like. Just follow Steps 3 through 5 in the preceding example.

You may have noticed the New button at the bottom of the screen. (No, that doesn't make you a new person — you're fine the way you are.) The New button opens the Edit Event dialog box. You can always use the Edit Event dialog box for entering a new appointment, which is frankly the most complete and detailed way to enter information, but I think it's a little cumbersome. You can read more about the Edit Event dialog box in the following sections.

186 Part III: PalmPilot and the Outside World

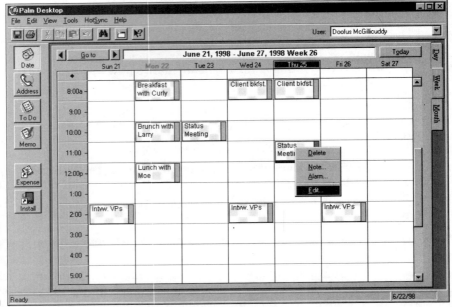

Figure 12-3: You can add appointments in the Week view of the Palm Desktop.

Repeating appointments

Anything worth doing is worth doing at least once a week — that's my opinion. Especially days off. Try to make a habit of those, won't you? And note them in your Palm Desktop, like this:

1. **With the Date Book visible, click the Day tab on the right edge of the screen (or press Alt+D for Windows or ⌘+D for Mac).**

   The Day view of your Date Book appears.

2. **Click the date of your appointment on the calendar on the right side of the screen.**

   The Date Book shows the appointments currently scheduled for that date.

3. **Click the appointment that you want to set as a repeating appointment.**

   The appointment's yellow box appears shadowed to show that you selected it.

4. **Click Edit at the bottom of the screen (or choose Edit⇨Edit Event).**

   The Edit Event dialog box opens, as shown in Figure 12-4.

Chapter 12: Operating the PalmPilot Desktop Program for Windows and Mac

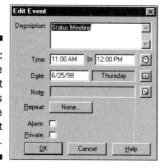

Figure 12-4: Change appointment details in the Edit Event dialog box.

5. **Click the button next to Repeat in the Edit Event dialog box.**

   The Change Repeat dialog box opens, as shown in Figure 12-5.

6. **Click the name of the repeat pattern that you desire.**

   The name that you choose is selected, and options for that pattern appear.

7. **Enter the choices that you desire for the repeat pattern you chose.**

   The choices that you make appear in the Change Repeat dialog box. Your choices are confirmed by the text box at the bottom of the dialog box.

8. **Click OK.**

   The Change Repeat dialog box closes.

9. **Click OK again.**

   The Edit Event dialog box closes, and a little circle appears next to your appointment to show that it repeats.

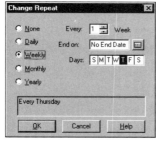

Figure 12-5: Do it again! Set up appointments that repeat as often as you want.

One tricky thing about repeating appointments is that every time you change one, the PalmPilot asks you whether you're just changing this one apppointment or the whole series. Don't be alarmed; just click the All button if you want to change all instances of the appointment, or click Current if you just want to change this instance of the appointment.

Making appointments private

Private appointments work pretty much the same way that private memos do (see "Making a memo private" later in the chapter) except that the check box in which you mark the appointment private isn't on the main screen; it's hidden. To find the check box to mark an appointment private, click the appointment to select it and click the Edit button at the bottom of the screen. That opens the Edit Event dialog box, which contains the Private check box.

When you mark an appointment private, a tiny key appears in the upper-left corner of the appointment box. You can hide all private records by choosing View⇨Hide Private Records. When you hide private records, a key appears in the toolbar. You can show private records again by choosing View⇨Show Private Records.

Deleting appointments

When you set up an appointment that you're not entirely sure about, you may tell a person you'll "pencil him in," which implies that you may erase him, too. All appointments in your PalmPilot are "penciled in" in a way, because it's so easy to erase them.

Take these steps to delete an appointment from your Palm Desktop:

1. **With the Date Book visible, click the Day tab on the right edge of the screen (or press Alt+D for Windows or ⌘+D for Mac).**

   The Day view of your Date Book appears.

   You can also choose the Week tab. If you prefer to view your whole week at a glance, jump ahead to Step 3.

2. **Click the date of your appointment on the calendar on the right side of the screen.**

   The Date Book shows the appointments currently scheduled for that date.

3. **Click the appointment that you want to delete.**

   The appointment's yellow box opens shadowed to show that you selected it.

4. **Click Delete (or choose Edit⇨Delete).**

   The Delete Datebook Event dialog box opens, as shown in Figure 12-6.

5. **Click OK if you want your appointment to disappear, or click Cancel if you have a change of heart.**

   If you leave the Archive box checked in the Delete Datebook Event dialog box, the appointment isn't lost forever; it automatically moves to an archive file where you can look it up at some future date.

Figure 12-6: Simply delete an undesirable date.

Arranging your Address Book

Keeping that little black book on a pocket computer is wonderfully efficient and amazingly quick. There's one big drawback to using a little computer for all that crucial stuff — what if you lose the thing! Yikes! Losing a contact lens is nothing compared to losing your personal organizer — not to mention how it can put a crimp into your social life!

Fortunately, you can maintain the whole mess on your desktop computer where it's all safe and sound and backed up. What are the chances of losing both your desktop computer and your PalmPilot at the same time? Do you really want to find out? I didn't think so.

To bring up your Address Book, just click the Address button on the left side of the screen, or choose View➪Address Book, and continue on to the following sections. You won't have a problem making sense of the Address Book; when you open it, you see a list of names to select from on the left side of the screen and full details of the person that you select on the right side.

Adding a new Address Book entry

You can keep track of as little or as much information as you want about each person in your address book. Just fill out the form, please.

To add a new entry to your Address Book on the Palm Desktop:

1. **With the Address Book visible, click New at the bottom of the screen (or choose Edit➪New Address).**

    The Edit Address dialog box opens.

2. **Type the last name of the contact in the Last Name text box.**

    The text appears in the Last Name text box, as shown in Figure 12-7.

3. **Enter the contact's first name, title, and company in the appropriate boxes.**

4. **Enter the contact's telephone number in the appropriate phone number box.**

    Your choices for telephone number are work, home, fax, and other.

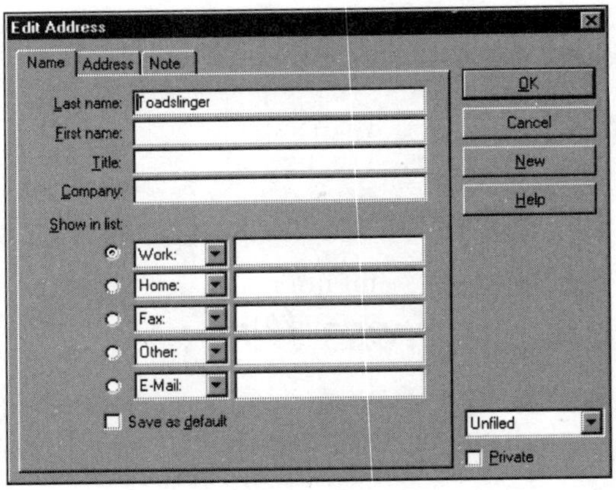

Part III: PalmPilot and the Outside World

Figure 12-7: To add a new address, fill in the form, please.

5. **Click the radio button to the left of the phone number that you want shown in the Address List.**

   The radio button that you click is blackened to show that you selected it.

6. **Click the Address tab at the top of the Edit Address dialog box.**

   The Address page of the Edit Address dialog box opens, as shown in Figure 12-8.

7. **Type the street address of your contact.**

   The person's street address appears in the Address box.

8. **Enter the contact's city, state, zip code, and country in the appropriate boxes.**

9. **Click OK.**

   The Edit Address dialog box closes.

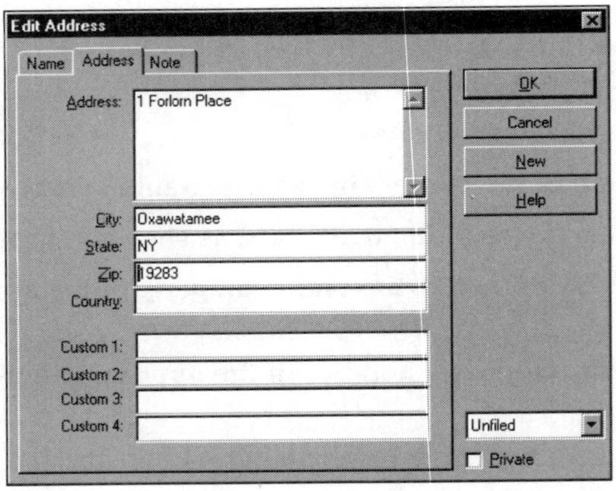

Figure 12-8: Put the street address in the big box and the city, state, and zip in the little boxes.

Chapter 12: Operating the PalmPilot Desktop Program for Windows and Mac   191

Although you can enter plenty of information in an Address Book entry, you can get away with just filling in one blank. Of course, if you just enter a phone number and not the name of the person at that phone number, you won't get much benefit other than a way to start a weird party game. It depends on what kind of parties you go to. I probably won't be there, thanks.

Editing an address record

I think that most people who carry PalmPilots are upwardly mobile, and so are most of the people that they know. Don't you? Of course. We both carry PalmPilots. What else would we think?

As you'd expect, all these upwardly mobile people are constantly moving to better jobs and better addresses, so plan on making lots of changes to your Address List. And, please, don't forget the little people.

These steps show you how to edit an address in your Palm Desktop:

1. **With the Address Book visible, double-click the name of the person whose record you want to change.**

   The Edit Address dialog box opens.

2. **Add new information the same way that you entered it originally.**

   For more information, see the preceding section "Adding a new Address Book entry."

3. **Select any information that you want to change and type the new information.**

   The text that you enter replaces the information that you selected.

4. **Click OK when you finish.**

   The Edit Address dialog box closes.

A big advantage to making your changes in the Palm Desktop rather than on the PalmPilot itself is that you can save the old address in your archive. Just select the address record, press Ctrl+C (Windows) or ⌘+C (Mac) to copy, and then Ctrl+V or ⌘+P to paste, and you'll have two identical records. If you delete one of the two and change the one that's left, you'll have the old address safely stored for posterity. To dig an old address out of your archive, see "Archiving Your PalmPilot Stuff" later in this chapter.

Attaching a note to an address record

"Always tell the truth," a wise person said, "it's the easiest thing to remember." If you can't always recall what you said to whom, you could probably benefit from keeping track of what you say along with a record of who you say it to. The perfect way to store these gems is in the form of notes in your Address Book. That way you won't get caught.

Follow these steps to attach a note to an address record in your Palm Desktop:

1. **With the Address Book visible, double-click the record that you want to annotate.**

   The Edit Address dialog box opens.

2. **Click the Note tab.**

   The Note page of the Edit Address dialog box appears, as shown in Figure 12-9.

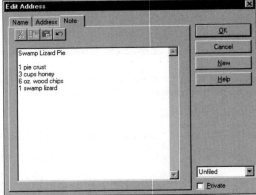

Figure 12-9: Notes have their own page in the Edit Address dialog box.

3. **Enter the text of your note.**

   The text that you type appears in the Note box.

4. **Click OK when you finish.**

   The Edit Address dialog box closes. To view your note, just click the person's name in the Address List; the note appears with the other contact information in the box at the right of the screen.

If you still can't remember what you said, keep your fingers crossed.

Finding the name you want

If you need to find a person's vital statistics quickly, you can just type the first few letters of the person's last name in the Look Up text box at the bottom of the screen. When you type a letter or two in the Look Up text box, the Palm Desktop highlights the first name in the list that starts with those letters. If that's not the exact name you're looking for, the one that you are looking for probably isn't far away. Keep typing letters until the name that you want to find is highlighted. You can open that person's address record by double-clicking his or her name.

Chapter 12: Operating the PalmPilot Desktop Program for Windows and Mac 193

Deleting a name

Some names just don't make your list anymore. It's sad but true. To gently, but firmly remove the name of someone who just isn't close to your inner microprocessor anymore, just click his or her name in your Address List and press Delete. A dialog box opens to make sure that you really want to do the deed; if you're sure, click OK.

If you change your mind, you can always restore any address record that you saved in an archive. See "Archiving Your PalmPilot Stuff," later in this chapter, for details.

Setting up custom fields

If you keep track of lots of people who have a few important things in common, it's useful to set up special fields in your Address Book to help you keep track of what you need to know. If you're a teacher, for example, you may want to keep track of each student's age or grade level. If you're a realtor, you may want to distinguish buyers from sellers and renters from landlords. Whatever your specialty, it's good to know that you can customize four of the Address Book fields for your own use.

These steps help you set up custom fields in the Palm Desktop:

1. **With the Address Book visible, choose Tools⇨Custom Field Labels.**

   The Custom Field Labels dialog box opens, as shown in Figure 12-10.

Figure 12-10: You can customize four fields in your Address Book.

2. **Type the name that you want to assign to the first custom field.**

   The name that you type appears in the box called Label 1.

3. **Press Tab and enter the name that you want to assign to each successive custom field.**

4. **Click OK.**

   The Custom Field Labels dialog box closes.

After you define the name of a custom field, all your address records will have a field by that name. For example, if you rename field 1 "Grade Level," every record in your address list will have a field by that name, even if the records aren't for students.

Doing stuff with your To Do's

Knowing what to do isn't enough if you don't remember to do it. The To Do List lets you add to your PalmPilot the items that you need to do so that the PalmPilot can remind you to do them.

To bring up your To Do List, just click the To Do button on the left side of the screen, or choose View⇨To Do List, and continue on to the following sections. The left side of the To Do screen looks a lot like the PalmPilot To Do screen. It's just a list of your To Do's. The right side shows details of the To Do that you selected.

Creating a To Do item

Nothing could be easier than entering a task in your To Do List. If only doing the tasks were so easy!

1. **With your To Do List visible, click New at the bottom of the screen (or choose Edit⇨New To Do).**

   A rectangle appears at the bottom of the To Do List, and the insertion point appears in the To Do text box on the right side of the screen, as shown in Figure 12-11.

2. **Type what you need to do in the To Do text box on the right.**

3. **Click the Apply button.**

   The name of your task appears in the To Do List on the left.

Setting the priority for a To Do item

With so many important things on your To Do List, how do you know what to do first? You need to set priorities. You have only the numbers 1 through 5 to assign as the priority for each task, but that's enough to make sure that you get to the really important things first.

Here's how to set the priority of a To Do item:

1. **With your To Do List visible, click the name of the To Do item for which you want to set a priority number.**

Chapter 12: Operating the PalmPilot Desktop Program for Windows and Mac

2. **Click one of the radio buttons next to the word Priority on the right side of the screen.**

   The radio button next to the number that you click is blackened to show which number you selected.

3. **Click the Apply button.**

   The priority that you assign appears next to your To Do item.

Another trick that you can try is to simply click the priority number in the To Do List. Clicking a priority number makes a list of priority numbers appear. You can choose the number that you want by picking it from the list with a single mouse click.

It's okay to have more than one To Do with the same priority. You can make every task your top priority or your bottom priority. Whatever you pick, it's *your* priority.

Assigning a category to a To Do item

Another way to keep track of what task you need to do next is to assign categories. For example, some tasks must be done at home, and others can be done only at work. When you're at the office, you don't need to remind yourself to mow the lawn (although if it gets you out of the office early, it's worth a try).

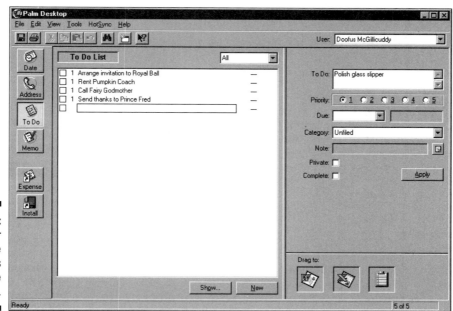

Figure 12-11: Whatever you type appears in the rectangle.

Part III: PalmPilot and the Outside World

To assign a category to a To Do item, follow these steps:

1. **With your To Do List visible, click the name of the To Do item to which you want to assign a category.**

2. **Click the Category box on the right side of the screen.**

   The drop-down list of available categories appears, as shown in Figure 12-12.

3. **Click the category that you want to assign to your To Do item.**

   The category that you click appears in the Category text box.

4. **Click the Apply button.**

   The priority that you assign appears next to your To Do item.

Adding categories

You can maintain your collection of categories either on your PalmPilot or on the Palm Desktop. Every time that you HotSync your data, the categories that you set up on your PalmPilot are mirrored on the Palm Desktop and vice versa.

Follow these steps to create a new category:

1. **With your To Do List visible, click the down-pointing arrow next to Category on the right side of the screen.**

   The drop-down list of available categories appears.

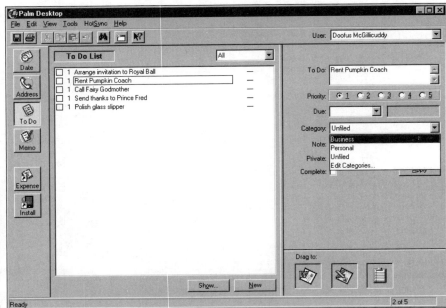

Figure 12-12: Some tasks are in a better category than others.

Chapter 12: Operating the PalmPilot Desktop Program for Windows and Mac   197

   2. Click Edit Categories.

   The Edit To Do Categories dialog box opens (see Figure 12-13).

   3. Click New.

   The New Category dialog box opens.

   4. Enter the name of the category that you want to add.

   The name that you enter appears in the New Category dialog box.

   5. Tap OK.

   The new category appears in the Edit To Do Categories dialog box.

   6. Tap OK again.

   The Edit To Do Categories dialog box closes.

Figure 12-13: Create new categories in the Edit To Do Categories dialog box.

Remember, you can have no more than 15 categories on your PalmPilot or in Palm Desktop. If you try to exceed 15 categories, the program adamantly (but nicely) refuses to add new categories.

Deleting categories

If you went wild and added some categories that you now regret, you can just zap your excess categories and get back to basics.

Follow these steps to delete a category:

   1. With your To Do List visible, click the down-pointing arrow next to Category on the right side of the screen.

   The drop-down list of available categories appears.

   2. Click Edit Categories.

   The Edit To Do Categories dialog box opens.

   3. Select the name of the category that you want to delete.

   The category that you tap is highlighted to show that you selected it.

Part III: PalmPilot and the Outside World

   4. **Click Delete.**

      The Delete Category dialog box opens, asking whether you want to move all items in the category to the Unfiled category or delete all items (see Figure 12-14).

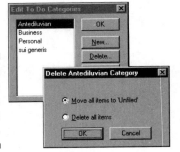

Figure 12-14: Rename 'em or remove 'em. Take your pick.

   5. **Choose either Move All Items to Unfiled or Delete All Items.**

      The circle next to the choice that you click appears darkened to show that you selected it.

   6. **Click OK.**

      The Delete Category dialog box closes, and your category is deleted.

   7. **Click OK.**

      The Edit To Do Categories dialog box closes.

At least when you delete a category on the Palm Desktop, you get a choice between deleting all the items in the category or sending all the items to the Unfiled category. On the PalmPilot itself, you can only send everything to Unfiled.

Renaming categories

Did you know that Whoopi Goldberg changed her name from Caryn Johnson? Go figure. Changing the names of your categories is easier than changing your name for show business, but it won't make you a star.

To rename a category, follow these steps:

   1. **With your To Do List visible, click the down-pointing arrow next to Category on the right side of the screen.**

      The drop-down list of available categories appears.

   2. **Click Edit Categories.**

      The Edit To Do Categories dialog box opens.

Chapter 12: Operating the PalmPilot Desktop Program for Windows and Mac

3. **Click the name of the category that you want to rename.**

   The name of the category is highlighted to show that you selected it.

4. **Click Rename.**

   The Rename Category dialog box opens (see Figure 12-15).

Figure 12-15: You can rename your categories any time.

5. **Enter the new name of the category that you want to change.**

   The name that you type replaces the old name in the Rename Category dialog box.

6. **Tap OK.**

   The name that you entered replaces the previous name of the category in the Edit To Do Categories dialog box.

7. **Tap OK again.**

   The Edit To Do Categories dialog box closes.

In case you were interested, Hal Linden started off as Harold Lipshitz, and Peter Marshall was originally named Pierre LaCock. But that's a totally different category.

Assigning a due date to a To Do item

Your To Do List can do more than tell you what tasks to do; it also helps you remember when to do them.

Use these steps to assign a due date to a To Do item:

1. **With your To Do List visible, click the name of the To Do item to which you want to assign a due date.**

2. **Click the down-pointing triangle to the right side of the Due text box on the right side of the screen.**

   A drop-down menu of available choices appears, including Today, Tomorrow, One Week Later, No Date, and Choose Date.

3. **Click the date that you want to assign to your To Do item.**

   If you picked anything other than Choose Date, the date that you picked appears in the Due text box, so you can click the Apply button and you're done.

4. **Select Choose Date if you need to assign a specific date to your task.**

   The Select Date dialog box opens.

5. **Click the date that you want to assign as your due date.**

   Figure 12-16 shows the date that I selected for my To Do item.

6. **Click OK.**

   The Select Date dialog box closes, and the date that you chose appears in the Due text box.

7. **Click Apply.**

Figure 12-16: Give your task its due date in the Select Date dialog box.

Unfortunately, the To Do List doesn't have reminders for the list itself, so you'll have to remember to look at your list from time to time.

Marking a To Do item private

You may have things to do that other people shouldn't know about. Shhh! Keep them under your hat — or at least under a password.

These steps show you how to mark a To Do item private on the Palm Desktop:

1. **With your To Do List visible, click the name of the To Do item that you want to mark private.**

2. **Click the Private check box on the right side of the screen.**

3. **Click the Apply button.**

   A little key appears next to your item in the To Do List to show that it's now marked private, as shown in Figure 12-17.

Chapter 12: Operating the PalmPilot Desktop Program for Windows and Mac

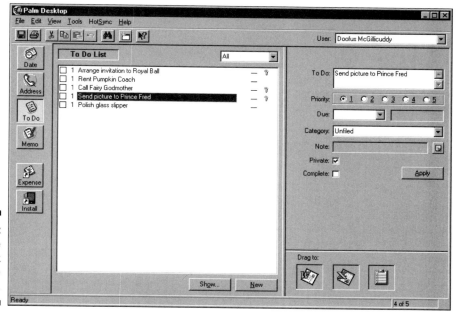

Figure 12-17: Those little keys mark your private tasks.

Of course, if you really want your private items to remain private, you should choose View➪Hide Private Records. That makes your private items invisible until you choose View➪Show Private Records. If you want to password-protect your private items, you have to set your password on the PalmPilot. For more about setting up passwords, see Chapter 3.

Attaching notes to To Do items

Of course, you know what you need to do and when you need to do it, but do you always remember how or why? Perhaps you just need a more detailed explanation of some part of the task, such as driving directions or a secret formula. If you need some elaboration on your task, add a note.

To add a note to a To Do item in the Palm Desktop, follow these steps:

1. **With your To Do List visible, click the name of the To Do item to which you want to attach a note.**

2. **Click the Note button to the right of the Note text box on the right side of the screen (it looks like a piece of paper with the bottom-right corner lifted up).**

   The Note Editor dialog box opens, as shown in Figure 12-18.

Part III: PalmPilot and the Outside World

Figure 12-18:
Make a note on what to do in your To Do.

3. **Type the text of your note.**

   The text that you type appears in the Note Editor dialog box.

4. **Click OK.**

   The Note Editor dialog box closes, and the same little piece of paper that's on the Note button appears next to the name of your To Do item to show that the item has a note attached.

You don't have to type lots of text into the note if you don't want to. You can always copy text out of another document on your desktop or from a Web page, and paste the text into the Note Editor dialog box.

Viewing items by category

If you make the effort to assign categories to your tasks, you'll get some real mileage from that feature by viewing your tasks according to the categories to which they belong. The name of the category that you're viewing is always shown at the top of the To Do List. If you click the name of the category that you're viewing, a drop-down list of the other categories appears. Just choose the category that you want to see.

Deleting a To Do item

Some tasks become unnecessary before you even do them. If you planned to water the lawn and it rains, you're in luck.

Use these steps to delete a To Do item in the Palm Desktop:

1. **With your To Do List visible, click the name of the To Do item that you want to delete.**

2. **Press Delete.**

   The Delete To Do Items dialog box opens, as shown in Figure 12-19.

3. **Click OK.**

   Your To Do item is deleted.

Chapter 12: Operating the PalmPilot Desktop Program for Windows and Mac 203

Figure 12-19:
Tasks can be completed or deleted. Take your pick.

The check box in the Delete To Do Items dialog box enables you to send deleted items to the archive for storage. I discuss how to deal with archived items at the end of this chapter.

Of course, if you actually did the task, your best bet is to mark the task complete. The little check box next to the name of the task is put there for that very reason. One click and you're the hero! Mission accomplished!

Setting preferences for your To Do List

Setting preferences is, well, a matter of preference. You don't need to make any changes at all in your To Do List preferences if you don't want to. But if you like your To Do List just so, you can change several little things.

To set your To Do list preferences in the Palm Desktop, follow these steps:

1. **With your To Do List visible, click the Show button at the bottom of the screen (or press Alt+O for Windows or ⌘+O for Mac).**

    The Show Options dialog box opens, as shown in Figure 12-20. Your To Do options for the Palm Desktop are identical to the To Do options on the PalmPilot itself, which I discuss in Chapter 6.

2. **Click the down-pointing triangle to the right of the Sort By text box to see your list of choices.**

    The drop-down list of sort options for your To Do List appears.

Figure 12-20:
When it comes to sorting tasks, you have several options.

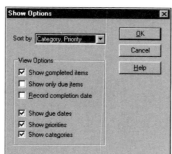

Part III: PalmPilot and the Outside World

3. **Choose the way that you want to sort your To Do List.**

   The choice that you click appears in the Sort By text box. The sort options on the Palm Desktop are identical to the choices on the PalmPilot, as I discuss in Chapter 6.

4. **Click the check boxes next to the options that you want for your To Do List.**

5. **Click OK.**

   The Show Options dialog box closes, and your To Do List reflects the preferences that you set up, as shown in Figure 12-21.

If you set up your preferences and then decide that you'd prefer something else, just change everything again.

Working with memos

The best reason to enter memos on the Palm Desktop rather than use Graffiti is that memos usually contain lots of text, and typing is much faster than scribbling with Graffiti or punching in individual letters on PalmPilot's on-screen keyboard. You can also copy and paste text to a memo from other desktop programs, such as your word processor.

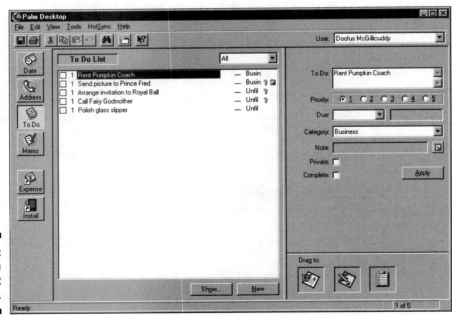

Figure 12-21: What you see is what you set.

Chapter 12: Operating the PalmPilot Desktop Program for Windows and Mac

To bring up your Memo Pad, just click the Memo button on the left side of the screen, or choose View⇨Memo Pad, and continue on to the following sections.

Creating a memo

Sometimes, you really need certain information that's not exactly an appointment and not exactly a To Do item, but you still need it on your PalmPilot. The simplest way to keep miscellaneous information on hand is to create a memo. Nothing could be easier.

Use these steps to create a new Memo on the Palm Desktop:

1. **With the Memo Pad visible, click New at the bottom of the screen (or choose Edit⇨New Memo).**

    A new line appears in your list of memos and the insertion point appears in the memo area on the right side of the screen.

2. **Type the text of your memo.**

    The text that you type appears in the memo area on the right side of the screen, as shown in Figure 12-22.

3. **Click the Apply button below the memo area.**

    The title of your memo appears in the list of memos on the left side of the screen.

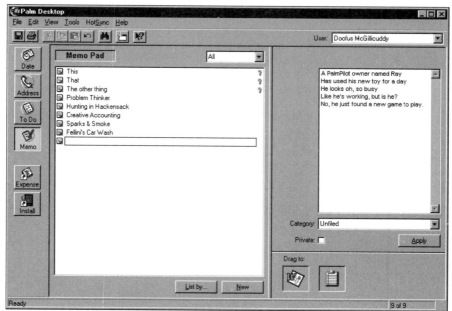

Figure 12-22: Type or copy whatever you like into a memo.

If you hate to type, you can also copy and paste text into your Memo Pad, too. Just select text from a word-processing document or even from the World Wide Web, press Crtl+C (Windows) or ⌘+C (Mac) to copy the text, then start the Palm Desktop Memo Pad, and press Ctrl+V (Windows) or ⌘+V (Mac) to paste the text right into the memo. You don't even need to create a new memo; the Palm Desktop figures out that you want a new memo and creates one automatically.

Reading a memo

You may not want to hang around reading your memos on the Palm Desktop because you can send them all to your PalmPilot, and then go sit in the park to read them. Even so, you may need to check what you put in your memos now and again, and fortunately, I can show you a way to do just that.

To read a memo, all you have to do is click the Memo Pad button on the left side of the screen (or choose View➪Memo Pad), and then click the memo that you want to see. Then read away!

If you need to read through all the memos on your desktop quickly, you can whip through the whole list by pressing the down arrow key. Each time that you press the down arrow key the next memo on the list appears in the memo area on the right side of the screen.

Printing a memo

Another really big thing that you can do from the desktop is print things. Yes, some people out there have clever schemes for beaming their PalmPilot data to especially well-equipped printers, but the whole scheme is still pretty tricky, and most printers aren't up to the job. Nearly everybody has printers hooked up to their desktop computers, so printing from the desktop is the quickest way to see your PalmPilot data on paper.

To print a memo from the Palm Desktop, follow these steps:

1. **With the Memo Pad visible, click the title of the memo that you want to print.**

    The text of the memo that you clicked appears in the memo area on the right side of the screen.

2. **Choose File➪Print (or press Ctrl+P for Windows or ⌘+P for Mac).**

    The Print dialog box opens.

3. **Click OK.**

    Your memo is printed.

Chapter 12: Operating the PalmPilot Desktop Program for Windows and Mac

The Palm Desktop doesn't let you do any fancy formatting of your memos; it's all plain vanilla. If you need to format and fiddle around with your text, you can drag the memo that you want to work with to the Microsoft Word icon at the bottom of the Palm Desktop for Windows screen. Dragging a memo to the Microsoft Word icon opens Word and copies your text into a new Word document that you can beautify as you please. You can also drag text to Excel if you wish, as I mention later in this chapter when I talk about the Drag To icons. If you don't have Microsoft Word installed on your desktop computer, you have to drag text to the clipboard icon, open any word processor or text editor, and paste the text into another document.

Editing a memo

If you use memos a lot, as I do, you'll certainly want to change a few of them now and then. The biggest advantage to keeping memos in an electronic form is that the text is so easy to change.

Follow these steps to edit a Memo on your Palm Desktop:

1. **With the Memo Pad visible, click the title of the memo that you want to edit.**

   The text of the memo that you clicked appears in the memo area on the right side of the screen.

2. **Click in the memo area on the right side of the screen at the point where you want to edit.**

   An insertion point appears where you clicked your mouse.

3. **Make any changes to the memo that you want.**

4. **Click the Apply button below the memo area.**

   Your changes are saved as part of your memo.

If you replace a large amount of the text in a memo, the text that you replace is ordinarily gone for good. Normally, that's fine by me, but sometimes you may want to save a copy of the original memo. One thing that you can do with memos on the Palm Desktop that you can't do on the PalmPilot itself is copy whole memos, and then just change one of them. To copy a whole memo, click the name of the memo to select it, press Ctrl+C to copy the memo, and then press Ctrl+V to paste it. You then have two identical memos. Just change one, and you have two different memos.

Categorizing a memo

Categories are particularly useful after you've collected more than a few dozen memos. Not only does categorizing make memos easier to find, it also lets you see your memo collection more easily on your PalmPilot, because that little screen can show only 11 memos at once.

Part III: PalmPilot and the Outside World

Use these steps to assign a category to a memo on the Palm Desktop:

1. **With the Memo Pad visible, click the title of the memo that you want to categorize.**

   The text of the memo that you clicked appears in the memo area on the right side of the screen.

2. **Click the category scroll-down button (the down-pointing triangle) below the memo text and choose the category that you want, as shown in Figure 12-23.**

   The category that you choose appears below your memo text.

If you want to create several memos in the same category, switch to that category, and then create the new memos. For example, if you switch to a view of your Business memos and start creating new memos, all the new memos are automatically assigned to the Business category.

Making a memo private

I'm sure that you have some things that you don't want just anybody to see, but you don't want to forget them yourself. You can mark certain memos private to protect them from prying eyes.

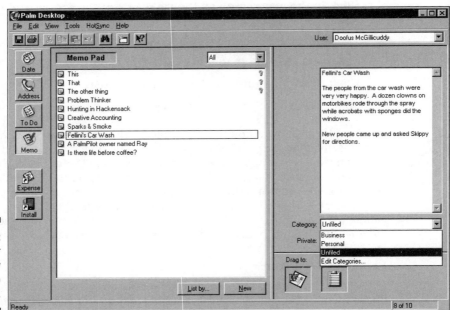

Figure 12-23: Change your category with just two clicks.

Chapter 12: Operating the PalmPilot Desktop Program for Windows and Mac

To mark a memo private in the Palm Desktop, follow these steps:

1. **With the Memo Pad visible, click the title of the memo that you want to mark as private.**

   The text of the memo that you clicked appears in the memo area on the right side of the screen.

2. **Click the Private check box below the memo text.**

   A check mark appears in the Private check box to show that this is a private memo (see Figure 12-24). A key also appears next to the subject of any memo that's marked private.

You can make all your private items disappear by choosing View⇨ Hide Private Records. If you want to make them reappear, choose View⇨ Show Private Records. Presto! If you want to be really sneaky, you can set a password on your PalmPilot to keep anyone from seeing your private records unless they know your password. For more on setting passwords, see Chapter 3.

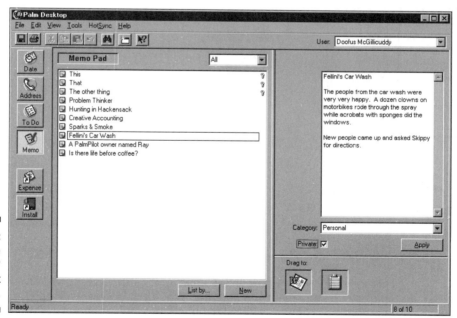

Figure 12-24: Do you have a secret? Mark it private.

Deleting a memo

You know how memos are — easy come, easy go. Especially go. Follow these steps to make your memos go away:

1. **With the Memo Pad visible, click the title of the memo that you want to delete.**

   The text of the memo that you clicked appears in the memo area on the right side of the screen.

2. **Choose Edit⇨Delete (or press Delete).**

   The Delete Memo Pad Items dialog box opens, as shown in Figure 12-25. If you put a check mark in the box next to Archive Deleted Memo Pad Items, your memo will be stored in an archive file.

3. **Click OK.**

   Poof! Your memo is gone.

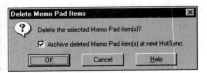

Figure 12-25:
The Delete Memo Pad Items dialog box makes sure that you want to delete that memo.

If you left the Archive box checked, you can go back and find the deleted memo at a later date. See the section, "Archiving Your PalmPilot Stuff," for more information.

What does that Expense button do?

Your PalmPilot includes an Expense application to help you track how much money you spend as you spend it. When you perform a HotSync, the information that you've gathered is pulled into a file on your desktop. Frankly, the program is pretty limited and is best for people who need to track business spending in order to file expense reports. Even for those people, the program has major drawbacks. It requires you to choose a description of each expenditure from a noncustomizable list of 28 choices ranging from Airfare to Telephone. It's pretty hard to make the Expense application useful if you can't enter the exact type of expenses that you incur.

You can start the Expense application by tapping the Applications soft button and tapping the Expense icon on your PalmPilot. Write in the amounts that you spend and pick the description that you think fits best. The program automatically assigns the current date to each expenditure unless you tap the date and pick another one from the calendar.

The Expense button on the Palm Desktop for Windows automatically starts up a special Excel spreadsheet that captures data that you've entered in the Expense application on your PalmPilot. If you don't have Excel installed on your Windows PC, the button is still present, but it doesn't do anything. Plenty of PalmPilot users have complained that the Expense program is too weak, so I hope that future versions will be more useful.

The Drag To icons

If you use Microsoft Word and Microsoft Excel on your desktop computer, the Palm Desktop for Windows displays a set of icons in the lower-right portion of the screen labeled Drag To (sorry, Mac users, you don't have these icons, either). Two of the icons look just like the icons for Microsoft Word and Microsoft Excel, and the third icon looks like a little clipboard. When you drag any item from the Palm Desktop to the Microsoft Word icon, Word opens and creates a copy of the item that you dragged and converts it to a Word document. Dragging an item to the Excel icon creates a copy of the item, formatted as an Excel spreadsheet. The most useful thing that you can do with this feature is to turn a memo into a Word document so that you can save, format, or print the text of the memo.

If you don't have Word or Excel installed on your computer, the Word and Excel icons don't appear. Even without Word or Excel, you can still drag items to the clipboard icon and then open a document in any word processor and choose Edit⇨Paste to insert the text that's on the clipboard.

Furnishing Your PalmPilot

What is a home, after all, without some furnishings? You may have a lovely breakfast nook, but eventually you'll want a dinette, at least. You can furnish your PalmPilot as lavishly (or sparingly) as you'd furnish your home. A few games, a spreadsheet, who knows what may strike your fancy.

Checking memory

Before you start adding things to your PalmPilot, you better make sure that you have room for the stuff. After all, a Palm III with 2MB of memory has less room for programs than a couple of your average floppy disks. A PalmPilot Professional has only 1MB of memory, or half the space of a Palm III. So, unlike my hall closet, which I seem to be able to cram anything into, your PalmPilot will protest if you try to put too much stuff on it.

You can see how much space is available on a Palm III by following these three steps:

1. **Tap the Applications soft button.**

    The applications list appears.

2. **Tap the Menu soft button.**

    The menu bar appears.

3. **Choose App⇨Info.**

    The Info screen appears. The line at the top of the Info screen says something like "Free Memory: 849K of 960K" (see Figure 12-26).

Figure 12-26: Before you install a new program, check your memory to see if you have enough room.

Most PalmPilot applications are pretty small, so as long as you have a few hundred kilobytes of memory (abbreviated *K* by computer geeks), you should be okay. But remember, every time that you add an item to one of the standard PalmPilot applications, like the Address Book or the Date Book, you tie up a bit more memory. So leave yourself some breathing room. You can free up some memory by either deleting applications, as I describe later

Chapter 12: Operating the PalmPilot Desktop Program for Windows and Mac

in this chapter, or by deleting bunches of items from the standard PalmPilot applications. The easiest way to delete records en masse is to use the Palm Desktop, as I describe in earlier sections of this chapter.

If you're still using a PalmPilot Professional or earlier model, the process for checking memory is a bit different because earlier PalmPilots have a separate Memory application. To check how much memory is available on those models, tap the Applications soft button and tap Memory.

You can upgrade the memory on your PalmPilot fairly easily, but it'll cost you a few bucks. A company called TRG specializes in selling extra memory for your PalmPilot. Check out Chapter 14 for more on upgrading.

Installing applications

Thousands of programmers are out there writing scads and scads of programs for the PalmPilot. You can get many programs over the Internet, and I include a sampling of particularly useful or fun programs on the CD that comes with this book. All that you need to do to install an application onto your PalmPilot is to copy the application to your desktop computer from the Internet or from the CD, and then locate that file with the Palm Install tool.

It's important to remember that the Palm Install Tool doesn't actually install applications; it *prepares* applications for installation. After picking an application with the Palm Install Tool, you need to perform a HotSync. Just place the PalmPilot in its cradle and press the HotSync button (for more on HotSyncing, see Chapter 11).

Using Palm Desktop for Windows

To install PalmPilot programs using Palm Desktop for Windows, follow these steps:

1. **Launch Palm Desktop.**
2. **Click the Install button on the left side of the screen, or choose View⇨Install.**

    The Palm Install Tool dialog box opens.

3. **Click Add (or press Alt+A).**

    The Open dialog box opens.

4. **Click the name of the file that you want to install.**

    The filename that you click is highlighted to show that you selected it (see Figure 12-27).

Part III: PalmPilot and the Outside World

Figure 12-27: Add new programs with the Palm Install Tool.

If you downloaded the application from the Internet or are installing applications from the CD, then browse until you find the application that you want to install.

 5. **Click Open.**

    The Open dialog box closes, and the filename that you picked is now listed in the Palm Install Tool dialog box.

 6. **Click Done.**

    Another dialog box opens telling you that the applications will be installed the next time that you HotSync.

 7. **Click OK.**

    The Palm Install Tool closes.

 8. **Press the HotSync button on the cradle of your PalmPilot.**

    The HotSync process begins, and the program is installed onto your PalmPilot.

Using Pilot Desktop for Macintosh

Use these steps to install PalmPilot programs by using the Pilot Desktop for Macintosh:

 1. **Open your Pilot Desktop 1.0 folder and double-click the InstallApp program.**

    The Pilot Install Tool dialog box opens, as shown in Figure 12-28.

 2. **Click Select to find the program file that you want to install.**

    The Open dialog box opens. Navigate until you find the program file that you want to install (see Figure 12-29).

 3. **Click Open.**

    The Open dialog box closes, and the file that you chose appears in the File Name box of the Pilot Install Tool dialog box.

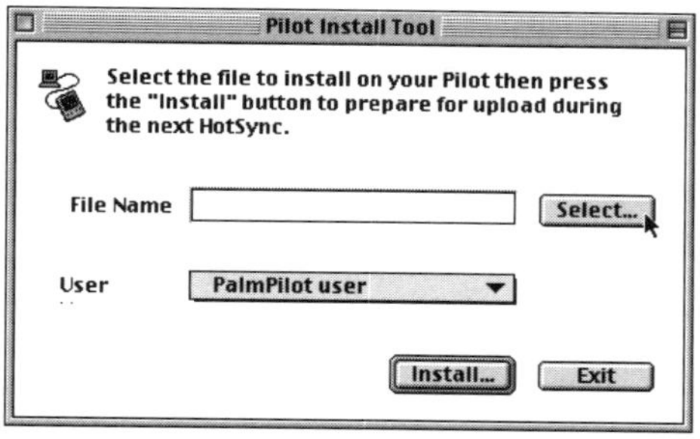

Chapter 12: Operating the PalmPilot Desktop Program for Windows and Mac 215

Figure 12-28: Install programs onto your PalmPilot from your Mac.

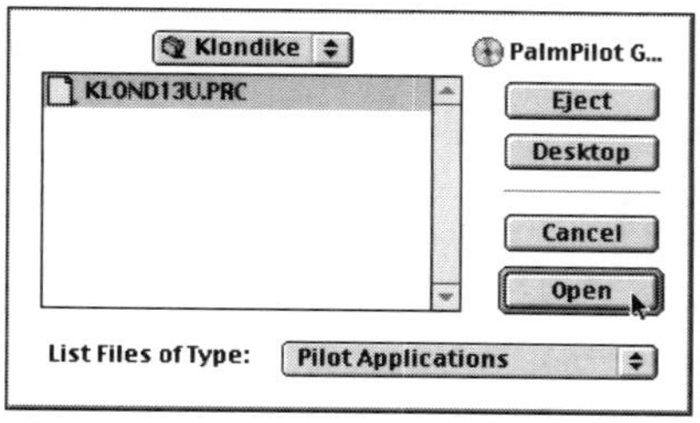

Figure 12-29: Locate the program you want to install on your Mac.

4. **Click Install.**

    The Ready to Install dialog box opens, telling you that the program will be installed onto your PalmPilot the next time that you HotSync.

5. **If you want to install another file, click Install Another File and repeat Steps 2 through 4.**

6. **If you're done, click Exit.**

    The Pilot Install Tool dialog box closes.

7. **Press the HotSync button on the cradle of your PalmPilot.**

    The HotSync process begins, and the program is installed onto your PalmPilot.

Deleting applications

Eventually, you may tire of your once-fashionable furnishings. I mean, orange shag carpet? Lava lamps? Please! Martha Stewart would send you straight to K-Mart!

Discarding unwanted applications from your PalmPilot is even easier than dumping those old Woodstock posters. You'll also be less embarrassed if someone catches you at it. You don't need to launch Palm Desktop to delete applications, either.

Part III: PalmPilot and the Outside World

Deleting applications on a Palm III

The process of deleting applications differs slightly on a Palm III from the way that it works on earlier models. Here's how to delete a program from a Palm III:

1. **Tap the Applications soft button.**

   The applications screen appears.

2. **Tap the Menu button.**

   The menu bar appears.

3. **Choose App⇨Delete.**

   The Delete screen appears, as shown in Figure 12-30.

Figure 12-30: Clear out the clutter by deleting unwanted applications.

4. **Tap the name of the application that you want to delete.**

   The name that you tap is highlighted to show that you selected it.

5. **Tap Delete.**

   The Delete Application dialog box opens.

6. **Tap Yes if you're sure. If you change your mind, tap No.**

   If you tap Yes, the application is deleted, and its name disappears from the list of applications in the Delete screen. If you tap No, the dialog box closes, and the application is still there.

7. **Tap Done.**

   The Delete screen closes.

Chapter 12: Operating the PalmPilot Desktop Program for Windows and Mac

Deleting applications on a PalmPilot Professional

On a PalmPilot Professional (or earlier model), you follow a slightly different process, which has an equally charming result: one less program cluttering up your PalmPilot.

To delete a program from a PalmPilot Professional (or earlier model):

1. **Tap the Applications soft button.**

    The applications screen appears.

2. **Tap Memory.**

    The Memory application opens.

3. **Tap Delete Apps.**

    The Delete Applications screen appears.

4. **Tap the name of the application that you want to delete.**

    The name that you tap is highlighted to show that you selected it.

5. **Tap Delete.**

    The Delete Application dialog box opens, as shown in Figure 12-31.

Figure 12-31: Zap pesky programs from the Delete Applications screen.

6. **Tap Yes if you're sure. If you change your mind, tap No.**

    If you tap Yes, the Delete Application dialog box closes, and your application is deleted. If you tap No, the dialog box closes, but the application is still there.

7. **Tap Done.**

    The Delete Application screen disappears.

There you are! And there it isn't! Your unwanted application is gone like platform shoes. Oops, I guess platform shoes have made a comeback. Well, you can always reinstall the applications using the same procedure in "Installing applications," earlier in this chapter.

Part III: PalmPilot and the Outside World

Protecting Your Turf

Sometimes the worst does happen; your little PalmPilot gets lost, stolen, or destroyed. You can always buy a new PalmPilot — that's the easy part. But what about all your data? Well, you're in luck — the Palm Desktop makes it easy to reinstall all your precious PalmPilot data.

Restoring PalmPilot data

In the best of times or in the worst of times, you may need to restore all your PalmPilot data. The best of times may be when you upgrade to a new PalmPilot model; the worst of times may be when you replace a lost, stolen, or destroyed PalmPilot. Either way, you can restore everything that was on your old PalmPilot with a simple HotSync, like this:

1. **Put your PalmPilot in its cradle.**

   Nothing happens. Psych!

2. **Press the HotSync button on the PalmPilot cradle.**

   The HotSync Manager on your desktop PC launches, and the Users dialog box opens on your desktop PC's screen.

3. **Click the name of the user whose data you want to install on the PalmPilot — it's probably your name.**

   The name that you click is highlighted to show that you selected it (see Figure 12-32).

Figure 12-32: Pick the name of the user whose data should go on this PalmPilot.

4. **Click OK (on the desktop).**

   The HotSync Progress dialog box opens. After a few minutes, the dialog box closes, your PalmPilot plays a tinny little fanfare, and a button labeled Reset appears on the screen.

Chapter 12: Operating the PalmPilot Desktop Program for Windows and Mac

5. **Tap the Reset button on the screen.**

   The General Preferences screen appears on your PalmPilot. You don't need to do anything in the General Preferences screen after a reset; you can either turn off the PalmPilot or go right on and use any application.

If you use one desktop computer to synchronize more than one PalmPilot, don't assign the same user name to more than one PalmPilot. The HotSync program can get confused and send the wrong data to the wrong PalmPilot, or worse yet, make data disappear.

Backing up your data

If you use only the programs that come in the box with your PalmPilot, you don't need to worry about backing up. If you HotSync regularly to keep your data current, you're covered. Your data from all the standard PalmPilot applications gets saved and archived by the Palm Desktop every time you HotSync. Of course, it's a good idea to backup the data on the desktop machine regularly as a general rule.

On the other hand, if you installed programs that don't come pre-installed on your PalmPilot, those programs may not automatically back themselves up like your standard PalmPilot apps do, so you need a backup program to keep those files safe. One program, called Backup Buddy, is available over the Internet to help you back up your nonstandard programs automatically. The program is shareware, which means that the author of the program asks you to send in the $15 registration fee voluntarily. You can contact him via e-mail at ahinds@poboxes.com. I think it's a good idea to register your shareware.

If all that you've added to your PalmPilot is a few games, I wouldn't worry about backing up. You need to be concerned with backups if you've added programs that add data themselves, like spreadsheets, databases, time and billing applications, or similar programs. If your PalmPilot was issued to you at work, you should check with your system administrator about whether you need to do anything special with backups.

Archiving Your PalmPilot Stuff

Your PalmPilot can hold only a fraction of the information that your desktop computer can. To save space on the PalmPilot, clearing things out on a regular basis is a good idea. The PalmPilot has a Purge function in the Date Book and To Do List that automatically gets rid of unneeded items and moves them to an archive file, if you want. For more about purging PalmPilot items, see Chapter 6.

Part III: PalmPilot and the Outside World

Viewing archived items

The Palm Desktop is the only place where you can open and view archived items. Even if you use another personal information manager, such as Microsoft Outlook or Lotus Organizer, to put items into your PalmPilot, you still need to look in the Palm Desktop to view your archived items.

These steps show you how to view your archived items in the Palm Desktop:

1. **Choose the type of archived item that you want to look at from the buttons on the left side of the screen (or from the View menu).**

   Calendar items are archived separately from items deleted from the Address Book, To Do List, or Memo Pad, so you need to open the part of the Palm Desktop that handles the type of item that you want to see.

2. **Choose File➪Open Archive.**

   The Open Archive dialog box opens, as shown in Figure 12-33.

Figure 12-33: Find those old deleted items by opening an archive file.

3. **Click the name of the archive file that you want to view.**

   Usually only one file appears on the archive list. If more than one archive file is listed and the archive that you open doesn't contain the item you want, repeat Steps 2 through 3 until you find the archive containing the item that you want.

4. **Click OK.**

   The items in the archive that you picked appear as a new list of items on your Palm Desktop.

If you're looking at the archive of items that are assigned to categories, the archive files will be organized by category — personal, business, or whatever you assign.

Chapter 12: Operating the PalmPilot Desktop Program for Windows and Mac

Returning an archived item to your PalmPilot

Another benefit to keeping archive files is to help you get back items that you accidentally delete. Don't be embarrassed — it happens to everybody.

To recover an item from an archive in the Palm Desktop, follow these steps:

1. **Choose the type of archived item that you want to recover from the buttons on the left side of the screen (or from the View menu).**

    Pick either Date Book, Address Book, To Do List, or Memo Pad.

2. **Choose File➪Open Archive.**

    The Open Archive dialog box opens.

3. **Click the name of the archive file that you want to view.**

    The file that you click is highlighted to show that you selected it.

4. **Click OK.**

    The items in the archive file that you picked are listed on the PalmPilot desktop.

5. **Click the item that you want to return to your PalmPilot.**

    The item that you click is highlighted to show that you selected it.

6. **Choose Edit➪Copy (or press Ctrl+C).**

    The item is copied to the clipboard. Nothing happens on the screen.

7. **Choose File➪Open Current.**

    Your collection of current items appears.

8. **Choose Edit➪Paste (or press Ctrl+V).**

    The item appears as part of your collection of current items.

9. **Place your PalmPilot in its cradle, and press the HotSync button on the cradle.**

    The HotSync dialog box opens and shows you the progress of your synchronization.

Remember, the whole reason for archiving items is to save space on your PalmPilot, so don't load old items back up to your PalmPilot unless you really need them.

Accommodating Multiple Users

Most people use a PalmPilot in conjunction with a desktop computer in order to simplify data entry and keep the data on their PalmPilots safe. But you don't have to limit yourself to one PalmPilot per computer. Palm Desktop enables you to synchronize PalmPilots with different users. The first time that you HotSync your PalmPilot, the HotSync Manager asks for your user name. The PalmPilot user name that you enter (or choose) is added to the list of user names in the Palm Desktop. Each time that you put a PalmPilot in the cradle attached to that desktop computer, the program recognizes which PalmPilot is in the cradle when you press the HotSync button. So after you've set up a computer to HotSync a particular PalmPilot, the desktop computer always knows which PalmPilot it's dealing with and synchronizes to that particular person's information.

It's not a good idea to set up multiple PalmPilot users on the same computer if you don't use the Palm Desktop program. It's possible to make your PalmPilot information synchronize to other programs, such as Microsoft Outlook or Act!, but you could encounter some confusion if you try to synchronize more than one PalmPilot to one of those programs. It's not impossible to use several PalmPilots with those programs; it's just not certain that everything will work right if you do it all through the same computer. If you want to host several PalmPilots on the same desktop PC, your best bet is to stick with the Palm Desktop.

The PalmPilot name game

Though all PalmPilots look pretty much alike in those little gray boxes, each one has one important difference — the name of the user. You can find out what name is assigned to the PalmPilot that you're using by tapping the Applications soft button and then tapping HotSync. The HotSync screen displays the name of the user assigned to it. A Palm III shows the user name in the upper-right corner of the screen. Older PalmPilots say "Welcome, *user name*." Also, when you perform a HotSync, the name of the user whose data is being synchronized appears in the HotSync Progress dialog box. You determine the PalmPilot user name the first time you perform a HotSync. If you try to HotSync a PalmPilot to a computer that hasn't seen a PalmPilot with that user name before, the HotSync Manager asks if you want to set up a new account for that user.

Chapter 13
Using the PalmPilot Modem

In This Chapter
- Explaining the basics
- Setting up your PalmPilot to use the PalmPilot Modem
- Using your modem to HotSync to your desktop computer
- Connecting to the Internet
- Sending and receiving Internet e-mail
- Browsing the World Wide Web
- Faxing

The amount of power that you can pack in a little bitty PalmPilot is amazing. But that's not all; snap on a PalmPilot Modem and look out! The modem adds only an inch or so to the length of your PalmPilot, but it extends the little gizmo's reach far enough to explore the entire Internet. The modem also enables you to exchange messages with people all over the world from nearly anywhere. Granted, a modem sets you back by about $129, but that's a small price to pay to put that much power in your pocket. You can also get a $19.95 PalmPilot modem cable that enables you to attach a standard external modem to your PalmPilot, but you need to be pretty savvy about setting up modems to make that work. I'd stick with the PalmPilot Modem.

PalmPilot Modem Basics

If you've just purchased a shiny new, store-bought PalmPilot and PalmPilot Modem, making them work together is fairly simple. When you see the PalmPilot and its modem together, you instinctively know how to attach them to one another. Just plug the modem into your PalmPilot the same way you plug the PalmPilot into its cradle and plug a phone line into the modem. The two work together seamlessly right from the get-go. After you've used your PalmPilot for a while, however, some settings may get changed or go awry. Here are the nitty-gritty details about the PalmPilot Modem in case you get into a pinch.

Setting up your modem

Your PalmPilot Modem doesn't need much attention. You can set it up in a snap. Here's the routine:

1. **Snap your PalmPilot into the modem.**

   The PalmPilot makes a slight snapping sound as it fits snugly into the modem.

2. **Plug a phone line into the modem.**

   The phone line snaps into your modem the same way that it does when you plug it into your phone.

Just feed your modem a new pair of batteries now and again and you're fine. The batteries fit behind the little door on the lower-front part of your modem case. Just slide the door downward to open the battery compartment.

The PalmPilot Modem's batteries power the modem for only about five hours of continuous operation. You can perform a Modem HotSync or check e-mail about 150 times on a single set of batteries. However, if you want to spend hours surfing the Web (yes, you can surf the Web with your PalmPilot; more about that in "Browsing the Web" at the end of this chapter), your modem will run out of battery power pretty fast. If you plan to run your modem for long periods of time, buy the optional AC adapter for the modem for $19.95 so that the modem draws power from your wall socket. Remember, the AC adapter powers only the modem, not the PalmPilot. If you plug your modem into an AC adapter, your PalmPilot could still run out of juice (although the PalmPilot runs a lot longer on a set of batteries than the modem does). So check the PalmPilot battery level every so often by tapping the Applications soft button and viewing your list of applications. A little battery-shaped icon at the top of the screen indicates the amount of power remaining in your battery.

International incidentals

Just like your hair dryer or your electric razor, the PalmPilot Modem is designed to be used in the United States and Canada. If you want to connect your PalmPilot modem to telephone systems outside North America, you may need to buy adapters and make special arrangements because the telephone lines and electrical outlets outside North America sometimes don't work with American electronics. I know of one company, called Road Warriors, that specializes in supplying gear to people who travel with computers. Check out the company's Web site at www.warrior.com for details on equipment that enables you to hook up a computer in any country on Earth.

Of course, you need to plug a telephone line into your PalmPilot Modem. A jack is located at the bottom of the case — it looks just like the jack on your home telephone. Simply unplug the wire that goes into your telephone and then plug it into your PalmPilot Modem.

All phone lines are not alike. Your home phone line is the right type of phone line to use with your modem. It's called an *analog* line, the old-fashioned kind of phone line. Another type of phone line that offices and hotels often use is called a *digital* line. *Do not plug your modem into a digital line!* In some cases plugging your modem into a digital line can damage the modem. Many hotels now have phones with a special jack on the side labeled *modem* or *data* in which you can safely plug your modem. If you're not sure whether a certain line is analog or digital, just ask. You can feel fairly confident that a phone line in a private home is safe. In an office, a phone line attached to a fax machine is also a good bet.

Setting up your PalmPilot to use the modem

After you snap your PalmPilot into the modem and plug in a suitable phone line, you're connected. Just tell your PalmPilot the type of modem that you're attaching and then enter the settings for the kinds of things that you want to do.

To set up your PalmPilot to work with a PalmPilot Modem, all you really need to do is plug your PalmPilot into the modem. The factory settings on a new PalmPilot enable it to run the PalmPilot Modem quite nicely. If your PalmPilot isn't factory-new, however, the settings may have been changed. To adjust the modem settings for a PalmPilot Pro or Palm III (or to make sure that your current settings are correct), follow these steps:

1. **Tap the Applications soft button.**

    The applications list appears, showing icons for all the programs installed on your PalmPilot.

2. **Tap the Prefs icon.**

    The Preferences screen appears.

3. **Tap the pull-down menu in the upper-right corner of the screen.**

    The list of preferences categories appears.

4. **Tap Modem.**

    The Modem Preferences screen appears, as shown in Figure 13-1.

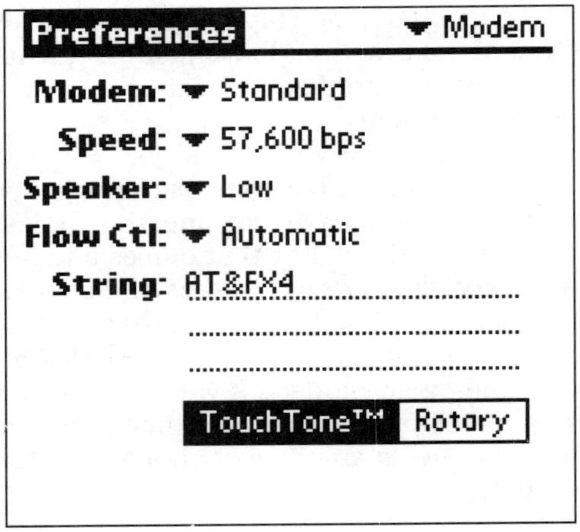

Figure 13-1: To reconfigure your modem, go to the Modem Preferences screen.

5. **Tap the triangle next to Modem on the first line of the screen.**

   A list of modems that you can use with your PalmPilot appears.

6. **Choose Palm US/Canada.**

   The words Palm US/Canada appear next to the word Modem.

   If you have a modem made by a different manufacturer, choose the appropriate modem.

7. **Tap the triangle next to Speed on the second line of the screen.**

   A list of numbers appears. Each number represents a different modem speed.

8. **Choose 57,600.**

9. **Tap the triangle next to Speaker on the third line of the screen.**

   A choice of speaker volumes appears. Choose either Off, Low, Medium or High. None of these settings makes the modem speaker obnoxiously loud, but if you absolutely can't stand the shrill sound of a modem making its connection, then choose Off.

10. **Choose the modem speaker volume that you prefer.**

    The volume that you choose appears next to Speaker.

11. **Tap the triangle next to Flow Ctl on the fourth line of the screen.**

    A list appears with the choices Automatic, On, and Off.

12. **Choose Automatic.**

    The word Automatic appears next to the words Flow Ctl.

13. **Choose the dialing method that you use for your telephone by tapping either TouchTone or Rotary at the bottom of the screen.**

    You know best which dialing method applies to your phone line. If you dial your phone with buttons, it's TouchTone. If you still have a dial on your phone, choose Rotary and call the Smithsonian. Your phone is a collector's item.

You can fiddle around with your modem settings a little bit without causing big problems in the way that it works, but be careful about changing too much. Modems have a way of getting fussy when you can't call someone for help, so after you get things working, leave the settings alone.

One item that you should definitely leave alone is the crazy characters on the String line, the ones that say something memorable like AT&FX4. That's a set of instructions that tells your modem how to do its work. If you change this string, you may mess up your modem. If you don't know what a modem setup string is, leave it alone.

Setting Up Your PalmPilot for a Modem HotSync

The main purpose of the PalmPilot Modem is to enable you to HotSync your PalmPilot with your desktop computer via a phone line. To successfully HotSync over the telephone, you need to set up your desktop computer as well as your PalmPilot in advance.

You can't perform a Modem HotSync to a specific desktop computer until you've completed at least one local HotSync with that computer. Doing a local HotSync is important because the HotSync Manager asks you to assign a user name to your PalmPilot, and it creates a set of files and folders dedicated to your PalmPilot. After you've completed a local HotSync, the HotSync Manager knows which PalmPilot it's dealing with each time you press the HotSync button, and it knows where to store information about your particular PalmPilot. If you haven't gone through the local HotSync process at least once, the HotSync Manager doesn't know what to do when it picks up the phone. For more on how to HotSync and set up your PalmPilot desktop program, see Chapter 11.

So if you plan to take your PalmPilot on your voyage to Mongolia and HotSync from there, you need to run a local HotSync before you go. Also, don't forget your passport and some sensible shoes.

Entering the Modem HotSync phone number

When you perform a Modem HotSync, your PalmPilot calls your desktop computer on the phone and then runs the HotSync program. The most important information that you need to supply is the phone number that your desktop computer answers.

To enter the HotSync phone number:

1. **Tap the Applications soft button.**

    The applications list appears, showing icons for all the programs installed on your PalmPilot.

2. **Tap the HotSync icon.**

    The HotSync screen appears. If you've never entered a HotSync phone number, the box below the Modem Sync icon says Enter Phone #; otherwise, the phone number that you've already entered appears there.

3. **Tap Enter Phone #.**

    The Phone Setup screen appears, as shown in Figure 13-2.

Figure 13-2: HotSync is smart, but you still need to tell it what phone number to call by entering the number in the Phone Setup screen.

Phone Setup

Phone #: 555-5685

☐ Dial prefix: 9,
☐ Disable call waiting: 1170,
☐ Use calling card:

(OK) (Cancel)

4. **Enter the phone number to which your desktop computer is connected, by using either the on-screen keyboard or Graffiti (see Chapter 2 for more on entering text).**

   The number that you enter appears on the Phone # line.

5. **If your phone system requires you to dial a prefix before making a call, tap the Dial Prefix check box and enter the prefix after Dial Prefix.**

   Some offices and hotels require you to dial an 8 or a 9 before making a call. Enter the number that your system requires on the Dial Prefix line.

6. **If you're using a calling card, tap the Use Calling Card check box and enter your calling card on the line below Use Calling Card and after the four commas.**

   The four commas make the modem wait a few seconds before dialing the calling card number, just like you do when you dial the calling card number yourself.

7. **Tap OK.**

Disabling call waiting

I don't understand why call waiting is so popular; I hate when people interrupt my phone conversations. Half the time the people interrupting my calls are selling products that I don't want.

Computers hate being interrupted by call waiting even more than I do. They often do crazy things when the little call-waiting beep sounds, but they never buy things from telemarketers. Fortunately, you can program your PalmPilot so that it disables call waiting before beginning a HotSync. Follow these steps just once to tell your PalmPilot to turn off call waiting:

1. **Tap the Applications soft button.**

   The applications list appears, showing icons for all the programs installed on your PalmPilot.

2. **Tap the HotSync icon.**

   The HotSync screen appears. The box below the Modem Sync icon displays either Enter Phone # or the last phone number that you entered.

3. **Tap the box below the Modem Sync icon.**

   The Phone Setup dialog box opens.

4. **Tap the box next to Disable Call Waiting.**

   A check mark appears in the box to indicate that you selected it.

To the right of Disable Call Waiting is the number 1170, which is usually the code that you dial to turn off call waiting. If the number used to turn off call waiting in your area is different, select the number that appears on-screen and then enter the number that does the trick in your locale.

5. **Tap OK.**

   The Phone Setup dialog box closes.

Setting up Palm Desktop for a Modem HotSync

Doing a HotSync over the telephone has the same result as running a HotSync directly from your desktop computer: It makes the contents of your PalmPilot identical to the contents of your Palm Desktop. If you have e-mail messages on your desktop computer, copies of those messages are transferred to your PalmPilot.

When your PalmPilot performs a Modem HotSync, it dials the phone number of your desktop computer. Your desktop computer then has to answer the phone when the PalmPilot calls. In order to be able to answer that call, your desktop computer must

- Have a modem.
- Be connected to a phone line.
- Be running when you call.
- Not be running any other communications program.
- Be configured to accept your call.

After that, it's easy! Because there are so many types of computers out there, I can't tell you how to configure yours to accept your call. Refer to your owner's manual for that. But here's how to configure your computer to wait for your Modem HotSync call:

1. **Start Palm Desktop.**

   Your Palm Desktop appears.

2. **Choose HotSync⇨Setup.**

   The Setup dialog box opens.

3. **Click the Modem tab.**

   The modem settings page appears, as shown in Figure 13-3.

Figure 13-3: Use the Modem tab to tell the HotSync Manager where your modem is installed so that it can answer the phone.

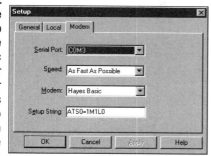

 4. **In the Serial Port list, choose the port to which your modem is assigned.**

    You can check which port your modem uses in Windows 95 or 98 by clicking the Start button, choosing Settings⇨Control Panel, and then double-clicking the Modems icon. After the Modems dialog box opens, click the Properties button. The properties page tells you which port your modem uses. The ports are named COM1 through COM4.

 5. **In the Speed box, choose As Fast As Possible.**

    I don't know why you'd want to pick anything else. The speed that you choose appears in the Speed box.

 6. **In the Modem box, choose the type of modem that you're using.**

    You can check what type of modem you're using in Windows 95 in the Control Panel, just like you checked the port in Step 4. If in doubt, Hayes Standard should work. The modem that you choose appears in the Modem box. The setup string for the modem that you pick automatically appears in the Setup String box. The setup string is the series of commands that your modem uses to configure itself, so don't mess with it.

 7. **Click OK.**

    The Setup dialog box closes.

 8. **Right-click the HotSync Manager icon in the taskbar.**

    The HotSync Manager icon is the little circle in the lower-right corner of your screen containing a red arrow and a blue arrow pointing in opposite directions. When you right-click the icon, the HotSync Manager menu appears.

 9. **If no check mark appears next to Modem, then choose Modem.**

    A check mark appears next to Modem, as shown in Figure 13-4, and then the menu disappears.

Figure 13-4:
Tell the HotSync Manager to answer the phone by clicking the HotSync icon in the Windows taskbar and then clicking Modem.

Now just leave your computer on and go your merry way.

However, I have both good news and bad news. The good news is that after you set up the HotSync Manager for a Modem HotSync, you can call up your desktop computer anytime to update your PalmPilot. The bad news is that nobody can receive phone calls on the phone line that your computer is connected to because the HotSync Manager answers *all* incoming calls. And you can't attach an answering machine to that computer. The HotSync Manager hogs the phone line whether your computer is running Windows or Mac OS.

The Modem HotSync trick is best for people who call phone numbers that are totally dedicated to taking calls from computers, like the phone numbers that many corporations have. If you need to HotSync by modem frequently, you may want to consider getting an extra phone line.

So, why bother doing a Modem HotSync at all? Because doing a HotSync, anytime, anywhere, backs up your data. After you're completely addicted to your PalmPilot (admit it, you're hooked already), you depend on the collection of information that you've amassed. If your PalmPilot falls from a gondola or gets rammed by a rhino in the course of your adventures, you can replace the PalmPilot with a wave of your credit card, but you could lose months trying to recreate the data.

PalmPilot on the Internet

With the PalmPilot Modem, you can connect to the Internet and do two of the things that make the Internet so popular: exchange e-mail and browse the Web. I won't pretend that the little PalmPilot navigates the Internet as

Chapter 13: Using the PalmPilot Modem

easily or impressively as your mighty desktop computer; the tiny gray screen shows you only so much. But like someone once said about a talking dog, no matter how well the trick is done, it's amazing to see it done at all.

You need some extra software to be able to exchange e-mail messages or browse Web pages, but the foundations are already on your PalmPilot to enable you to access the Internet and take advantage of what it offers. The Palm III includes something called TCP/IP, which is the language spoken by all computers connected to the Internet. You never actually see TCP/IP, but if you try to connect a computer to the Internet without TCP/IP, nothing happens.

Setting up your Internet connection

Before you do anything on the Internet, you need to get connected. You'll need something called an *ISP,* or Internet Service Provider. An ISP is a company like Netcom or CompuServe that gives you a phone number that you dial to connect to the Internet. You may be able to use the same ISP that you use to connect your desktop computer to the Internet; just enter the same information in the Network Preferences program on your PalmPilot, and you're on your way. Check with your ISP to see if you can connect your PalmPilot to the Internet through your ISP's servers.

When you set up your Internet connection, you also need to set up your modem as I describe in "Setting up your PalmPilot to use the modem," earlier in this chapter.

To set up your PalmPilot to dial your ISP:

1. **Tap the Applications soft button.**

    The applications list appears, showing icons for all the programs installed on your PalmPilot.

2. **Tap the Prefs icon.**

    The Preferences screen appears.

3. **Tap the pull-down menu in the upper-right corner of the screen.**

    The list of preferences categories appears.

4. **Tap Network.**

    The Network Preferences screen appears, as shown in Figure 13-5.

5. **Tap the triangle next to the word Service.**

    A list of the services with which the PalmPilot is ready to connect appears.

6. **Tap the name of the Internet Service Provider that you use.**

    The name of the service that you tap appears next to the word Service.

234 Part III: PalmPilot and the Outside World

Figure 13-5: The Network Preferences screen is where you tell your PalmPilot how to connect to the Internet.

If your ISP doesn't appear, call up your ISP's tech-support area and see what the folks there recommend.

 7. **Enter your user name on the User Name line by using either the on-screen keyboard or Graffiti (see Chapter 2 for more on entering text).**

If the User Name line is blank, just tap the line and enter your user name. If temporary text appears on the User Name line, select the text and then enter your user name.

 8. **Tap the box next to the word Password.**

The Password dialog box opens, as shown in Figure 13-6.

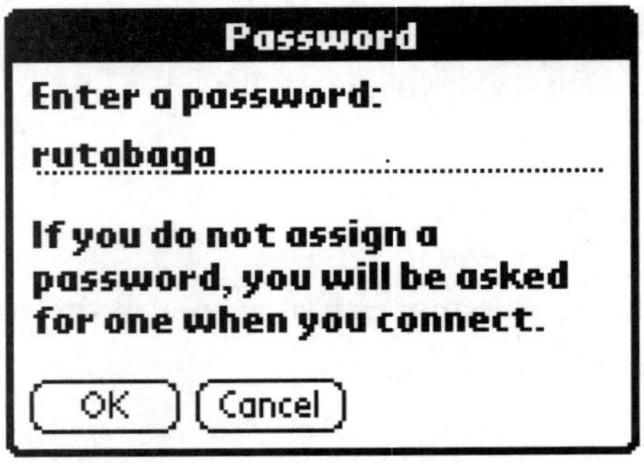

Figure 13-6: Enter your Internet password in the Password dialog box.

Chapter 13: Using the PalmPilot Modem 235

9. **Enter your password.**

   The password that you enter appears in the Password dialog box.

10. **Tap OK.**

    The Password dialog box closes.

11. **Tap the box next to Phone.**

    The Phone setup screen appears.

12. **Enter the phone number of your Internet Service Provider by using either the on-screen keyboard or Graffiti (see Chapter 2 for more about entering text).**

    The phone number that you enter appears on the Phone # line. You can also set up a dial prefix and a calling card number exactly the same way that I describe earlier in this chapter.

13. **Tap OK.**

    The Phone Setup screen closes.

After you set up your network preferences, you probably won't have to mess with them again except to change the ISP phone number when you're traveling. Of course, many ISPs have toll-free 800 numbers that you can use everywhere. So, you can travel anywhere in North America without changing the phone number.

The Connect button at the bottom of the Network Preferences screen actually makes the modem dial the phone number that you've entered and connects you to the Internet. You don't usually need to tap the Connect button because the e-mail program or the web browser that you normally use starts up your connection automatically. In a pinch, though, you can return to the Network Preferences screen and tap Connect to force your PalmPilot to connect to the Internet. After you're connected, that same button says Disconnect, so you can tap the Disconnect button to force your PalmPilot to disconnect from the Internet.

Tapping the Details button opens a screen that shows some of the nitty-gritty details that your PalmPilot needs to know to connect to the Internet. I can't think of any reason that you'd change those settings, so leave them alone.

Sending and receiving REAL e-mail

The PalmPilot mail program, which is pre-installed on every PalmPilot Professional and Palm III, synchronizes e-mail with the e-mail program on your desktop computer. Unless a message has successfully arrived on your desktop, you can't synchronize it to your PalmPilot.

This setup can be a problem if you plan to use your PalmPilot to get your e-mail while you're on the road, because the HotSync Manager needs to hog your modem 24 hours a day. And if the HotSync Manager ties up your modem all the time while you're travelling, your desktop e-mail program can't dial out to get your messages. So for many people, the Modem HotSync feature keeps everything on their PalmPilots current *except* their e-mail.

One solution to this problem is to set up your PalmPilot to go right to the source and act like a real computer, getting real e-mail from the Internet. If you set up your PalmPilot to connect to the Internet as I describe in the previous section, you can use a program like HandMail or MultiMail to go out to the Internet and pick up your messages.

Setting up a PalmPilot Internet e-mail program

You can use several e-mail programs to send and receive e-mail through your PalmPilot the same way that a conventional desktop e-mail system does. One option is to use MultiMail Pro, a commercial e-mail program. In this section, I show you how to use this particular program, but most e-mail programs require the same sort of setup routine. The details differ, but the general idea is the same: You need to tell the e-mail program which computer on the Internet holds your e-mail and what user name and password enable you to access your mail.

Before you set up an e-mail program to get your messages, you need to install the e-mail program itself. (See Chapter 11 for details on installing programs to your PalmPilot.) You also need to know how your mail system assigns names to itself and to you. Check with your ISP's technical support people.

Of course, if you were a good little Net surfer, you wrote all that information down when you set up your desktop e-mail program, so you may not have to call your ISP. But if you're like me (and who wouldn't want to be like me?), you probably prefer to talk to those friendly people in the middle of nowhere who sit all day and answer phone calls from people like us. Ask 'em if they have a PalmPilot, too! Who knows, you could make a new friend and exchange e-mail on your PalmPilots. Hoo, boy! There's a big time!

Here's how to set up MultiMail Pro to get e-mail:

1. **After you've installed MultiMail Pro (or the e-mail program of your choice), tap the Applications soft button.**

    The applications list appears, showing icons for all the programs installed on your PalmPilot.

Chapter 13: Using the PalmPilot Modem 237

2. **Tap the MultiMail icon (or the icon for whatever other e-mail program you may be using).**

   The MultiMail screen appears, as shown in Figure 13-7.

Figure 13-7:
MultiMail is one of several e-mail programs that you can use to send and receive Internet e-mail with your PalmPilot.

3. **Tap Menu.**

   The menu bar appears.

4. **Choose Options⇨Mail Server.**

   The Mail Server screen appears, as shown in Figure 13-8. Mail servers are the kinds of computers on the Internet that hold mail. Your e-mail program picks up mail from these computers.

5. **Tap the number of the mailbox that you want to set up.**

   You can set up more than one mailbox in many e-mail programs. MultiMail enables you to set up four mailboxes. If you haven't set up any mailboxes yet, tap the number 1.

6. **Enter the name of your mail server on the Server line by using either the on-screen keyboard or Graffiti (see Chapter 2 for more on entering text).**

Figure 13-8: In the Mail Server screen, you tell your e-mail program where to deliver your mail.

You can get this information from the tech support people at your ISP. And ask those nice people how the weather is wherever they are.

TIP: If you don't want to wait on hold for an hour with your ISP, another way to get this information is to check the settings of your desktop e-mail program. Odds are, you entered the same information there that you have to enter here.

7. **Enter the name of your mailbox on the Mailbox line by using either the on-screen keyboard or Graffiti.**

   Your mailbox name is usually the part of your e-mail address that comes before the @ sign. For example, if your e-mail address is snorkle66@dive.com, your mailbox name is probably snorkle66. Check with your ISP to be sure.

8. **If *Blank* or *Unassigned* appears on the Password line, tap the box in which the word Unassigned appears and then enter your password.**

   Again, your tech support gurus know all this stuff, so be nice to them and ask politely.

9. **Tap OK.**

   If your tech support people say that's all you need, you're done. Some systems require other settings.

After you set up a mailbox, you're ready to go.

PalmPilot and AOL mail

America Online (AOL) is by far the most popular online service, but it's a screaming pain in the neck when it comes to managing e-mail. Most of the terms that I've heard people use to describe AOL's mail system are unfit to be printed here. The folks at AOL have promised to make improvements to their e-mail system, but they haven't followed up on those promises so far.

The people who created HandMail have solved the AOL mail problem; they've developed a version of their program that enables you to send and receive your AOL e-mail via your PalmPilot. The program costs $49, a bit more than I wish it would, but it's well worth the money if you exchange lots of mail over AOL.

Not only is reading your e-mail more convenient on a PalmPilot than on a desktop computer, but a real e-mail program like HandMail gives you lots of e-mail management tools that aren't available on the AOL desktop program, such as the ability to use rules to send incoming mail to different mailboxes and look up e-mail addresses from your PalmPilot Address Book. You can visit the makers of HandMail at the company's Web site at www.smartcodesoft.com.

Sending and receiving PalmPilot Internet e-mail

Your PalmPilot isn't always connected to your phone line. Otherwise, you'd have to walk all over town with a really, really, really long phone cord dragging around behind you. You can create or read PalmPilot e-mail anywhere, anytime, but to actually send the messages, you need to make sure that your PalmPilot is plugged into the modem and that the modem is plugged into a phone line. Then give your e-mail program the command to send and receive messages. HandMail requires you to tap Menu, and then choose Mail⇨Send and Retrieve. MultiMail, another popular package, has a Send/Receive button on the main screen.

Browsing the Web

So you can't believe that you can surf the Internet on your PalmPilot? Well, it's true. Granted, most Web sites look pretty poor on that teensy little screen, but you can find a lot of text on the Internet, too, and text looks fine on a little bitty screen.

Of course, there's a catch. Before you can surf the Web with your PalmPilot, you need two things: an Internet connection and a web browser. In "Setting up your Internet connection" earlier in this chapter, I show you how to connect to the Internet. You also need to get a web browser and install it on your PalmPilot.

I've tried two web browsers that I like: HandWeb from Smartcode Software (www.smartcodesoft.com) — the company that also created HandMail (see the previous section) — and ProxiWeb. HandWeb is pretty simple and works a lot like the web browsers that you may use on your desktop computer, such as Netscape Navigator and the one made by that other company (MicroSomething?). The HandWeb program's main shortcoming is that it doesn't do enough to make Web pages look good on that tiny gray screen.

ProxiWeb uses something called a proxy server, which means that it shows you everything on the Web through its computer; its computer interprets the pages that you request to make them look better on the PalmPilot screen. Although this process makes the pages look better on your PalmPilot, the loading time for each page is slow. ProxiWeb manages to interpret some graphics, but fancy features such as frames and animation that many advanced Web sites use just disappear on a PalmPilot web browser. The browsers that I've mentioned here don't let you bookmark pages the way you do in a desktop web browser. You can save the URL of a Web page by entering it in a list of favorite pages, but you can't really capture the address easily.

PalmPilot web browsing is very primitive at this point, but I expect rapid progress in the near future.

Sending a Fax with Your PalmPilot

Why would you want to send a fax from a PalmPilot? Because hundreds of millions of fax machines exist in the world. Not everyone is equipped to receive e-mail yet, but many people have the capability to receive a fax.

Obviously, you can't receive a fax on your PalmPilot. Not yet anyway. I'm sure that someday you'll see papers flying out of people's pockets when their PalmPilots get an urgent fax, but that isn't possible yet.

The same folks who created HandMail sell a fax program called HandFax. For $49.95, you can buy the program and fax messages from your Memo Pad via your PalmPilot Modem.

Part IV
Extending the Life of Your PalmPilot

In this part . . .

You can't stop PalmPilot progress (not that you would want to). The list of new features and functions for the PalmPilot is growing, and you'll certainly want to upgrade now and then. This part shows you how to upgrade to the latest model when the time comes.

Chapter 14
Upward Mobility — Upgrading Your PalmPilot

In This Chapter
▶ Figuring out which version of Palm OS you're using
▶ Upgrading your Palm OS
▶ Installing a new memory card in your PalmPilot
▶ Upgrading your Palm III
▶ Upgrading your desktop program

I spend this entire book discussing the PalmPilot Professional and Palm III while scarcely mentioning the hallowed ancestors of these models, the PalmPilot 1000, PalmPilot 5000, and PalmPilot Personal. What am I, anti-progress? Have I forgotten the sacrifices of the early adopters who bought their PalmPilots 18 long months ago? Not at all.

All PalmPilots are upgradeable — even the very first ones. Sometimes you just need to install some software, other times you swap a tiny memory card, but you can always upgrade to the latest features. So rather than belabor every page with boring distinctions about which model did what, I focus on the latest models. My suggestion: Anyone with a PalmPilot Personal or earlier model should upgrade to either a PalmPilot Professional or Palm III and stop suffering. Life is short, and upgrades are easy.

Upgrading Made Easy

You can upgrade three elements of your PalmPilot:

✔ The operating system (or Palm OS)
✔ The memory card
✔ The desktop program

> ## The Wizard of OS
>
> Every computer, even the PalmPilot, has something called an *operating system* to direct all the activities of the machine. Computer nerds often classify computers by the type of operating system they use. Windows is the best-known operating system; it's the successor to DOS, the system used on the original IBM PC. Dozens of different companies manufacture Windows computers, but you refer to any of them as Windows machines. You used to be able to say the same thing about the Macintosh; Apple allowed several clone makers to manufacture machines similar to the Macintosh that ran the Mac OS. All these clones were also called Macs. However, Apple pulled the plug on the Mac clone makers, so only Apple makes Macs these days.
>
> Computers that run the same operating system do the same things, more or less, and run the same programs. Every so often the companies that write operating systems improve their products and issue new versions of their operating systems. Microsoft made a big splash when it released a new version of Windows a few years back, called Windows 95. The company made a smaller splash with the more recent release of Windows 98. Apple also peps up its operating system now and again, offering System 7, followed by System 7.5, and then Mac OS 8.
>
> The PalmPilot also has its very own operating system, called the Palm OS. When the Palm people release a new PalmPilot, they often release a new version of their operating system as well. The release of the Palm III coincided with the release of a new operating system, Palm OS 3.0. The most advanced Palm OS available at this writing is Palm OS 3.01, which you can find on the PalmPilot Web site at www.palmpilot.com.

You need to know these two essential things about upgrading your PalmPilot:

- Any PalmPilot can be upgraded by installing a new memory card.
- Any PalmPilot can work with any version of the Palm Desktop.

That's it. If you don't have the latest PalmPilot version, you can upgrade your PalmPilot to make it the latest version. Likewise, if you don't have the latest version of the desktop, you can upgrade that as well. Simple? Of course!

Upgrading Your PalmPilot

Before you tackle a Palm OS upgrade, you need to know which version of Palm OS you're using. Here's how:

1. **Press the Date Book hard button (or any of the other hard buttons).**

    The Date Book application appears.

Chapter 14: Upward Mobility — Upgrading Your PalmPilot

2. **Tap Menu.**

    The menu bar appears.

3. **Choose Options⇨About Date Book.**

    The About Date Book screen appears, as shown in Figure 14-1. The Palm OS version number appears on the left side of the screen.

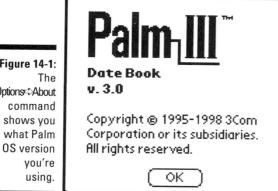

Figure 14-1: The Options⇨About command shows you what Palm OS version you're using.

If your Palm OS version number is less than 3.0, you can buy and install the Palm 2MB upgrade card to give your PalmPilot all the latest features (more about the upgrade card later in this chapter).

Installing a new version of the Palm OS

The simplest way to upgrade your PalmPilot is to install the latest version of the Palm OS, the operating system that all the PalmPilot programs rely upon. The Palm people offer constant improvements to the Palm OS and post the new improvements, called patches, on the Internet. You can check out their Web site at `www.palmpilot.3com.com/custsupp/downloads/indexdl.html` for the latest information about Palm OS patches (see Figure 14-2).

Although you can install a patch to the operating system of any PalmPilot, you can use patches only for the operating system made for the level of PalmPilot hardware you're using. For a PalmPilot 1000, you can use only Palm OS 1.0 and the patches that go with it — versions 1.1, 1.2, and so on. For a PalmPilot Personal or PalmPilot Professional, you use Palm OS 2.0 and the patches numbered 2.1, 2.2, and so on. If you want to make your Palm OS jump a whole level, from Palm OS 2.0 to Palm OS 3.0, you need to install a memory card that can handle Palm OS 3.0, which turns your unit into a Palm III.

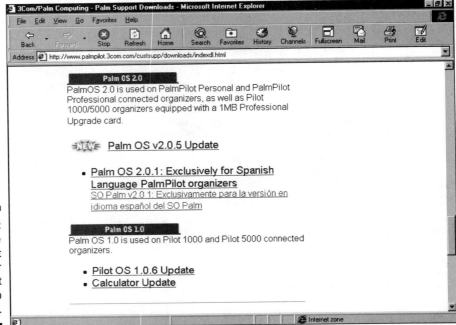

Figure 14-2: Check the PalmPilot Web site for the latest upgrades to Palm OS.

If you do choose to download a patch to upgrade your Palm OS, you need to install it just like you install any other PalmPilot program with the Palm Install Tool. See Chapter 12 for more in installing applications.

Installing a new memory card into a pre-Palm III model

What separates the Professionals from the Personals (in the PalmPilot world, anyway) is a tiny circuit board called the *memory card*. The memory card is a bit smaller than a corn chip (but not as edible, so don't dip it in guacamole). If you take the memory card out of a PalmPilot Personal and install the Palm III card, *voilà,* you have a Palm III! Actually, you have something that thinks like a Palm III in the body of a PalmPilot Personal. It's like a brain transplant; the thinking improves but the body stays the same (unless you're the Frankenstein monster, in which case you probably have more immediate problems). You can upgrade a PalmPilot Personal so that it becomes a Palm III, but you won't have the handy backlight for reading your screen in the dark; that feature is available on the PalmPilot Professional and later models.

Chapter 14: Upward Mobility — Upgrading Your PalmPilot

The Palm people sell the Palm III upgrade card for about $130, at the time of this writing. Be aware, though, that PalmPilot prices change quickly as new models come out.

The first few PalmPilot models were designed so that you could easily upgrade them. They even have doors on the backs of their cases for swapping memory cards with very little fuss.

If you're comfortable swapping electronic components, upgrading your PalmPilot will be a snap for you. If you're anxious about fiddling with chips, just take your time and follow these steps:

1. **Perform a full HotSync to back up your information.**

   You lose all your data when you change your memory card, so make sure that the copy on your PC is current. For more about performing a HotSync, see Chapter 11. Also, if you've installed a lot of add-on programs, you lose them, too. You might want to check out a program called Backup Buddy, which I mention in Chapter 12, for help in saving and restoring third-party programs.

2. **Lay your PalmPilot face down on a table or any other smooth, flat surface.**

   The two access doors are located on the back of the unit.

3. **Clear static by touching the metal backplate of your computer.**

   A good jolt of static electricity can damage the tiny memory card.

4. **Remove the battery door.**

5. **Remove the batteries.**

   Would you have a brain transplant with no anesthesia? Of course not.

6. **Remove the large access door at the top of your PalmPilot.**

   Often, you can simply press on the door and slide it upward and off the PalmPilot case. You can release the door by pressing a straightened paper clip into the hole just below the door (the hole that's *not* marked Reset). The memory card is in a white mounting bracket.

7. **Turn your PalmPilot so that the memory card faces you.**

   You'll find the card a bit easier to remove that way.

8. **Press outward on the two small metal tabs on each side of the memory card to release it and then tilt the card from the top.**

   After you slightly tilt the card away from the bracket, it's free and ready to be removed.

9. **Pull the memory card out of your PalmPilot.**

   Wiggle the card a little to free it up as you remove it.

Part IV: Extending the Life of Your PalmPilot

10. **Store the old memory card in a safe place.**

    If anything goes wrong with the new card, you can put the old one back in.

11. **Insert the new memory card into exactly the same position in which the old card sat.**

    Snap the new card into the brackets. If it's a Palm III memory card, make sure the two little infrared bulbs point toward the top of the PalmPilot case.

12. **Reinstall the batteries.**

    The battery door should snap tightly shut.

13. **Press the power switch to see if your PalmPilot turns on and runs.**

    If you've seated the memory card in properly, the unit should run perfectly. If the unit fails to run, gently press the memory card into the bracket to ensure that it's seated correctly.

14. **Reinstall the memory door (or install the new memory door if you've installed a Palm III memory card).**

    The memory door snaps tightly shut.

Once you've replaced the memory card, you have what amounts to a brand-new PalmPilot with no data. You can perform another HotSync to restore all the information in the standard PalmPilot applications.

If you had third-party applications installed before you upgraded, you need to reinstall them with the Palm Install Tool. See Chapter 11 for more about installing applications.

Although your PalmPilot is pretty hardy, be sure to do an upgrade in a reasonably safe, clean location. Don't change memory cards in a sandstorm or underwater. And try to avoid swapping memory cards while riding your motorcycle (especially if you're driving); you could lose the card and be unable to find it. What would the other Hell's Angels think if you couldn't start your PalmPilot?

Upgrading a Palm III

According to a PalmPilot legend, when Jeff Hawkins was inventing the PalmPilot, he cut a little block of wood about the size of a PalmPilot and walked around with it in his pocket to see if it was the right size to write on. So it's not surprising that the first few PalmPilot models were all shaped like a little block of wood.

Chapter 14: Upward Mobility — Upgrading Your PalmPilot   249

By the time the Palm III came out, the company was bigger, and it had been purchased by the huge 3Com Corporation. I guess that the big outfit had some designers on staff who thought that the homely little-block-of-wood look was not exactly chic. So they applied something called industrial design to the little PalmPilot and came up with a new look: the slightly-rounded-little-block-of-wood look. Personally, I liked the old look better; the stylus was easier to get to, and the old machine fit cleanly into the PalmPilot cradle and modem.

Also, the Palm III has no door for the memory card because the new design requires that the memory go in sideways. So, the physical process for changing the memory card in a Palm III is different than the process for changing the memory card in any other PalmPilot. Here's the routine:

1. **Perform a full HotSync to back up your information.**

   You lose all your data when you change your memory card, so make sure that the copy on your PC is current. You also lose any add-on programs that you installed. See Chapter 12 for more about backing up third-party programs.

2. **Lay your PalmPilot face down on a table or any other smooth, flat surface.**

   Four screws are visible on the back of the unit.

3. **Clear static by touching the metal backplate of your computer.**

   A good jolt of static electricity can damage the tiny memory card.

4. **Open the battery door.**

5. **Remove the batteries.**

   I'm told that you can get away with removing only one battery, but why not go all the way?

6. **Remove the four screws on the back of your PalmPilot and remove the back of the case.**

   The entire back of the PalmPilot case comes off, revealing the memory card inside. The memory card sits sideways inside the PalmPilot case. It's a little green circuit card about the size of two postage stamps. That sounds small, but it's the biggest thing you'll see inside the PalmPilot case.

7. **Turn your PalmPilot so that the memory card faces you.**

   The card is a bit easier to remove that way.

8. **Press outward on the two small metal tabs on each side of the memory card to release it and then tilt the card from the top.**

   After you slightly tilt the card away from the bracket, it's free and ready to be removed.

9. **Pull the memory card out of your PalmPilot.**

   Wiggle the card a little to free it up as you remove it.

10. **Store the old memory card in a safe place.**

    If anything goes wrong with the new card, you can put the old one back in.

11. **Insert the new memory card into exactly the same position in which the old card sat.**

    Snap the new card into the brackets.

12. **Reinstall the back of the case and replace the four screws.**

    The case snaps on tightly.

13. **Reinstall the batteries.**

    The battery door should snap tightly shut.

14. **Press the power switch to see if the PalmPilot turns on and runs.**

    If you've seated the memory card properly, the unit should run perfectly. If the unit fails to run, reopen the case and reseat the memory card.

After you complete your upgrade, you need to perform another HotSync to restore your data. You also need to reinstall any programs you'd added to your PalmPilot before the upgrade. See Chapter 11 for more on HotSyncing and Chapter 12 for more on installing applications.

Of course, as I write this, the Palm people don't offer an upgrade card for the Palm III, because Palm III is the top of the line. But a few months is an eternity in PalmPilot time, so you may encounter other options by the time you read this book. If I had ESP, I'd tell you what those options will be, but if I *really* had ESP, I wouldn't be writing this; I'd make zillions winning all the lotteries and I'd retire to Fiji.

But I'm not saying that you can't upgrade a Palm III right now. A company called TRG offers an upgrade card for a Palm III called the SuperPilot Memory Board. The SuperPilot board uses the same Palm OS 3.0 that comes standard with the Palm III, but the SuperPilot can increase the total memory of your PalmPilot to as much as 8MB. See Chapter 16 for more about the SuperPilot board. You may think that 8MB sounds like a lot of memory, considering that you started out with 2MB or less, but if you have a large address list or if you do ambitious things on your PalmPilot, you can use up space in a jiffy.

Upgrading the PalmPilot Desktop Program

You can upgrade the Palm Desktop for Windows for free by downloading the latest version from the PalmPilot Web site at www.palmpilot.3com.com. At this writing, the Palm Desktop 3.0 is the latest version, so if that's what you have, you don't have any reason to upgrade.

To see which version of the Palm Desktop you're currently using, open your desktop program and choose Help⇨About. If you're using version 3.0, you'll see the screen shown in Figure 14-3. If you're using a previous version of the desktop program and you're using Windows 95, 98, or NT, you'd be better off upgrading to version 3.0. Remember that you can use any version of the desktop program with any PalmPilot model.

Figure 14-3: You can upgrade the Palm Desktop for free, so you might as well get the latest version.

Macintosh users have been virtually ignored by the Palm people — at least until very recently. Early in 1998, they released the MacPac, which includes the Pilot Desktop 1.0, which does essentially the same things that Palm Desktop does, but it's not very pretty, especially the HotSync process.

While the Palm Desktop for Windows steadily improved, the only update Mac users had was the much-needed Conduit Manager Update 1.01, which cleaned up the HotSync process quite a bit, though it's still not as easy as the single-button Windows method (see Chapter 11 for more on HotSyncing to both platforms).

However, Macofiles have reason for hope: Palm recently purchased Claris Organizer from Apple and plans to use that as its Mac desktop program, replacing the functional, albeit sad Pilot Desktop. Claris Organizer (renamed Palm Desktop for the Macintosh) is a feature-rich personal information manager that may make Windows users envious for a change. The program wasn't available for review at the time of this writing, so we'll have to see if it fixes the unwieldy HotSync process. But keep your eyes on the PalmPilot Web site at `www.palmpilot.3com.com` for more information.

For more on installing, performing a HotSync to, and operating the desktop programs for both Windows and Macintosh, see Chapters 11 and 12.

Chapter 15
PalmPilot Software by Profession

In This Chapter

▶ Finding the right software for your job

*N*early anyone who can get out of bed in the morning can find some use for a PalmPilot. As long as you need to keep track of people, tasks, or ideas, you can take advantage of PalmPilot software. In this chapter, I list specific professions that can benefit from specially designed PalmPilot software. I know some professionals, however, who rely on their PalmPilots without any extra software; a rabbi in New Jersey, actors in Hollywood, and farmers in Mississippi all get something special from the little computers in their pockets. I apologize if I leave out your profession, but if I do, you can search for PalmPilot software by checking the list of Web sites and other resources in Appendix A at the back of this book. Several products mentioned here require you to install a product called Jfile first. For more about Jfile, see the manufacturer's Web site at www.land-j.com. The program costs $19.95 to register. You can also use a competing database called MobileDB from Mobile Generation Software at www.mobilegeneration.com.

Some of the software listed in this chapter is free. Some titles are offered as *shareware,* which means that the people who created the program rely on your honor to send in a donation in exchange for the product. Some programs are demos, which work for free for a limited time, and then you have to buy a copy. Quite a few of these programs are real, live, cash-on-the-barrelhead commercial software. I list prices and terms wherever possible, but you may want to check with the manufacturer to confirm the price and find out how to use the program.

Architect/Building Professional

Putting up a building means putting up with zillions of details. **Punch List** (www.punchlist.com) is a program that helps you track the details of large projects and make sure that everything is done on time and in order. Designed for professionals in the construction industry, Punch List synchronizes with your desktop PC and enables you to maintain lists of tasks that need to be done, along with the names of the people who are supposed to do them. By using Punch List on your PalmPilot, you collect information at the building site; then when you HotSync to your desktop, the desktop portion of Punch List automatically sends faxes to your subcontractors with task lists and notes about uncompleted tasks. Punch List is commercial software from Strata Systems that costs $179 for each user. You can reach the company by phone at 888-336-3652.

Athletic Coach

When Vince Lombardi said, "Winning isn't everything, it's the only thing," nobody dared to say "That's meaningless, Coach!" Would you? If you're a coach who wants to give your team meaningful information, get a copy of the **Athlete's Calculator** from Steven's Creek Software (www.stevenscreek.com). It's free for one-time use, but you need to pay $14.95 for the registered version. This program enables you to rattle off statistics about time, distance, and pace, and also perform calculations on the spot. Now you can demand 110 percent from your athletes and scream when you only get 109 percent.

Bartender

Every purveyor of potent potables needs a collection of recipes for popular concoctions. **Drinks,** shown in Figure 15-1, is a collection of 145 recipes for drinks, ranging from an Alabama Slammer to a Zombie. Because Drinks is a Jfile database, you need to install the Jfile program before taking advantage of your newfound repertoire. If you want to customize the collection, you can add recipes for beverages of your own invention. You can download Drinks from www.palmcentral.com and use it for free.

Couch Potato

I won't mention any names, but many people need help in the diet and exercise departments. **DietLog** from SoftCare Clinical Informatics (www.dietlog.com) is the most popular PalmPilot program for munch-management. Research shows that nothing shocks you into good behavior faster than recalling just how badly you've eaten in the recent past. DietLog helps you track your food intake and set suitable diet goals for your age, sex, height, and weight. You can download a free trial copy of DietLog, which runs for 15 days. If you haven't given up on your diet by then, you can order the full-featured version for $59; just call 800-676-7793. I plan to start using DietLog . . . tomorrow.

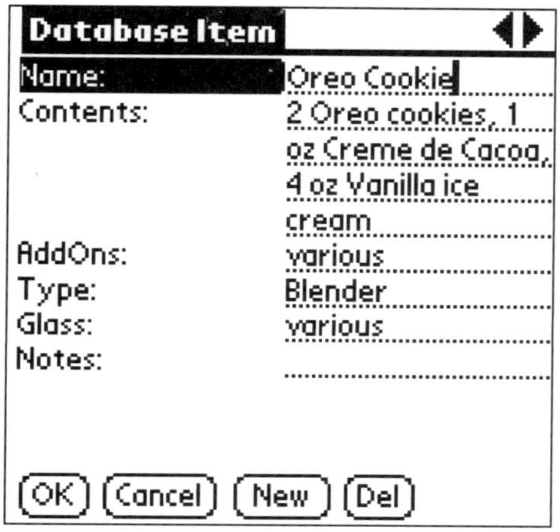

Figure 15-1: When your customers want more than a shot and a beer, look up something more interesting in the Drinks list.

Electrical Engineer

EE Toolkit can help electrical engineers perform many of the routine calculations involved in building electronic projects. It can calculate the resistance of resistors, the capacity of capacitors, and perform many other useful electronic tasks. You can even draw pictures on a built-in doodle pad. Hey! Even I can handle that! You can download a free, 14-day trial version from the designers' Web site at www.mindspring.com/~jgrand/eetoolkit.htm. If you haven't electrocuted yourself after two weeks, contact Pilot Gear HQ at www.pilotgear.com to buy the $20 high-powered version.

Help Desk Technician

Remedy Help Desk from Remedy Corp. is part of an elaborate system that you use to track and manage computer problems in a large organization. If you've ever worked as a computer-help-desk person, you know how much trivial information you need to organize and keep current. You also need to know how many times technicians visit a certain computer and how many things are done to that machine. Remedy Help Desk enables field technicians to enter information about problems and solutions while in the field, and then update the big company database by performing a simple HotSync. For more about Remedy Help Desk, see www.remedy.com.

Lawyer

Perry Mason may have spent all his time orating in courtrooms, but real lawyers have to spend time keeping track of documents and tracking their billable hours. **Amicus Attorney** is part of a Practice Management system that's designed to help lawyers run their businesses and track their billings accurately on a desktop computer or office network. The program includes a link to your PalmPilot so that you can document billable activities as you perform them. Unless you're the kind of lawyer who works for free, Amicus Attorney can help you stay on top of your business. Contact Gavel & Gown Software at www.amicus.ca.

Manager

PalmProject is a simple program that enables you to keep track of tasks that occur in sequence, as shown in Figure 15-2. If you're making a movie, for example, you need to write a script, then hire a director, then cast actors, then shoot the film, and so on. PalmProject enables you to enter up to 99 tasks, each of which can be linked to an earlier task. You can display lists of required resources and milestones and choose either a five-day workweek or a seven-day workweek. If you're a Microsoft Project user, you can also export projects from PalmProject and run them in Microsoft Project, which enables you to create elaborate flowcharts and reports. You can visit www.pda-ware.com for a free trial version of PalmProject, or buy the full-featured version for $19.95 at www.pilotgear.com.

Minister

Yes, your PalmPilot even has room for the Good Book. You can download a free copy of the King James version from PalmCentral (www.palmcentral.com) — 1.2MB of pure inspiration. If you don't have a Palm III, you probably don't have room for 1.2MB of inspiration, so you need to check out the King James version that's split up into five sections; even a little bit of inspiration goes a long way. You can also find devotional text from a variety of religions at the PalmCentral Web site and around the PalmPilot Web ring.

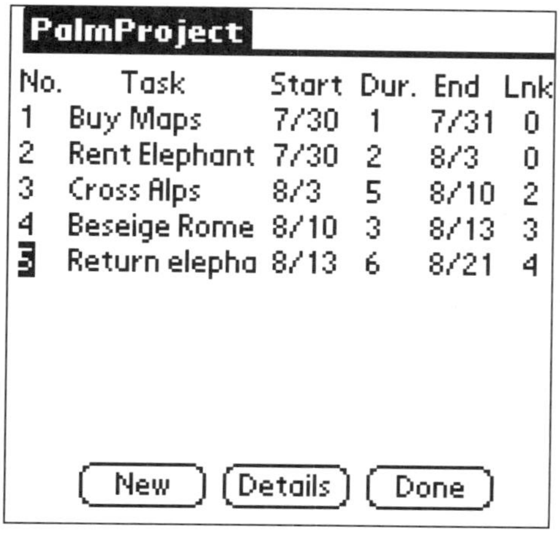

Figure 15-2: Plan before you Act! Good planning can give you a competitive edge.

```
PalmProject
No.  Task          Start  Dur.  End   Lnk
 1   Buy Maps      7/30   1     7/31  0
 2   Rent Elephant 7/30   2     8/3   0
 3   Cross Alps    8/3    5     8/10  2
 4   Beseige Rome  8/10   3     8/13  3
 5   Return elepha 8/13   6     8/21  4

   ( New )  ( Details )  ( Done )
```

Molecular Biologist

OligoCalc is a tool for molecular biologists. According to Ray's PalmCentral archive, it's a "calculator for molecular biologists who have to deal with oligonucleotide synthesis and purification. You will get the most common physical characteristics of oligonucleotides — extinction coefficient, molecular weight, etc." Yeah, well, whatever that is, OligoCalc does it for free. Download a copy at www.palmcentral.com.

Musician

You may be used to the on-screen keyboard that lets you enter text, but **PocketSynth** gives you an on-screen piano keyboard, shown in Figure 15-3, for composing melodies and then playing them back. You can enter one-part tunes as simple as "Yankee Doodle" or as complex as Beethoven's "Fifth Symphony" by tapping a tiny piano keyboard. If you value your sanity, stick with simple tunes like "Yankee Doodle" because that itty-bitty keyboard will drive you nuts. PocketSynth includes a variable metronome that enables you to play your songs at whatever speed you like. Of course, everything that you play on PocketSynth sounds like the squeaky little tones that always come out of your PalmPilot, but if you've ever wanted to hear your PalmPilot whistling "Dixie," PocketSynth can make it happen. Developer Eric Cheng offers PocketSynth on his Web site at www.echeng.com/Pilot/index.html. Suggested fee is $10.

Figure 15-3: Compose your first sonata on your PalmPilot by using PocketSynth.

New York City Taxi Driver

Unlike nice, orderly cities, New York City's system of street addresses is totally nonsensical. I could give you examples, but why bother when you can make sense of it all with **NY CrossTown 1.5** from True North, Inc. (northisup.com). For only $12, you can instantly come up with the nearest cross street from any avenue address or find the nearest avenue to any street address. If you don't need NY CrossTown because you never visit the Big Apple (or you have a chauffeur), count your blessings.

Parent

Are your kids bugging you to buy a new puppy? Or are they just bugging you? Distract the little darlings with a **DigiPet**. DigiPet, shown in Figure 15-4, is the PalmPilot version of those popular electronic pet keychains. Your little electronic beast has many of the charming qualities of a real pet, including the need to eat, get sick, demand your attention at all hours, and have "accidents." DigiPet is available in English and Japanese versions. The program was developed by Shuji Fukumoto and is available at www.wakuwaku.ne.jp/shuji or from www.palmcentral.com. And best of all, it's free.

Figure 15-4: DigiPet can keep you busy for hours, whether you like it or not. Remember, parents, it's only a game. This DigiPet is friendly, but not the brightest beast.

Physician

More PalmPilot medical programs are available than you can shake a scalpel at. Several companies offer programs that enable doctors to keep track of patient data and update patients' records from the bedside. **Mobile Medical Data** at www.medcomsys.com is one of the better-known products for keeping patient records. Another product called Auto Doc (www.autodoc.com) tracks patient records, and most amazing of all, claims to understand doctors' handwriting 100 percent of the time. That's something I've got to see.

Pilot

The fact that PalmPilots are so popular with airplane pilots is no surprise. **AirCalc** is one of many PalmPilot applications designed to perform the kinds of calculations that airplane pilots need. You can calculate such things as True Altitude (TALT), True Airspeed (TAS), and Mach Number (MN), as shown in Figure 15-5. Unfortunately, AirCalc can't handle frequent flyer miles. Another favorite program is **AvCheck,** a simple checklist program that reminds you to complete every step of your preflight preparations so that you don't skip anything essential, such as fuel or parachutes. If you're the type who makes checklists before you go on vacation, you can use AvCheck for that purpose, too, and create your own checklists on your desktop computer by using the AvCheck converter. You also may want to have your little checklist obsession checked out by a shrink. The program is available from the developer's Web site at www.infoequipt.com. The Personal version costs $29.95, and the Professional version (for flight schools and fleet operators) runs $59.99.

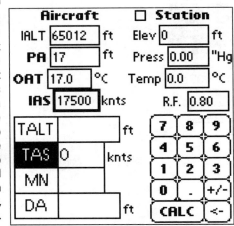

Figure 15-5: AirCalc figures out the more important calculations that you need while flying. Try to make the plane go up quickly and down slowly, please.

Psychic

Are you a real psychic? If you're really a psychic, you know who you are. Naturally, all psychics who are worth their crystal balls need to play a little Tarot to blow off steam between seances; those cosmic vibrations can get pretty intense. The **Tarot Assistant,** available from Seapoint Software (www.seapoint.net), deals and interprets pentacles, swords, and cups in a flash, and keeps unsavory psychics from dealing wizards from the bottom of the deck. The program is a text-only offering, no pictures, sorry. Because you're psychic, you know that you can also find the program at the PalmCentral Web site at www.palmcentral.com. But if you were really a psychic, you wouldn't need to read this because you'd already know.

Salesperson

Sales people are people people, so the standard PalmPilot programs, especially the Address Book, are a must for anyone in sales. But the standard PalmPilot applications lack the powerful contact management and sales automation features that you find in desktop programs like Goldmine and Act! Fortunately, you can set up both of those programs to send their most important information to your PalmPilot. Most of the best sales automation programs include a PalmPilot link, so all you need to do is ask the manufacturer how to use your sales program with a PalmPilot.

Stock Broker/Investor

If you have megabucks tied up in the stock market, you want up-to-the-minute news about what's happening on Wall Street. Years ago, you needed an expensive stock ticker to get the latest from the exchanges, but now you can use a PalmPilot equipped with **Reuters Market Clip** and a Novatel Wireless Modem to give you the very latest stock info, no matter where you are. Trade stocks from roadside, poolside, or fireside. Becoming a PalmPilot investment mogul isn't all that expensive; the whole package, including the wireless modem and the PalmPilot, runs only $699 plus $115 per month for wireless service. That's small change compared to your enormous capital gains, right? If you're a professional broker or dealer, you have to pay additional exchange fees as well. Contact Reuters at www.marketclip.reuters.com or call 888-9STOCKS.

Teacher

Who says memorization is boring and old-fashioned? Okay, maybe it's old-fashioned, but you can make memorization fun by using one of the flashcard programs available for your PalmPilot. One of the most versatile programs, **Flash!**, imports lists of text from your Memo Pad and converts them into a system that you can use to drill students on collections of facts. The program even has a quiz mode that automatically generates a multiple-choice test and keeps track of the number of right and wrong answers you choose, as shown in Figure 15-6. You can download a free demo of Flash! from homunculus.dragonfire.net/flash.html. Jaime Quinn, the author of Flash!, asks you to send him a voluntary donation of $14.95 or have a meal in his favorite restaurant in Mexico. Another popular memorization program is called **JTutor**, from Land J Technologies, the same company that offers Jfile. The company's Web site is located at www.land-j.com.

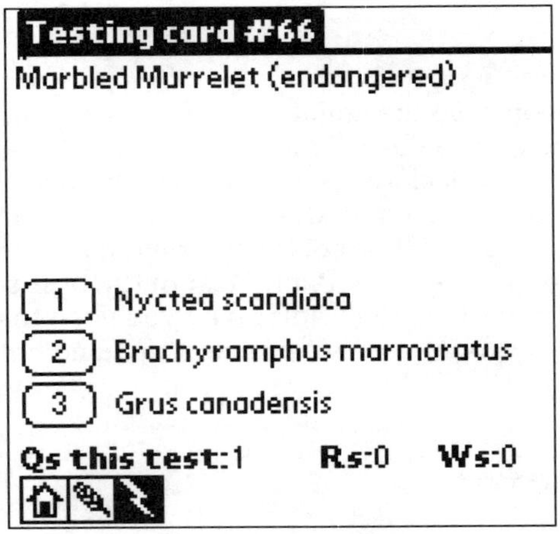

Figure 15-6: Get ready to win that big TV game show by drilling trivia with Flash! "I'll take birds for $100, Alex."

```
Testing card #66
Marbled Murrelet (endangered)

  1   Nyctea scandiaca
  2   Brachyramphus marmoratus
  3   Grus canadensis

Qs this test:1    Rs:0    Ws:0
```

Telemarketer

If you make a lot of phone calls, trying to figure out where you're calling by looking at an unfamiliar area code can be tough. The free Area Codes database at PalmCentral (www.palmcentral.com) can help you figure out where you're calling when your fingers do the walking. The program can't help telemarketers know when to call people in order to catch them during dinner or while they're in the shower, but most telephone sales people already have that trick down to a science. You need to install Jfile, the PalmPilot database program, before using the Area Code list.

Travel Agent

You didn't become a travel agent because you like to sit at home; you like to go places, the farther the better. When you travel to a foreign country, you may need to ask for help to find a hotel room, restaurant, or restroom. **Small Talk** is an electronic phrasebook that helps you get what you need when you don't speak another country's language. I even know of some travel agents who lend (or give) their clients a PalmPilot equipped with the program to keep their customers happy. See Chapter 18 for more about Small Talk, or point your web browser to www.conceptkitchen.com. The program costs $49.95 for two languages or $79.95 for all five languages. Currently available languages include English, French, Spanish, German, and Italian.

Writer

The PalmPilot is a gift for this writer; I always get my best ideas when I'm farthest from a computer. The most useful type of writer's tool is the outliner, a program that automatically organizes a series of thoughts into a numbered list. One of the most popular PalmPilot outliners is called **BrainForest Mobile Edition** and costs $30 to register. BrainForest enables you to quickly pull together an outline of your thoughts lickety split, as shown in Figure 15-7, and arrange them in several different outlines. After you empty your thoughts into the outliner, you can rearrange the outline by dragging and dropping any item to the location(s) where you want it. BrainForest is only one popular outliner; another popular outliner is **Thought Mill,** which is $17.95 from Hands High software. Both products are available at www.palmcentral.com.

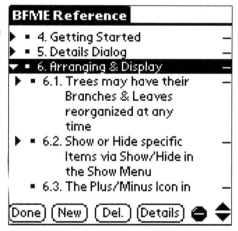

Figure 15-7: Put your thoughts into logical order with a PalmPilot outliner like BrainForest. Linear thinking! What a concept!

Part V
The Part of Tens

In this part . . .

I just spent a whole book telling you what your PalmPilot can do; now, I tell you the few things your PalmPilot can't do — believe me, it's a short list. In this part, I also tell you about some cool stuff — both hardware and software — that you can add to your PalmPilot to make it even more productive.

Chapter 16
Ten Things You Can't Do with a PalmPilot... Yet

In This Chapter
▶ Running on AC power . . . not
▶ Recharging batteries in the cradle . . . nope
▶ Viewing two programs at the same time . . . I wish
▶ Linking items between programs . . . a pipe dream
▶ Searching and replacing text . . . wouldn't it be nice?
▶ Recording voice notes . . . not that I would use this anyway
▶ Creating recurring To Do items . . . please, please, please

You can make your PalmPilot do a surprising number of tasks for you, considering how little the bugger is. But you may expect to be able to do certain things that just aren't on the menu yet. Here, I tell you about ten things that you can't do with a PalmPilot . . . yet. You can be sure that thousands of programmers are toiling away in basements and garages to come up with products that expand the PalmPilot's repertoire, so don't be surprised if many of these gaps are filled in fairly quickly.

Run on AC Power

A PalmPilot can get plenty of use out of a pair of AAA batteries, so you probably wouldn't want to plug the thing into a wall socket . . . unless the batteries die. Murphy's Law guarantees that your batteries will die just when you're farthest from the convenience store. Your best bet: Keep a pair of spare batteries around all the time. Some PalmPilot carrying cases even have room for an extra set of batteries, so don't be caught without juice. If your batteries run down so far that your PalmPilot won't start, leave the old batteries in until you have a new set. A PalmPilot holds its data when the batteries are too low to turn the PalmPilot on, but if you take those batteries out for more than 30 seconds, your data will be lost.

Recharge Batteries in the Cradle

Leaving your PalmPilot in the cradle does NOT recharge the batteries. As a matter of fact, batteries drain faster when the PalmPilot is in its cradle than when you're just carrying it around. Rumor has it that the people who make the PalmPilot will fix this problem in the future and will include a rechargeable battery, but for the moment, if you own a Palm III or an earlier model, only put the PalmPilot in its cradle when you're actually performing a HotSync.

View Two Programs at the Same Time

PalmPilot programs have windows and buttons that remind you a little bit of common Windows or Macintosh programs. However, you can look at two different programs at the same time on a Mac or Windows PC; you can't do anything like that with a PalmPilot. I don't know how you'd make sense of what you'd see on that tiny screen if you tried to display two programs at once, but I wouldn't mind sometimes seeing my appointments and To Do's at the same time. Right now, it's one at a time, please.

Link Items between Programs

Not only are you limited to seeing one program at a time, but you can't link items in one PalmPilot program to items in another PalmPilot program. I would find it very handy if I could link an appointment in my Date Book with a person in my Address Book. That way, when the reminder for the appointment pops up on my PalmPilot, I could hop right over to the person's address record to jog my memory about who the person is and why we're meeting.

Search and Replace Text

The Memo Pad is just a convenient place to enter and save text; it's not a word processor. You can use the PalmPilot Find program to look up items that contain a certain word, but can't do some of the more clever word-processing tricks, like search and replace, that you can with popular word processors like Microsoft Word.

Record Voice Notes

Some competing hand-held computers include a little microphone that enables you to dictate short notes to yourself by simply talking. Later on, you can listen to what you recorded and write down what you said. Personally, I don't want a feature like that, not when I can scribble a quick memo to myself in Graffiti. But the Windows CE devices offer it anyway. Voice recording is a cute feature, I guess, but voice recordings chew up lots of memory, and they always make you sound like you're underwater. Besides, those Windows CE machines still aren't PalmPilots. 'Nuff said.

Create an Appointment That Spans Two or More Dates

Say you work the graveyard shift in an office, factory, or heaven knows, even a graveyard (I'm not ready to write *PalmPilot For Vampires* just yet). If you plan to hold a meeting that starts at 11:30 p.m. and ends at 1:00 a.m., you're out of luck. PalmPilot appointments can happen only during the span of a single day. You'd have to break up your meeting when the clock strikes midnight and start again. And try to finish your meeting before sunrise when the werewolves all go home.

Use Superscripts and Subscripts

If you're the mad-professor type who frequently shouts "Eureka!" and then jots down something like $E=mc^2$, you won't be able to enter the superscript number *2* for your formula just yet. You can enter all sorts of foreign accents and special characters, but you can't enter superscript and subscript. Most people don't create footnotes or mathematical formulas on a PalmPilot all that often, but those who do have to wait for a future version of PalmPilot. Then you can really shout "Eureka!"

Create Recurring To Do Items

You can't create recurring To Do items with your PalmPilot or the Palm Desktop program, but you can synchronize your PalmPilot with another desktop program that lets you create *recurring tasks,* which are To Do items that repeat at regular intervals. The task of filing your quarterly tax payment is an example of a recurring task. If you enter that kind of task in your PalmPilot, you can't just enter the task once and then tell your PalmPilot to make it recurring. Your only choice is to enter the task in January, April, July, and October. Fortunately, if you enter the task in a different desktop program that allows recurring tasks, the PalmPilot automatically repeats what it sees on the desktop.

Assign Multiple Categories to One Item

If you have items that could fit into more than one category, you'll have to pick just one. For example, if you have a Key Customer category and a Business category, you might want a name to appear in both categories. Sorry, no can do.

Categorizing Dates

Do you want to categorize your appointments just like you categorize the Tasks in your To Do List? Sorry! No can do! Some desktop organizers, such as Microsoft Outlook, can do the job for you, but the category information doesn't show up on the PalmPilot. PalmPilot developers plan to add this feature in the future.

Other Things a PalmPilot Can't Do

There are quite a few things I wish a PalmPilot could help me do, but sadly, I'm on my own. Here are a few problems that nobody even pretends a PalmPilot can solve, although I believe I've heard of other products that are supposed to fit the bill:

- Wash away the gray in just five minutes
- Get the red out
- Help you lose weight while eating all you want
- Give dandruff the brush off
- Save 50 percent on all your long-distance calls
- Balance your energy
- Discover your Inner Warrior (or your Inner Geek)
- Seize the day
- Purify your blood
- Open the secrets of your Inner Mind

Chapter 17
Ten Nifty PalmPilot Accessories

In This Chapter
- WriteRight
- Brain Wash
- Karma Cloth
- Extra styluses
- Card Scanner
- UniMount
- SuperPilot Memory Board
- Tripmate GPS receiver
- Wireless Minstrel modem
- Cases

As citizens of a consumer-based society, we all have an important responsibility: TO BUY STUFF! Thank heavens you bought this book. But don't stop there; buy another copy, and then check out the list below to see which PalmPilot gewgaws you simply can't live without. Remember, your economy depends on you!

WriteRight

Because it has virtually no moving parts, your PalmPilot has almost nothing that can wear out except the screen itself. After you've scribbled a few millions words of Graffiti, the plastic screen can take quite a beating. You can add an extra layer of plastic to your PalmPilot screen to reduce wear and tear. Some people stick plain old transparent adhesive tape to the Graffiti area — a perfectly adequate solution, but the tape can be tricky to remove. I prefer WriteRight Screen Enhancements overlays — little sticky pieces of plastic cut to fit your PalmPilot screen perfectly. The people at

Concept Kitchen, the manufacturer of WriteRight, recommend changing the adhesive-backed overlay once a month. In addition to reducing wear, WriteRights cut down glare. Less glare means that your screen is easier to read, but you can't check your look in your PalmPilot screen anymore to make sure you don't have anything stuck in your teeth. Bummer!

Brain Wash

Also from Concept Kitchen, Brain Wash is a screen-cleaning system for getting the grime off your PalmPilot screen without using any nasty abrasives or chemicals that could scratch or cloud your screen. Brain Wash actually consists of two items: a moist towelette and dry towelette. First, wash off your screen with the moist towlette, and then follow up with the dry towelette. Of course, you could just dab some window cleaner on a paper towel, but what fun would that be? Use Brain Wash to make your screen so bright that you can see yourself, and then apply a WriteRight to cut out that nasty reflection.

Karma Cloth

Now and then a nice buffing can remove that annoying dust and grime from your PalmPilot screen. Karma Cloth, another product cooked up by Concept Kitchen, is perfect for giving your screen a quick touchup; it can even remove minor scratches. The Karma Cloth contains some protective substances that make your PalmPilot screen clearer and smoother, and therefore easier to use. And, of course, a Karma Cloth can bring you good luck if you rub your screen just right.

Extra Styluses

You can find scads of new and improved styluses (or is that styli?) for your PalmPilot, many of them made by the same folks who make fancy and expensive writing pens. If you want a stylus that displays your taste, class, and distinction, check out the better office supply stores. If you want a plain old stylus that fits in the little stylus well on your PalmPilot, you can get a three-pack of plastic styluses for about five bucks. Check with the merchant who sold you your PalmPilot. If you own a Palm III, you can also get very chic colored lids and styluses to match your wardrobe. Ooh la la!

Card Scanner

Corex Technologies makes two products for entering business card data into your PalmPilot: software for scanning business cards from any scanner (called CardScan 3.0) and a special scanner that's perfectly sized for business card scanning (called CardScan Plus 300). If you travel to attend trade shows or conferences regularly and need to get business card info entered into your PalmPilot and desktop contact manager in a hurry, the Corex card scanner can help you. The scanner doesn't attach directly to your PalmPilot; you attach the scanner to the desktop or laptop computer that you use as the host for your PalmPilot. Scan your collection of business cards into the host computer first. When all the cards are entered into the host computer, put your PalmPilot in its cradle and do a HotSync.

UniMount

For those who frequently use a PalmPilot in the car, Revolv Design Company makes a special device called the UniMount to keep your PalmPilot easy to see and use on the road. Now, I don't recommend using your PalmPilot while driving, but when you're stopped, you might want to consult your PalmPilot for the address of the person you're going to see, or their phone number if you plan to call from your car phone. And speaking of telephones, you can also attach your cell phone to the UniMount right next to your PalmPilot to make a little mobile office for yourself. All you need now is a water cooler.

SuperPilot Memory Board

You can upgrade any PalmPilot to hold as much as 8MB of data by using the SuperPilot Memory Board from the Technology Resource Group. That's enough memory to store the names and addresses of over 80,000 of your closest friends. Of course, the thing costs $300, more than you may have paid for your PalmPilot in the first place, but sometimes you just can't get along without lots of memory.

DeLorme TripMate GPS Receiver

Loading a map onto your PalmPilot is great, but having your PalmPilot show you your current location on the map is even cooler. For that you need a receiver that can pinpoint your location by using signals from navigational satellites called the Global Positioning System, or GPS. The Tripmate GPS receiver is a tad smaller than the PalmPilot and has its own battery power. When you connect the Tripmate GPS receiver to a PalmPilot running DeLorme Street Atlas USA (included with the receiver), your PalmPilot can show you exactly where you're located and how to reach your destination. You can even keep track of your speed, time, heading, and elevation. About the only thing it can't tell you is how far you are from the next restroom. I think that requires a different type of satellite.

Minstrel Wireless Modem

Normally, you only need one wire to do everything you need to do with a PalmPilot: the wire from your PalmPilot cradle to your desktop computer. With the Minstrel wireless modem (from Novatel Wireless), you can cut that down to no wires at all, and what a difference it makes! Sit by the pool and read your e-mail, surf the Web while sitting on the beach, check your stock portfolio while waiting for the movie to start — there's no end to what you can do. Of course, you have to pop another $399, plus the cost of using the special type of wireless service that the Minstrel modem uses (called CDPD). You can't count on being able to use the Minstrel wireless modem everywhere, because the CDPD network doesn't cover the entire Earth or even the whole United States, but if you're in an area that's covered by CDPD, you can go completely cordless. When you do, send me an e-mail; I'll be by the pool.

Cases

It seems that everyone — from the very classy Coach leather works to inmates at the Funny Farm — is turning out wallets that can store and protect your PalmPilot. Personally, I use something called the Co-Pilot from E&B Cases, because it has room for cash and a few cards, but it's still small enough to keep in my front pocket. You can check out the E&B people at www.ebcases.com. Another popular case manufacturer is RhinoSkin, at www.rhinoskin.com. RhinoSkin's best-known product is a titanium PalmPilot case that looks like it was torn off a tank and could probably survive being shot from a cannon. I prefer a softer, gentler PalmPilot case.

Chapter 18
Ten Ultracool Commercial Software Programs for the PalmPilot

In This Chapter
- T9
- QuickSheet
- FlashBuilderIII
- Forms programs
- Actioneer
- Delorme Street Atlas
- CardScan
- Small Talk
- HandFax
- Syncronization programs

Behind the PalmPilot's friendly face is a real computer waiting to take on the work that you want to do. All you need to add is the right software.

Many of the better PalmPilot programs aren't available as shareware; you have to buy the program up-front. In this chapter, I give you a sampling of the commercial, pay-before-you-play programs that I consider worth paying for. You can find many more than this; software companies release new programs every day, but I put these programs at the top of the class.

I include a selection of the more popular shareware programs on the CD that comes with this book. You can check out Appendix C for a list of programs on the CD.

T9

Some folks take to using Graffiti the way a cowboy takes to riding a horse. Others would rather not horse around with Graffiti at all. That's why a product called T9 (from Tegic Communications) was invented — to offer a familiar telephone-style keypad for entering text (see Figure 18-1), just like how you enter those famous alphabetic phone numbers, such as 1-800-FLOWERS. The people who invented T9 also sell the program to cellular telephone manufacturers so that people can send e-mail from their cell phones more easily. (Some cell-phone makers are also buying the PalmPilot operating system. Don't be surprised if you see a PalmPilot Phone any day now.) I find Graffiti faster on the whole, because I've had a lot of practice, but if you want to start entering text into your PalmPilot in a jiffy, you can pick up using the T9 keyboard in a flash.

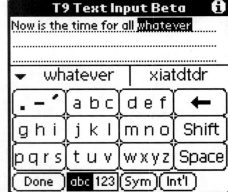

Figure 18-1: With T9, you can let your fingers do the talking.

QuickSheet

Spreadsheets were the first really popular programs for desktop personal computers back in the darkest days of DOS. QuickSheet (from Cutting Edge Software) is the first really useable spreadsheet for the PalmPilot. You can get a shareware spreadsheet called TinySheet that only costs you a few bucks, but if you do any serious work with spreadsheets and you want to do any of that work on your PalmPilot, it's worth spending $49.95 for QuickSheet instead. You can synchronize QuickSheet to an Excel 5.0 or greater spreadsheet on your desktop computer to take advantage of the collection of work you've amassed over the years. You won't find the kind of power in QuickSheet that you do in major desktop programs like Excel. There aren't nearly as many automated functions in QuickSheet, and there's no autofill or drag-and-drop copying, but if you ever need to carry around and update a tiny version of your most important spreadsheet, QuickSheet gives you a way to do it for only $49.95.

FlashBuilderIII

Gloria Vanderbuilt didn't say, "You can never be too thin or too rich or have too much memory on your PalmPilot," but she could have. As I write this, you can only buy PalmPilots with up to 2MB of memory for storing addresses, appointments, programs, or whatever you store. That's a reasonable amount of memory at first, but you can fill the thing up without much effort, especially with the help of your desktop computer or a good e-mail program.

The engineers at TRG specialize in building things that help expand the capacity of the PalmPilot. FlashBuilderIII ($49.95) takes advantage of the fact that your Palm III has some "hidden" (or flash) memory, where the PalmPilot saves its most important programs like the standard applications and the operating system. If you buy FlashBuilderIII, you can store some of the programs you've added to your Palm III in flash memory, which is like adding 40 percent to your available memory. If you need a little extra memory and only want to spend a little extra money, FlashbuilderIII is just the ticket. FlashBuilderIII works only with Palm III. If you upgrade an earlier PalmPilot with a Palm III upgrade card, either from 3Com or from TRG, you can use FlashBuilderIII just as if you had a real Palm III.

Forms Programs

The more you do with your PalmPilot, the more you want to do. If, sooner or later, the standard PalmPilot applications don't do it for you anymore, you may have to resort to a do-it-yourself solution. If you're not ready to turn into a programmer (I'm certainly not), you can use other programs to create simple forms for entering and managing data on your PalmPilot. You actually need to create your forms on a PC running Windows 95 or later, but you can install the forms you create onto the PalmPilot.

Pendragon Forms (from Pendragon Software) is the simplest and least expensive of the forms programs available. You can choose from a limited assortment of predesigned forms (for an example, see Figure 18-2) and link those forms to a file on your PC or to a Microsoft Access database. If you want to make your fortune writing slick programs that you can sell to other PalmPilot users, Pendragon Forms probably isn't for you. But if you just need a quick way to catalog your collection of rare tulip bulbs, Pendragon Forms can get you there easily.

The other important forms program is called Satellite Forms 2.0 Developer Addition from SoftMagic Corp. A step up from the price and performance ladder of Pendragon Forms, Satellite Forms enables you to build your own forms from scratch and write real programs (see Figure 18-3) that you can install as separate programs that show up as icons in your PalmPilot's applications list. Don't expect to master Satellite Forms in a single sitting; the program comes with two thick manuals to tell you how to create applications. Still, if you have ambitious ideas about creating programs for the PalmPilot, but you're not ambitious enough to actually learn programming, Satellite Forms is for you.

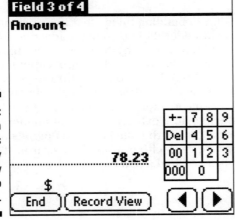

Figure 18-2: Pendragon Forms helps you easily create new ways to enter data.

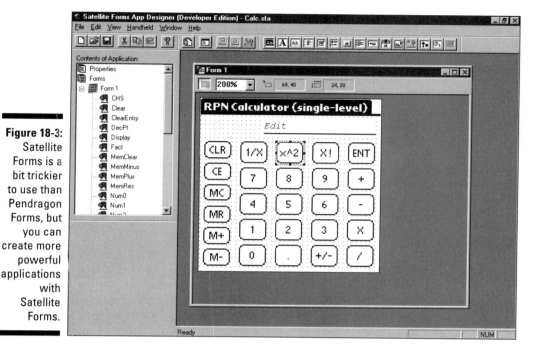

Figure 18-3: Satellite Forms is a bit trickier to use than Pendragon Forms, but you can create more powerful applications with Satellite Forms.

Actioneer for the Palm Computing Environment

Wouldn't it be nice if you could just use plain English to enter notes about your upcoming tasks and appointments and have your PalmPilot sort out which PalmPilot application gets the entry? Actioneer does exactly that for you. Just start up Actioneer and then enter plain text like "Meet Bob Monday 9 am" (see Figure 18-4). Actioneer automatically creates an event called "Meet Bob Monday 9 am" in your calendar. You can define keywords to help Actioneer automatically send items containing certain words to the application or category you desire. You still need to know how to use the standard PalmPilot applications to see the things you've entered, but at least you can rely on plain English when you're adding information. If you're an Outlook user, you can get a desktop version of Actioneer that performs the same magic on the information you enter into Outlook.

Figure 18-4: Actioneer translates your plain English entries and creates items in the proper PalmPilot program.

Delorme Street Atlas

Having someone's street address on your PalmPilot is even more useful when you can find the street on a map. The Delorme Street Atlas software links up to your PalmPilot and gives you a copy of a street map and driving directions right on your PalmPilot, along with your list of names and addresses. The product actually runs on your desktop computer, which means that you can print the maps and include parts of the map in other documents. If you want to add the DeLorme TripMate GPS Receiver that I mention in Chapter 17, your PalmPilot can show you your current location on a map via a satellite signal. How cool is that?

CardScan

Face the facts: Some people still don't own a Palm III. That means that when you go to conferences or trade shows, most people give you conventional business cards instead of beaming their cards to your PalmPilot. Until that unfortunate problem is fixed, you need a quick way to enter business cards in your PalmPilot. The CardScan software (from Corex Technologies Corp.), which you can buy for $49 or get for free along with a CardScan Plus 300 business card scanner, reads the text on all those business cards and creates contact records in your favorite personal information manager.

Unfortunately, there's no way to connect the scanner directly to the PalmPilot and cut out the middleman; however, you can use the Corex software with any scanner you want.

Small Talk

Small Talk (from Concept Kitchen) is an interactive electronic language translator for people who travel frequently. I'd call Small Talk a phrase book rather than a translator, because it only translates a handful of sentences that cover the most common situations a traveler might encounter, such as checking into a hotel, finding transportation, ordering a meal, and so on (see Figure 18-5). You can't use Small Talk to translate today's Parisian newspapers, but you can use it to help order *escargots*.

Figure 18-5: Small Talk makes your PalmPilot serve as an electronic phrase book.

HandFax

If you have the PalmPilot Modem, you can turn your PalmPilot into a pocket-sized fax machine with HandFax from Smartcode Software (www.smartcodesoft.com). Fax any item from your Memo Pad to any standard fax machine and include your own cover page. You don't even have to remember the person's fax number; just look up the number in your Address Book.

I include a demo version of HandFax on the CD that comes with this book. For more on using the PalmPilot Modem, check out Chapter 13.

Synchronization Programs

The folks who invented the PalmPilot were smart enough to make the PalmPilot work with the programs that you already have on your Windows PC. You may already have a PIM (personal information manager) that you're attached to (or stuck with) for good reasons. As the PalmPilot has caught on, more and more companies that make PIMs are offering ways to link those PIMs to the PalmPilot. Other companies are making their fortunes by creating ways to connect your PalmPilot to programs from companies that don't want to support the PalmPilot (yes, Microsoft, how did you know?).

The Palm Desktop program that comes with your PalmPilot talks directly to your PalmPilot every time you hit the HotSync button (for more about HotSyncing, see Chapter 11). Because the PalmPilot was made to talk to the Palm Desktop, you don't need another program to act as a go-between. But if you're already using a different program for your PIM, such as Microsoft Outlook or ACT!, you need a program to translate and move information between your Windows PC and your PalmPilot. Several programs, called *conduits* or *synchronizing tools,* can do the job for Windows users.

Unfortunately, as of this writing, Mac users are pretty much stuck with the Pilot Desktop for all their PIM action. However, hope is on the horizon. The Palm people have made available a conduit developer's kit for their upcoming new version of the desktop program so that the conduit makers can create conduits for the popular (and not-so-popular) Macintosh PIMs. Keep an eye on the 3Com Web site at www.palmpilot.3com.com for more information.

Windows users can choose between three well-known conduit programs. These programs all do a similar job, but each offers a slightly different set of features at a different price. Here they are:

- **PocketMirror for Outlook 97 from Chapura:** This is the least expensive synchronization program; in fact, you get a copy of the program free with the purchase of a Palm III. If you buy your own copy of PocketMirror, it runs $39.95. PocketMirror can only synchronize your PalmPilot with Microsoft Outlook 97/98 and offers relatively few of the more advanced features that competitors offer, but many people don't use the more advanced features, so PocketMirror is a perfectly good choice.

Chapter 18: Ten Ultracool Commercial Software Programs for the PalmPilot 283

- **Desktop To Go from DataViz, Inc.:** This program costs about $49 and synchronizes a PalmPilot to only Microsoft Outlook 97/98 and Schedule+, but it enables you to do a couple of fancy things when you synchronize that you can't do with PocketMirror, such as tell Outlook to send information from your Outlook custom fields to certain fields on your PalmPilot. Because almost nobody uses more than one type of PIM, Desktop To Go does a fine job of synchronizing your PalmPilot. You can also use Desktop To Go to synchronize a limited date range in your Date Book so that you spend less time waiting for your PalmPilot to finish synchronizing. For example, if you have 100 appointments in your schedule, spread out over the next year, your HotSync will take longer than if you only have a few appointments scheduled in the next week. You might want to tell the conduit to synchronize only the appointments for the next week to speed up the HotSync process.

- **IntelliSync from Puma Technology:** IntelliSync is the most powerful and best-known conduit available for the PalmPilot, and it costs the most. At $69.95, IntelliSync enables your PalmPilot to trade information with just about every major personal information manager out there, including Goldmine, Ecco, and Lotus Organizer. If you're an Outlook user, IntelliSync also lets you synchronize your PalmPilot to any Outlook folders you choose, and it also retains the categories that you assign to your items in Outlook when those items turn up on your PalmPilot. IntelliSync is overkill if you use Outlook only in the simplest way, but if you're an Outlook power user or you use organizers other than Outlook, IntelliSync is indispensable.

- For more on Microsoft Outlook, check out *Microsoft Outlook 98 For Dummies,* written by yours truly and published by IDG Books Worldwide, Inc.

- You can also find IntelliSync products for synchronizing handheld computers with Web sites, laptop computers with desktop computers, and heaven knows what else. If they made a product that synchronized your VCR with your popcorn popper, I wouldn't be surprised.

Before you rush out and buy a special program to synchronize your PalmPilot with your PIM, check with the people who make your PIM to see if you can get a free conduit for the program you use. For example, the people who make ACT! offer a special program to link their product with the PalmPilot. In fact, ACT! 4.0 includes a PalmPilot link right on the CD with the program. Ecco is another well-known PIM that includes a PalmPilot link.

Unfortunately, I can't cover how to use your other PIM in this book; this is a book about the PalmPilot, after all. But don't fret; if you work with another PIM and would like to know more about it, try to find a *...For Dummies* book on the subject. Odds are, one exists.

The three most popular PIMs have books devoted to them. I wrote a book on Microsoft Outlook, cleverly entitled *Microsoft Outlook 98 For Dummies,* which, as you might guess, I highly recommend. For ACT! users, Jeffrey J. Mayer wrote a great book just for you called *ACT! 4 For Windows For Dummies.* And Lotus Organizer, which remains popular after years as one of the top PIMs, is covered in *Lotus SmartSuite Millennium Edition For Dummies* by Michael Meadhra and Jan Weingarten. All these books are published by IDG Books Worldwide, Inc.

Appendix A
Internet Resources for the PalmPilot

Time flies quickly in the technology business! Every few weeks a smashing new program for the PalmPilot turns up from some emerging software genius. Every few months, the geniuses at Palm release a whole new PalmPilot. How can you possibly keep up? Your best bet for staying abreast of developments is to turn to the Internet. You can find thousands of sources of PalmPilot information on the Internet; this appendix includes a list of my favorites.

The PalmPilot Web Ring

This is the place to start. If I were to give you a list of all the Web sites devoted to the PalmPilot, the list would number in the hundreds, but it would be out of date by the time you read it. A great place to begin your Internet search for PalmPilot Web sites is the PalmPilot Web Ring, which you can access at the 3Com Web site at www.palmpilot.3com.com. The PalmPilot Web Ring is a chain of hundreds of Web sites that advise PalmPilot users on how to get the most from their hand-held computer. If you explore the Web Ring long enough, you'll encounter all the other sites that I mention in this appendix.

Calvin's PalmPilot FAQ

www.pilotfaq.com

Calvin Parker maintains one of the oldest and best-known lists of questions and answers about using the PalmPilot. The site is a bit geeky, but it's simple and well organized, and it contains more information about using the PalmPilot than you could ever want to know.

InSync Online

```
www.insync-palm.com
```

The Palm people at 3Com run an Internet mailing list called InSync Online, which sends regular messages describing tips, tricks, and special offers for PalmPilot users. You can sign up at the InSync Web site.

Palm Central

```
www.palmcentral.com
```

Palm Central is my favorite source for the latest, greatest, and strangest software available for the PalmPilot. At one time called Ray's Pilot Files, Palm Central offers downloadable copies of every kind of PalmPilot software, from scientific calculators to a database of the birthdays of every Beanie Baby.

PalmOS.com

```
www.palmos.com
```

A useful Web site and software archive, PalmOS.com includes reviews of products and software carefully organized into categories. And, best of all, it offers a discussion group where you can put in your two cents.

The PalmPilot Newsgroups

```
comp.sys.palmtops.pilot
alt.comp.sys.palmpilot
```

Gee, what funny-looking Web site addresses. Well, that's because they aren't Web addresses; they're the addresses for two PalmPilot newsgroups. The Internet has thousands of online discussion forums called *newsgroups,* in which people post and reply to questions, opinions, and announcements on nearly every conceivable topic. You can read any newsgroup through a news-reading program, such as Microsoft Outlook Express, or by pointing your browser at `www.dejanews.com` and searching for the word PalmPilot.

PalmPower Magazine

www.palmpower.com

I read PalmPower Magazine daily. Every morning, PalmPower lists up to a half-dozen stories of interest to PalmPilot users around the Web. Also, the editors of the site prepare monthly features about PalmPilot technology and reviews of new PalmPilot accessories. If you want to follow what goes on in the PalmPilot universe on a daily basis, PalmPower is an important resource.

PDA Dash

www.pdadash.com

Some people call the PalmPilot a PDA, meaning *Personal Digital Assistant*, not *Public Display of Affection* (you know, the kind that you used to get in trouble for in high school — if you were really lucky). Of course, there's nothing wrong with displaying your affection for your PalmPilot, within reason. Anyway, the PDA Dash Web site is devoted to the latest news about Personal Digital Assistants. PDA Dash discusses the PalmPilot as well as the Psion palmtop computers, Rex personal organizers, Windows CE products, and the late Apple Newton. The site is run by Concept Kitchen, a firm that sells some of the accessories that I mention elsewhere in this book.

Pilot Gear H.Q.

www.pilotgear.com

Part newspaper, part online store, Pilot Gear is the most likely place to find information about accessories that you can buy for your PalmPilot. The folks at Pilot Gear gladly take your credit card number over the phone or the Web and sell you anything from a PalmPilot modem cable to a fancy leather jacket with a pocket that's just the right size to hold your PalmPilot.

Pilot Zone

www.pilotzone.com

Like Palm Central, the Pilot Zone is an extensive list of downloadable software for your PalmPilot. The Pilot Zone list isn't as exhaustive as the one at Palm Central, but the editors of the site evaluate each listed program and apply their own rating system, awarding one to five airplanes to each program, depending on how much each product impresses them.

3Com

www.palmpilot.3com.com

Point your browser to the PalmPilot manufacturer's Web site for the official word on PalmPilot products, upgrades, and links. You can find a complete collection of articles, Web site links, and the latest versions of all the software that you need to keep your PalmPilot in tip-top condition. The 3Com Web site also features links to the Web sites of other companies that manufacture software and accessories for the PalmPilot.

Appendix B
Troubleshooting Tips

My PalmPilots have rarely given me problems, except when I've messed something up, like letting the batteries run out. That's not to say that nothing can ever go wrong, but most common PalmPilot problems have simple solutions.

Screen Taps Don't Work

Sometimes when you tap a button on the PalmPilot screen, absolutely nothing happens. That's because the PalmPilot software gets a little out of whack over time and can't determine exactly where you're tapping. To fix this problem, tap the Applications soft button and pick the Prefs application. Choose Digitizer in the upper-right corner of the Prefs application. The Digitizer puts a series of X-shaped targets on your screen and prompts you to tap the center of each target. When you tap each target, your PalmPilot gets readjusted to the relationship between the figures that it displays on the screen and where you tap.

My Screen Is Blank

What could be more alarming than to turn on your PalmPilot only to see — nothing! A blank screen may be something serious, but it also may be something simple, such as having the contrast set too low. Turn the little contrast wheel on the left side of your PalmPilot to see if it makes an image appear on your screen. If changing the contrast doesn't fix the problem, try putting in fresh batteries.

The Menu Button Doesn't Work

If you tap the Menu soft button and nothing happens, the most likely explanation is that no menus are available for the screen that you're viewing. Not all screens have menus. For example, when a dialog box is open, you can't look at a menu until you finish using that dialog box and close the box.

My PalmPilot Won't Turn Off

If you can't make your PalmPilot switch applications and it won't turn off, chances are you have a misbehaving program. The standard PalmPilot programs (Date Book, Address Book, To Do List, and Memo Pad) almost never misbehave, but some programs that you find on the Web can be finicky that way. If your PalmPilot program is frozen, your only solution is to perform a soft reset, which has the same effect as turning your PalmPilot off and turning it back on again. To perform a soft reset, unbend a paper clip and press it into the hole in the back of your PalmPilot case that's labeled Reset. That normally closes all programs and restarts your PalmPilot. A soft reset doesn't lose your data; however, a hard reset erases all the data on the PalmPilot. See Chapter 1 for more about resetting before performing either kind of reset.

The Hard Buttons Stick

If the hard buttons at the bottom of your PalmPilot stick, you can get the PalmPilot people to repair or replace your PalmPilot. Contact 3Com's technical support folks at 847-676-1441 for details on getting your PalmPilot fixed. If your one-year warranty is still in effect, you can get your PalmPilot fixed for free; otherwise a flat $100 charge applies.

Graffiti Is Always Wrong

I've found that Graffiti often fails to understand my entries, but most of the time my handwriting is to blame. Sometimes, however, all that I need to do is recalibrate my PalmPilot rather than go back to the first grade for penmanship classes. To recalibrate your PalmPilot, tap the Applications soft button, tap the Prefs application, and then choose Digitizer from the pull-down list in the upper-right corner of the screen. Follow the prompts that ask you to tap each X-shaped target as it appears.

If running the digitizer doesn't fix your Graffiti problems, make sure that you make each character as large as possible and keep your lines as straight as possible. Of course, there's always that penmanship class. You'll see me there — I'm the one in the corner with the dunce cap.

My Screen Is Too Dark

The PalmPilot screen is often tricky to read when there's too much light (or too little). If you find the screen hard to read, adjust the contrast by turning the contrast wheel on the left side of your PalmPilot case. If adjusting the contrast doesn't do the trick and you're using the PalmPilot in a fairly dim environment, turn on the backlight by holding down the power button for two seconds.

My PalmPilot Won't Start

If you drop your PalmPilot and it won't start afterward, the memory card may have shaken loose. The memory card is the heart, soul, and brains of your PalmPilot. If the brains of your PalmPilot get shaken loose, it can have problems, just as any of us would. To reseat the memory card, open the memory door (or remove the back of the case, if you have a Palm III), and then press very gently on the memory card to make it sit more snugly in its fitting.

Beaming Fails

Remember, beaming works only between a pair of Palm IIIs that are switched on, pointed at one another, and within about 3 feet of each other. You also need to make sure that the beaming feature is enabled on both units. To check if beaming is activated, tap the Applications soft button, tap the Prefs application, choose the General option, and make sure that the last line of the General Preferences screen says Beam Receive On. If beaming is off, tap the triangle next to Receive and pick On from the drop-down list.

I Got a "Fatal Exception" Error

If you like to try out lots of free software, as I do, now and again you get a program that misbehaves. The result of a misbehaving program is sometimes an error message that says "Fatal exception." You should be able to press the power switch and turn off your PalmPilot, and then turn it right back on. If hitting the power switch doesn't work, unbend a paper clip and press it into the hole marked Reset on the back of your PalmPilot.

Appendix C
About the CD

So, just what is that shiny, round thing stuck to the inside back cover of this book? A coaster? A mini-frisbee? The newest Pearl Jam CD?

No, not quite. It's even better. I've included a selection of my favorite PalmPilot software, plus some software to help you get on the Internet (if you're not already on it). Here are a few highlights from the *PalmPilot For Dummies* CD-ROM:

- Jfile, the leading database program for the PalmPilot
- TealPaint, a versatile PalmPilot painting and drawing program
- A collection of software that you can install on your PalmPilot for business and pleasure

System Requirements

To use the CD, make sure your computer meets the minimum system requirements listed below. If your computer doesn't match up to most of these requirements, you may have problems using the contents of the CD.

- A PC with a 486 or faster processor, or a Mac OS computer with a 68030 or faster processor.
- Microsoft Windows 3.1 or later, or Mac OS system software 7.5 or later.
- At least 8MB of total RAM installed on your computer. For best performance, we recommend that Windows 95/98–equipped PCs and Mac OS computers with PowerPC processors have at least 16MB of RAM installed.
- At least 120MB (Windows) or 55MB (Mac) of hard drive space available to install all the software from this CD. (You'll need less space if you don't install every program.)
- A CD-ROM drive — double-speed (2x) or faster.

PalmPilot For Dummies

- Recommended: A sound card for PCs. (Mac OS computers have built-in sound support.)
- Recommended: A monitor capable of displaying at least 256 colors or grayscale.
- Recommended: A modem with a speed of at least 14,400 bps.

If you need more information on the basics, check out *PCs For Dummies,* 6th Edition, by Dan Gookin; *Macs For Dummies,* 6th Edition by David Pogue; *Windows 95 For Dummies,* 2nd Edition and *Windows 98 For Dummies* by Andy Rathbone; or *Windows 3.11 For Dummies,* 4th Edition, by Andy Rathbone (all published by IDG Books Worldwide, Inc.).

Using the CD

1. **Double-click the file called License.txt.**

   This file contains the end-user license that you agree to by using the CD. When you're done reading the license, close the program (most likely NotePad) that displayed the file.

2. **Double-click the file called Readme.txt.**

   This file contains instructions about installing the software from this CD. It might be helpful to leave this text file open while you use the CD.

3. **Double-click the folder for the software you are interested in.**

   Be sure to read the descriptions of the programs in the next section of this appendix (much of this information also shows up in the Readme file). These descriptions give you more precise information about the programs' folder names and about finding and running the installer program.

4. **Find the file called Setup.exe, or Install.exe, or something similar, and double-click that file.**

   The program's installer walks you through the process of setting up your new software.

How to use the CD using the Mac OS

To install the items from the CD to your hard drive, follow these steps:

1. **Insert the CD into your computer's CD-ROM drive.**

   In a moment, an icon representing the CD that you just inserted appears on your Mac desktop. The icon looks like a CD-ROM.

2. **Double-click the CD icon to show the CD's contents.**
3. **Double-click the Read Me First icon.**

   This text file contains information about the CD's programs and any last-minute instructions you need to know about installing the programs on the CD that we don't cover in this appendix.

4. **Open your browser.**

   If you don't have a browser, the CD includes the two most popular ones for your convenience — Microsoft Internet Explorer and Netscape Communicator.

5. **With the browser runnning click File⇨Open and select the CD entitled *PalmPilot For Dummies*.**

6. **Some programs come with installer programs — with those you simply open the program's folder on the CD and double-click the icon with the words *Install* or *Installer*. Others have a .PRC file that you have to install with the InstallApp tool. See Chapter 12 for more on installing applications.**

   Once you've installed the programs that you want, you can eject the CD. Carefully place it back in the plastic jacket of the book for safekeeping.

What You'll Find

Here's a summary of the cool stuff you can find on this CD. Most of the software listed here will run on any PalmPilot, but a few won't run with Palm OS 1.0. If you haven't upgraded and you want to take full advantage of this CD, see Chapter 14 for more on upgrading. I've noted when certain programs won't run with Palm OS 1.0.

Financial tools

FCPlus Professional

FC Plus is an advanced financial calculator for working out loans, leases, annuities, depreciation, and other big money matters. Doesn't work with Palm OS 1.0.

Qmate

Quicken users will be happy to know that they can enter their financial data on a PalmPilot and then HotSync and import the data to Quicken. I think Qmate could be a lot easier to use, but if your Quicken data is really important to you, Qmate can help you enter data from the field.

Time Expense Auto Keeper (TEAK)

Gas, oil, repairs, and mileage all go into TEAK so that you know the overall cost of operating your auto.

Fun and games

Blackjack

A PalmPilot version of the casino favorite, BlackJack deals the cards and takes your bets as you try to beat the house. Legal in all 50 states.

Eliza, Pilot Psychologist

Eliza is a computerized shrink who answers the questions you answer with more questions, just like some real shrinks. Eliza is purely for entertainment; anyone who considers Eliza the equivalent of real psychotherapy needs to have his head examined.

Jpack

The people at J-Land have wrapped up a collection of their most popular programs in Jpack. The collection includes the following:

- **Jfile** is the leading database program for the PalmPilot. You can find ready-made Jfile databases covering everything from drink recipes to chemical elements.
- **Jshopper** is a shopping list organizer. Arrange your list by store at up to ten different stores. Keep up with coupons, too.
- **Jtutor** is a flash card program for memorizing information and drilling you to improve recall.
- **Jookerie** is a game derived from the classic dictionary game in which people make up definitions of words to try to fool their opponents.
- **Jstones**, described as an addictive board game, demands that you earn points by placing markers, called "stones," on a playing board according to an elaborate set of rules.

Klondike

A solitaire game for those moments when a database just won't do.

Language Dictionary

A multilingual dictionary that translates between a variety of foreign languages. Doesn't work with Palm OS 1.0.

Words Per Minute

When you get so good at Graffiti that you think, "Hey! I'm good!" find out how good you really are. WPM checks how fast you enter Graffiti in test sentences. I'm sorry to say, WPM does reduce your score for mistakes. Rats!

Internet tools

AvantGo Desktop and Web Client

If you want to read your favorite Web pages from your PalmPilot while riding the train to work, you can use AvantGo to download selected pages to your desktop computer and then HotSync them to your PalmPilot to view everything later. AvantGo includes a desktop client and PalmPilot application that work together.

HandMail

HandMail is an e-mail package that you can use with your PalmPilot Modem to send and receive real e-mail to an Internet account, rather than just to copy messages from your desktop computer. The program requires you to have your own Internet connection and e-mail account.

HandWeb

It's hard to believe that you can actually browse the World Wide Web on your PalmPilot, but with HandWeb, you can. Frankly, Web browsing on a PalmPilot is pretty frustrating, and the PalmPilot Modem is pretty slow, but with HandWeb it's possible, at least.

Microsoft Internet Explorer

Internet Explorer is one of the two big cheeses in web browsers. To check out the newest updates on IE, please visit Microsoft's Web site at www.microsoft.com/ie.

Important note: This software, if run under Windows NT 4.0, requires Service Pack 3 to run. If you don't have Service Pack 3, please visit the Microsoft Web site at www.microsoft.com. If you do, or after installing it, continue the installation and follow the prompts on your screen to install the NT version of Internet Explorer.

MindSpring Internet Access

In case you don't have a connection to the information superhighway, the CD includes sign-on software for MindSpring Internet Access, an Internet Service Provider.

After you are signed on, one of the first places you can check out is the MindSpring Web site at www.mindspring.com. You need a credit card to sign up with MindSpring Internet Access.

Important note: If you already have an Internet Service Provider, please note that MindSpring Internet Access software makes changes to your computer's current Internet configuration and may replace your current settings. These changes may stop you from being able to access the Internet through your current provider.

Netscape Communicator

Netscape Communicator is a suite of programs that includes the other big cheese in web browsers, Netscape Navigator. To check for the newest updates of Communicator, please visit Netscape's Web site at www.netscape.com.

Palmeta Mail

If you have an older PalmPilot that didn't include the Mail program, Palmeta Mail compensates by pulling messages from your desktop e-mail program and turning each into a memo on your PalmPilot. Palmeta Mail equires Windows 95 or Windows NT 4.0.

Multimedia

AportisDoc

The best known of the document reader programs, AportisDoc enables you to store and read whole books and short stories on your PalmPilot. You can also bookmark whatever you're reading so that you can pick up reading where you left off.

Image Viewer

You can display photographs on your PalmPilot with the help of Image Viewer. Most photos look pretty rough on the PalmPilot screen, but you may still have your reasons for wanting to see pictures on the PalmPilot. I know of a PalmPilot-toting couple who keep their wedding pictures on their PalmPilots. Isn't that romantic?

TealPaint

The premiere drawing program for the PalmPilot, TealPaint enables you to create your own artistic masterpieces, capture screens from other PalmPilot programs, and send them all to your Window 95 desktop computer to be used in conventional graphics programs like Corel or Adobe Illustrator.

Organizational tools

Action Names
Action Names enhances the PalmPilot calendar, contact, and To Do programs by letting you link the names of people to the activities that involve them. Doesn't work with Palm OS 1.0.

Actioneer
You don't need to switch between the PalmPilot applications to enter your appointments and To Do's if you have Actioneer. You can enter plain English statements like "Call Bob tomorrow at 2 p.m." into Actioneer and let the program create the appointment or To Do as necessary. Actioneer also offers a similar program for users of Microsoft Outlook.

AreaCoder
It seems like the phone company changes everybody's area code every couple of weeks, which makes for a lot of work when you're maintaining a list of contacts. AreaCoder searches for and replaces changed area codes in your PalmPilot Address Book.

BrainForest
You can find several outliner programs for the PalmPilot; BrainForest is one of the best known. Organize your thoughts into "trees" with "branches" and "leaves" that you can move, copy, sort, and delete. Doesn't work with Palm OS 1.0.

BugMe!
When you want to be reminded to get back to something in an hour or so, enter a quick note in BugMe!, and the note will set off a PalmPilot alarm to remind you about it.

PhoneLog
PhoneLog helps you keep track of phone calls you've made and received according to length, time, and category. Doesn't work with Palm OS 1.0.

Punch List
See Chapter 15 for more about this advanced project manager.

TealGlance
For a quick summary of your next appointments and To Do's, as well as the current time and battery level every time you start your PalmPilot, install TealGlance. Doesn't work with Palm OS 1.0.

ThoughtMill

Another outliner, ThoughtMill automatically turns the text you enter into a structured outline that you can expand, collapse, or export to the Memo Pad. Doesn't work with Palm OS 1.0.

TimeReporter

TimeReporter is a tool for people who earn a living through hourly billings. Record the time you spend on all your various clients and projects on the job using TimeReporter.

World Time

See the current time and date in over 260 different cities, countries, and time zones, from Alaska to Zaire and back.

Synchronization tools

Desktop to Go

Desktop to Go is one of the three major synchronization programs that connect your PalmPilot to Microsoft Outlook. Desktop to Go is quick and simple and lets you use either Microsoft Outlook or Microsoft Schedule+ in lieu of your PalmPilot desktop program.

PROFS-AutoPilot

If you *really* like to accessorize, you can get an IBM mainframe to go with your PalmPilot and use PROFS-AutoPilot to synchronize with the PROFS personal organizer on the mainframe. For the PalmPilot owner who has everything.

UnDupe

When the HotSync process messes up and creates two of everything on your PalmPilot, UnDupe automatically converts your double vision back to normal.

Utilities

FlashBuilder III for the Palm III

The Palm III has a secret area of memory, called flash memory, that programs can't use without the help of FlashBuilder. Under the right circumstances, you can get as much as 40 percent more space to use on your PalmPilot. Not all PalmPilot programs take well to being loaded into flash memory, but if the programs you use agree with Flash Builder, you're in business.

HandFax

Your PalmPilot Modem can send faxes if you have a suitable fax program to do the work. HandFax enables you to fax items from your Memo Pad to any normal fax machine. At the moment, you can't receive faxes and you can't send graphics to a PalmPilot.

MakeDoc

Doc files are special compressed text files that you can store and read on your PalmPilot. You can store lengthy documents, even whole books (short ones) in Doc format and read them with the help of a reader like AportisDoc (also on this CD). MakeDoc is a Windows program that enables you to create your own Doc files from files on your PC.

PalmPrint

Like the name suggests, PalmPrint is designed to give your PalmPilot the ability to send text to a printer. Early versions of PalmPrint could send a print job to a printer with the help of a wire and a special converter. The people who dreamed up PalmPrint have a new version that lets you beam print jobs from a Palm III to an IR-based printer. Pretty slick.

Satellite Forms

You don't need to be a programmer to create your own applications for the PalmPilot if you use Satellite Forms. For more about Satellite Forms and other forms programs, see Chapter 18.

TealEcho

When the task of learning Graffiti eludes you, TealEcho can help by tracing out the image of whatever you draw in the Graffiti drawing area so that you can see what you've done. Many Graffiti gurus recommend TealEcho. You must install HackMaster for this to work.

TealMagnify

That tiny typeface in the PalmPilot display can be pretty tough to read. TealMagnify adds a magnifying glass to let you zero in on text you can't make out. You need to install HackMaster before TealMagnify can work.

If You've Got Problems (Of the CD Kind)

The PalmPilot programs that we include on the CD run on any PalmPilot running Palm OS 2.0 or later and most run with Palm OS 1.0, as long as you can get them installed from your desktop computer. What happens on the desktop computer could be another story.

When it comes to running the CD, the two likeliest problems that you may encounter are that you don't have enough memory (RAM) for the programs you want to use, or you have other programs running that are affecting the installation or running of a program. If you get error messages like `Not enough memory` or `Setup cannot continue`, try one or more of these remedies and then try using the software again:

- ✔ Turn off any antivirus software that you have on your computer. Installers sometimes mimic virus activity and may make your computer incorrectly believe that it's being infected by a virus.

- ✔ Close all running programs. The more programs you run, the less memory is available to other programs. Installers also typically update files and programs. So if you keep other programs running, installation may not work properly.

- ✔ Have your local computer store add more RAM to your computer. This is, admittedly, a drastic and somewhat expensive step. However, if you have a Windows 95/98 PC or a Mac OS computer with a PowerPC or G3 chip, adding more memory can really help the speed of your computer and allow more programs to run at the same time. This may include closing the CD interface and running a product's installation program from Windows Explorer.

- ✔ If push comes to shove, just run the Palm Install Tool from Windows (or InstallApp from a Mac), and double-click the name of the program you want to install. If you can't get the CD to run, you may still be able to install PalmPilot programs directly.

If you still have trouble installing the items from the CD, please call the IDG Books Worldwide Customer Service phone number: 800-762-2974 (outside the U.S.: 317-596-5430).

Index

• Symbols •
@ sign in Graffiti, 40

• A •
AC adapter for modem, 224
AC power, 267
accessories
　Brain Wash screen-cleaning system, 272
　business card scanners, 273, 280–281
　cases, 274
　Karma Cloth, 272
　Minstrel wireless modem, 274
　styluses, 272
　SuperPilot Memory Board, 250, 273
　TripMate GPS receiver, 273–274, 280
　UniMount (for your car), 273
　WriteRight Screen Enhancements overlays, 271–272
ACT! 4 For Windows For Dummies, 284
ACT! 4.0 PalmPilot link, 261, 283
Action Names, 299
Actioneer, 279–280, 299
addictiveness of PalmPilot, 1
add-on software
　Action Names, 299
　Actioneer, 279–280, 299
　AirCalc, 259
　for airplane pilots, 259–260
　Amicus Attorney, 256
　AportisDoc, 143, 298
　for architects, 253–254
　Area Codes database, 262
　AreaCoder, 299
　Athlete's Calculator, 254
　Auto Doc, 259
　AvantGo, 297
　AvCheck, 259–260
　for bartenders, 254, 255
　BlackJack, 296
　BrainForest, 263, 299
　BugMe!, 299
　CardScan, 280–281
　on the CD-ROM, 12, 295–301
　for coaches, 254
　for couch potatoes, 254
　Delorme Street Atlas, 274, 280
　Desktop To Go, 283, 300
　DietLog, 254
　DigiPet, 258–259
　Drinks, 254, 255
　EE Toolkit, 255
　for electrical engineers, 255
　Eliza, Pilot Psychologist, 296
　FCPlus Professional, 295
　financial tools on CD-ROM, 295
　Flash!, 261, 262
　FlashBuilder III for Palm III, 277, 300
　forms programs, 277–279, 301
　games on CD-ROM, 296
　HandFax, 240, 281–282, 301
　HandStamp Pro, 297
　HandWeb, 297
　for help desk technicians, 255–256
　Image Viewer, 298
　installing, 213–215
　Internet tools on CD-ROM, 297–298
　Jpack, 296
　JTutor, 261, 296
　King James version of the Bible, 256
　Klondike, 296

language dictionary, 296
for lawyers, 256
MakeDoc, 301
for managers, 256, 257
for ministers, 256
Mobile Medical Data, 259
for molecular biologists, 257
for musicians, 257–258
for New York City taxi drivers, 258
NY CrossTown 1.5, 258
OligoCalc, 257
organizational tools on CD-ROM, 299–300
Palmeta Mail, 298
PalmPrint, 144, 301
PalmProject, 256, 257
for parents, 258–259
PhoneLog, 299
for physicians, 259
PocketSynth, 257–258
by profession, 253–263
PROFS-AutoPilot, 300
for psychics, 260
Punch List, 253–254, 299
QuickSheet, 276–277
Qmate, 295
Remedy Help Desk, 255–256
Reuters Market Clip, 261
for salespeople, 261
Satellite Forms, 278–279, 301
Small Talk, 262, 281
for stockbrokers, 261
synchronization programs, 282–283
synchronization tools on CD-ROM, 300
T9, 46, 276
Tarot Assistant, 260
for teachers, 261–262
TealEcho, 301
TealGlance, 299
TealMagnify, 301

TealPaint, 298
for telemarketers, 262
ThoughtMill, 263, 300
Time Expense Auto Keeper (TEAK), 295
TimeReporter, 300
for travel agents, 262
UnDupe, 300
utilities on CD-ROM, 300–301
Words Per Minute, 296
World Time, 300
for writers, 263, 299, 300
Address Book, Palm Desktop
  adding new entries to, 189–191
  attaching note to address record, 191–192
  deleting name in, 193
  editing address records in, 191
  finding name in, 192
  setting up custom fields in, 193–194
Address Book, PalmPilot
  accessing, 73–74
  attaching note to address record, 79–80
  defined, 25
  deleting a name from, 84–85
  deleting a note from address record, 85–86
  editing an address record, 78–79
  entering names into, 74–77
  finding name in, 82–84
  hard button, 14, 73–74
  marking business card, 81–82
  setting preferences in, 86–87
  setting up custom fields, 87–88
Address Edit screen, 75–77
Address List, 73–74
Address View screen, 78
AirCalc program, 259, 260
airplane pilots, add-on software for, 259–260

Index

alarm sound, 52, 135
alarms
  BugMe! (on CD-ROM), 299
  on PalmPilot, 128–130
alphabet, Graffiti, 34–36
America Online (AOL) e-mail system, 239
Amicus Attorney, 251
analog line, 225
AportisDoc, 143, 298
appendixes in this book, 4–5
  About the CD (Appendix C), 293–302
  Internet resources for PalmPilot (Appendix A), 285–288
  troubleshooting tips (Appendix B), 289–292
AppHack program, 64
Apple's operating systems, 244
application hard buttons, 14–15
application timesavers, 67–69
applications
  beaming, 142–143
  defined, 14
  deleting, 215–217
  installing add-on, 213–215
  opening, 14–15, 20–21
applications on PalmPilot, pre-installed
  Address Book, 25, 73–88
  Calculator, 25
  Date Book, 25–26, 121–136
  defined, 24
  Expense, 26, 27, 210–211
  Giraffe game, 26, 27
  HotSync, 20, 26. *See also* HotSyncing
  Mail, 26, 145–163
  Memo Pad, 28, 109–120
  Preferences, 28, 29, 47–56
  Security, 28, 30, 56–60
  To Do List, 28, 89–107
Applications soft button, 19–21

appointments in Palm Desktop Date Book
  adding appointments in, 185
  Day view of, 183–184
  deleting, 188–189
  Month view of, 184
  private, 188
  repeating, 186–187
  Week view of, 184
appointments in PalmPilot Date Book
  deleting, 133–134
  dragging and dropping, 68–69, 123–124
  entering, 125–128
  private, 132
  purging, 136
  repeating, 130–132
appointments that span two or more dates, 269
architects, add-on software for, 253–254
archive copy of To Do items, 103
archive files
  purging and moving items to, 219
  returning an archived item to PalmPilot, 221
  viewing, 220
Area Codes database, 262
AreaCoder (on CD-ROM), 299
Athlete's Calculator program, 254
attaching notes
  to address records, 79–80
  to To-Do items, 93–94
attachments, e-mail, 146, 163
attorneys, add-on software for, 256
Auto Doc program, 259
automobiles
  Time Expense Auto Keeper (TEAK), 295
  Unimount for, 273
Auto-off interval, 50–51
AvantGo (on CD-ROM), 297
AvCheck program, 259–260

• B •

BackHack program, 64
backing up data, 219
backlight
  as drain on batteries, 16, 30
  turning on, 16
  versions of PalmPilot with, 24
backspace character, Graffiti, 37
Backup Buddy program, 219, 247
bartenders, add-on software for, 254
batteries, PalmPilot
  Auto-off for saving, 50–51
  backlight as drain on, 16, 30
  changing, 30
  dates and dead batteries, 50
  duration of, 1, 21, 30
  rechargeable, 31
  spare, 267
batteries, PalmPilot Modem, 224
battery icon in applications list, 21
BCCs, blind copies, 155–156
beaming a business card, 66
  setting up PalmPilot for, 81–82
beaming feature, Palm III
  defined, 53, 81, 137–138
  future of, 144
  receiving an application, 143
  receiving a category, 141–142
  receiving an item, 139–140
  sending an application, 142–143
  sending a category, 140–141
  sending an item, 138–139
  troubleshooting tips for, 291
  turning off, 53
beaming memos, 120
beaming To Do's, 98–99
Bible, King James version of, 256
BlackJack, 296
blank screen, 289
blind copies of e-mail messages, 155–156
Bogglet, 143

Brain Wash screen-cleaning system, 272
BrainForest outliner program, 263, 299
browsing the Web, 239–240
  with HandWeb (on CD-ROM), 240, 297
  with Microsoft Internet Explorer, 297
  with ProxiWeb, 240
BugMe!, 299
business cards
  beaming, 66
  marking, 81–82
  scanning, 273, 280–281
buttons
  Address Book button, 14
  Date Book button, 14, 121
  defined, 6, 14
  hard, 14–15
  Memo Pad button, 14, 15
  power button, 16
  Reset button, 16–17
  Scroll buttons, 14, 15
  soft, 19–23
  To Do List button, 14, 15, 90
Buttons Preferences screen, 53–54

• C •

Calculator program, Athlete's, 254
Calculator program, PalmPilot, 25
Calculator soft button, 19, 21–22
calendar views in PalmPilot Date Book
  Daily view, 122
  Month view, 124–125
  Week view, 123–124
call waiting, 229–230
Calvin's PalmPilot FAQ, 285
capital letters in Graffiti, 38–39
CardScan 3.0, 273, 280–281
CardScan Plus 300, 273, 280
cars
  Time Expense Auto Keeper (TEAK), 295
  Unimount for, 273

Index

cases to hold PalmPilot, 274
categories, assigning
  adding multiple items to a category, 69
  assigning multiple categories to one item (no can do), 270
  in Palm Desktop To Do List, 195–196
categories, beaming and receiving, 140–142
categories in To Do List
  adding, 96
  available, 95
  changing, 67, 95
  deleting, 96–97
  renaming, 97–98
categorizing
  dates (no can do), 270
  memos, 114
  memos on Palm Desktop, 207–208
CD-ROM, 5, 12
  financial tools on, 295
  fun and games on, 296
  Internet tools on, 297–298
  multimedia tools on, 298
  organizational tools on, 299–300
  problems with running, 301–302
  synchronization tools on, 300
  system requirements for, 293–294
  utilities on, 300–301
  using, 294
  using CD with Mac OS, 294–295
CDPD network, 274
checking memory, 212–213
checking the time, 66
Cheng, Eric, 257
choosing, defined, 6
Claris Organizer, 168, 252
cleaning PalmPilot screen
  with Brain Wash, 272
  with Karma Cloth, 272
clicking, defined, 6
Co-Pilot case, 274

coaches, add-on software for, 254
Command Shift stroke in Graffiti, 39
commercial software programs for PalmPilot.
  See also add-on software
  Actioneer, 279–280, 299
  CardScan, 280–281
  Delorme Street Atlas, 274, 280
  FlashBuilderIII, 277, 300
  forms programs, 277–279
  HandFax, 240, 281–282, 301
  QuickSheet, 276–277
  Small Talk, 262, 281
  synchronization programs, 282–283
  T9, 46, 276
completed tasks, 102
Concept Kitchen firm
  Brain Wash from, 272
  Karma Cloth from, 272
  PDA Dash Web site run by, 287
  Small Talk from, 262, 281
  WriteRights from, 271–272
Conduit Manager 1.01 Updater, 172, 251
Conduit Manager Updater dialog box, 176
conduits
  defined, 179, 282
  Desktop To Go, 283, 300
  IntelliSync, 283
  PocketMirror, 282
construction industry professionals, software for, 253–254
contact management software, 261
contrast wheel, 16
  fixing blank screen with, 289
  fixing too dark screen with, 291
copying and pasting text, 69
Corex Technologies, 273, 280
couch potatoes, add-on software for, 254
countries, formats corresponding with, 55–56

cradle
  HotSync button on, 178–179
  storing PalmPilot in, 31
Create User Account dialog box, 170
cursor, Graffiti, 36–38
custom fields in
  Palm Desktop Address Book, 193–194
  PalmPilot Address Book, 87–88
cutting, copying, and pasting, 69
Cutting Edge Software, 276

• D •

Daily view, Date Book
  in Palm Desktop, 183–184
  in PalmPilot, 122–123
dash character in Graffiti, 40
Date Book, Palm Desktop
  adding appointments in, 185
  Day view of, 183–184
  deleting appointments in, 188–189
  Month view of, 184
  private appointments in, 188
  repeating appointments in, 186–187
  Week view of, 184
Date Book, PalmPilot
  adding appointments to, 125–128
  alarms, 128–130
  button, 14, 121
  defined, 25–26
  deleting appointments in, 133–134
  dragging and dropping, 68–69, 123–124
  icon for, 20
  private appointments in, 132
  purging appointments in, 136
  repeating appointments in, 130–132
  setting preferences in, 134–135
  uncluttering screen in, 68
  views, 122–125
date, setting the, 49–50
Delete Event dialog box, 133–134

Delete Items dialog box, 103
Delete Memo dialog box, 116–117
Delete Message dialog box, 153
Deleted Items folder, 153, 155
deleting
  appointment in Date Book, 133–134
  category in To Do List, 96–97
  e-mail, 153–155
  forgotten password, 58–59
  name from Address Book, 84–85
  note from address record, 85–86
  note in To Do List program, 103–104
  ShortCut, 63
  memos, 116–117
  text in Graffiti, 37
  To Do item, 39, 102–103
deleting applications, 215
  on a Palm III, 216
  on a PalmPilot Professional, 217
DeLorme Street Atlas software, 274, 280
desktop computers
  defined, 5
  HotSyncing PalmPilot with, 29–30, 178–179
  PalmPilots versus, 15
desktop programs
  HotSyncing to, 178–179
  installing Palm Desktop for Windows, 167–171
  installing Pilot Desktop for Macintosh, 172–178
  upgrading Palm Desktop, 251–252
  using Palm Desktop Address Book, 189–194
  using Palm Desktop Date Book, 183–189
  using Palm Desktop Memo Pad, 206–210
  using Palm Desktop To Do List, 194–204
Desktop To Go program, 283, 300
details for a To Do item, 91–93

Index

dialog boxes, defined, 6
dictation, 269
dictionary on CD-ROM, multilingual, 296
DietLog program, 254
DigiPet, 258–259
digital line, 225
Digitizer
  for Graffiti problems, 290–291
  for screen taps that don't work, 289
display area, 17–19
doctors, add-on software for, 259
double-clicking, defined, 6
downloading latest version of Palm Desktop for Windows, 251
dragging, defined, 6
dragging and dropping appointments, 123–124
  as a timesaver, 68–69
drawing program for PalmPilot, 298
Drinks database, 254, 255
due dates for tasks, 92

• E •

E&B Cases, 274
e-mail attachments, 146, 163
e-mail program, HandMail, 146, 239
e-mail program, MultiMail Pro, 236–239
e-mail program, PalmPilot's
  creating a message in, 147–149
  customizing, 158–163
  defined, 26, 146
  deleting a message in, 153–154
  desktop mail program needed for, 146
  forwarding a message in, 152–153
  icon for, 20
  purging deleted messages in, 154–155
  reading a message in, 149–150
  replying to a message in, 150–151
  saving drafts in, 155
  sending and receiving real e-mail directly, 235–239
  sending a blind copy, 155–156
  signatures, 161–162
  sorting messages in, 157
e-mail systems that work with PalmPilot, 171
  HandMail, 146, 239
  MultiMail Pro, 236–239
Ecco personal information manager, 283
Edit commands
  Edit⇨Copy, 69
  Edit⇨Cut, 69
  Edit⇨Graffiti Help, 36
  Edit⇨Paste, 69
  Edit⇨Undo, 101
editing memos
  on Palm Desktop, 207
  on PalmPilot, 112–113
editing ShortCuts, 62–63
EE Toolkit, 255
electrical engineers, add-on software for, 255
Eliza, Pilot Psychologist, 296
entering names
  into Palm Desktop Address Book, 189–191
  into PalmPilot Address Book, 74–77
entering text
  with GoType, 46
  with on-screen keyboard, 44–45
  with T9 system, 46, 276
entering text in Graffiti area, 23
  alphabet for, 34–36
  backspace character, 37
  capital letters, 38–39
  punctuation, 40
  return character, 37–38
  space character, 37
erasing all your data, 17

error messages
  "Fatal exception" error, 292
  when running the CD, 302
Eudora, 171
Event Details dialog box, 129
Excel, 183, 211
  dragging text to, 207
Expense button on Palm Desktop, 183, 211
Expense program
  defined, 26, 27
  icon for, 20
  usefulness of, 210–211
Explorer, Internet, 297
Extended Shift character in Graffiti, 39

• F •

"Fatal exception" error, 292
faxing from PalmPilot
  with demo version of HandFax on CD, 282, 301
  with HandFax commercial program, 240, 281
FCPlus Professional, 295
File menu commands
  File⇨Open Archive, 220
  File⇨Print, 206
Filed folder, 154
filtering e-mail messages, 160–161
financial tools on CD-ROM, 295
Find soft button, 19, 22–23
finding and replacing text (no can do), 268
finding names in Address Book, 82–84
finger versus stylus, 66
fish loop, Graffiti, 42–43
fixing problems in PalmPilot
  beaming failures, 291
  blank screens, 289
  "Fatal exception" errors, 292
  Graffiti problems, 290–291
  hard buttons that stick, 290
  menu buttons that don't work, 290
  PalmPilots that won't start, 291
  PalmPilots that won't turn off, 290
  screen taps that don't work, 289
  too dark screen, 291
Flash! program, 261–262
FlashBuilder for Palm III, 277, 300
fonts, changing, 118
foreign language electronic phrasebook, 262, 281
forgotten passwords, 58–59
Format Preferences screen, 55–56
forms programs, 277
  Pendragon Forms, 278
  Satellite Forms, 278–279, 301
forwarding e-mail, 152–153
free add-on software
  Area Codes database, 262
  DigiPet, 258–259
  Drinks, 254, 255
  King James version of the Bible, 256
  OligoCalc, 257
Fukumoto, Shuji, 258
Fulghum, Robert, 93
fun and games on CD-ROM, 296

• G •

game sounds, 52
games on CD-ROM, 296
Gavel & Gown Software, 256
General Preferences screen
  accessing, 47–48
  adjusting sound with, 52
  defined, 29
  turning off beaming feature with, 53
general timesavers, 65–67
gifts, PalmPilots as, 2
Giraffe game, 26, 27
Global Positioning System (GPS), 273
Go To icon, Date Book, 125

Goldmine, 261
Gookin, Dan, 294
GoType, LandWare's, 46
Graffiti, 3
  capital letters in, 38–39
  cursor, 36–38
  fish loop, 42–43
  Help, 35–36, 70
  letters and numbers, 34–36, 41
  on PalmPilot screen, 23
  punctuation, 40
  ShortCuts, 43–44
  timesavers, 70
  whiz secrets, 40–41
  Words Per Minute program for, 296
  writing area, 34

• H •

HackMaster, 64
hacks, defined, 63–64
HandFax program
  on the CD, 301
  demo version of, 282
  faxing with, 240, 281
HandMail program, 146, 239
Hands High software, 263
HandStamp Pro (on CD-ROM), 297
HandWeb (on CD-ROM), 240, 297
hard buttons
  Address Book button, 14, 73–74
  Date Book button, 14, 121
  defined, 6, 14
  Memo Pad button, 14, 15
  To Do List button, 14, 15, 90
hard buttons that stick, 290
hard reset, 17, 290
Hawkins, Jeff, 248
headers, e-mail, 150
Help, PalmPilot
  Graffiti Help screen, 35–36, 70
  troubleshooting tips, 289–292

help desk technicians, add-on software
    for, 255–256
Hide Records dialog box, 59–60
hiding private items, 59–60
highlighting, defined, 6
HotSync button, 178–179
HotSync e-mail options, 158–159
  filtering, 160–161
  truncating, 162–163
HotSync program
  defined, 20, 26
  restoring PalmPilot data with, 218–219
HotSyncing
  actual process of, 178–179
  defined, 4, 29–30
  with Palm Desktop for Windows,
    167–171
  with Pilot Desktop for Macintosh,
    172–178
  setting up PalmPilot for Modem
    HotSync, 227–232

• I •

IBM WorkPad, 2–3, 24
icons, Drag To, 211
icons for PalmPilot applications, 20
icons used in this book, 7
IDG Books Worldwide Customer Service
    phone number, 302
Image Viewer, 298
imitators, PalmPilot, 12
Inbox, e-mail, 154
infrared (IR) port, 81
Install icon on Palm Desktop 3.0, 183
installing add-on software. *See also* add-
    on software
  using Palm Desktop for Windows,
    213–214
  using Pilot Desktop for Macintosh,
    214–215

installing new memory card in pre-Palm III model, 246–248
installing Palm Desktop for Windows, 167
  connecting cradle to PC before, 168–169
  steps for, 169–171
installing Pilot Desktop for Macintosh
  connecting cradle to Mac before, 172–173
  Hotsyncing with a Mac, 177–178
  steps for, 173–176
InSync Online, 286
IntelliSync products, 283
international characters, 45
Internet
  connecting to, 232–235
  surfing, 239–240
Internet e-mail program
  setting up, 236–238
  using, 239
Internet Explorer, Microsoft, 297
Internet resources
  Calvin's PalmPilot FAQ, 285
  InSync Online, 286
  newsgroups, 286
  Palm Central, 286
  PalmOS.com, 286
  PalmPilot newsgroups, 286
  PalmPilot Web Ring, 285
  PalmPower Magazine, 287
  PDA Dash, 287
  Pilot Gear H.Q., 255, 287
  Pilot Zone, 288
  3Com, 288
Internet Service Provider (ISP)
  defined, 233
  MindSpring Internet Access, 297–298
  setting up PalmPilot to dial your ISP, 233–235
Internet tools on CD-ROM, 297–298
inventor of PalmPilot, 248

• J •

Jfile
  defined, 253, 296
  for Drinks program, 254
  in Jpack, 296
  from Land J Technologies, 261
Jookerie, 296
Jpack, 296
Jshopper, 296
Jstones, 296
JTutor program, 261, 296

• K •

Karma Cloth, 272
keyboards
  GoType, 46
  on-screen, 44–45
  piano, 257–258
  T9, 46, 276
King James version of the Bible, 256
Klondike, 296

• L •

Land J Technologies, 253, 261
LandWare Web site, 46
language dictionary on CD-ROM, 296
latest version of Palm Desktop for Windows, 251
latest version of PalmPilot, 2
Launch Bar, Palm Desktop, 182
launching applications in PalmPilot
  Address Book, 73–74
  with application hard buttons, 14–15
  with Applications soft button, 20–21
  Date Book, 121
  Expense application, 211
  HotSync Manager, 178–179

Memo Pad, 109–110
Preferences application, 47–48
Security application, 56–57
To Do List, 90
lawyers, add-on software for, 256
letters in Graffiti
  alphabet on Help screen, 35–36
  capital, 38–39
  fish loop for letters K, Y, and X, 42–43
  secret tricks for making, 41
  single stroke of the stylus for, 34–35
  writing area for, 34
limitations of PalmPilot, 267–270
linking items between programs
    (no can do), 268
Lombardi, Vince, 254
looking up
  addresses and phone numbers,
      106–107
  e-mail addresses, 147
Lotus Notes 171
*Lotus SmartSuite Millennium Edition For
    Dummies,* 284

• M •

Mac OS 8 For Dummies, 5
Mac serial ports, 172, 174
Macintosh platforms, 5
Macintosh, Pilot Desktop for
  installing, 172–178
  upgrading, 251–252
MacPac, 168, 172, 251
Macs For Dummies, 5, 294
Magazine, PalmPower, 287
mail, AOL, 239
Mail, Palmeta, 298
Mail program, PalmPilot
  creating a message in, 147–149
  customizing, 158–163
  defined, 26, 146
  deleting a message in, 153–154
  desktop mail program needed for, 146
  forwarding a message in, 152–153
  icon for, 20
  purging deleted messages in, 154–155
  reading a message in, 149–150
  replying to a message in, 150–151
  saving drafts in, 155
  sending a blind copy, 155–156
  signatures, 161–162
  sorting messages in, 157
MakeDoc program, 301
managers, add-on software for, 256
manufacturer of PalmPilot, 168
marking completed To Do's
  in Palm Desktop, 203
  in PalmPilot, 102
marking memos private
  in Palm Desktop, 209
  in PalmPilot, 115–116
Mayer, Jeffrey J., 284
Meadhra, Michael, 284
medical programs, PalmPilot, 259
Memo Details dialog box, 115
Memo Pad, PalmPilot
  beaming memos, 120
  categorizing memos, 114
  changing fonts in, 118
  creating new memos, 110–111
  defined, 3, 28
  deleting memos, 116–117
  editing memos, 112–113
  faxing messages from, 240, 281–282,
      301
  hard button, 14, 15, 109–110
  private memos, 115–116
  reading memos, 111–112
  setting preferences for, 118–119
  viewing memos by category, 117–118

memory
  checking, 212–213
  in different PalmPilot versions, 24
  FlashBuilder III for expanding, 277, 300
Memory application, defined, 20
memory board, SuperPilot, 250, 273
memory card
  changing Palm III's, 248–250
  defined, 246
  installing new card in pre-Palm III model, 246–248
  reseating memory card for PalmPilot that won't start, 291
memos on Palm Desktop
  categorizing, 207–208
  deleting, 210
  editing, 207
  entering, 204–206
  printing, 206–207
  private, 208–209
  reading, 206
memos on PalmPilot
  beaming, 120
  categorizing, 114
  changing fonts for, 118
  creating new, 110–111
  deleting, 116–117
  editing, 112–113
  private, 115–116
  reading, 111–112
  setting preferences for, 118–119
  viewing memos by category, 117–118
menu commands, 6
Menu soft button, 19, 21
Menu soft buttons that don't work, 290
Microsoft Excel, 183, 211
  dragging text to, 207
Microsoft Exchange, 171
Microsoft Internet Explorer, 297
Microsoft Outlook, 171, 179
Microsoft Outlook 98 For Dummies, 283, 284

Microsoft Word
  dragging memos into, 207
  icon on Palm Desktop, 211
Microsoft's Web site, 297
MindSpring Internet Access, 297–298
MindSpring Web site, 297
ministers, add-on software for, 256
Minstrel Modem, 146
Minstrel wireless modem, 274
mistakes, undoing, 101
Mobile Generation Software, 253
Mobile Medical Data program, 259
models, PalmPilot, 2, 23–24
  Palm III, 2, 4, 13, 24. *See also* Palm III
  PalmPilot 1000, 24
  PalmPilot 5000, 24
  PalmPilot Personal, 24
  PalmPilot Professional, 24, 81
modem port, Mac, 172–173
modem setup string, 227
Modem, PalmPilot
  batteries, 224
  browsing the Web with, 239–240
  connecting to Internet with, 232–235
  cost of, 223
  faxing with, 240
  outside North America, 224
  performing a Modem HotSync, 227–232
  setting up, 224–225
  setting up PalmPilot to use, 225–227
Modem HotSync
  disabling call waiting, 229–230
  entering Modem HotSync phone number, 228–229
  after local HotSync, 227
  setting up Palm Desktop for, 230–232
molecular biologists, OligoCalc for, 257
Month view, Date Book, 124–125
multilingual dictionary on CD-ROM, 296
MultiMail Pro, setting up, 236–239
multimedia tools on CD-ROM, 298
multiple users, accommodating, 222
musicians, PocketSynth for, 257–258

Index

• N •

name, user, 170, 175, 222
names in Address Book
  adding, 75
  in Address List, 74
  assigning categories to, 83
  deleting, 84–85
  finding, 82–83
Netscape Communicator, 298
Netscape Navigator, 298
Netscape Web site, 298
Network Preferences screen, 233–235
New York City taxi drivers, add-on software for, 258
newsgroups, PalmPilot, 286
Note screen, 79–80
notes in PalmPilot, 94
  attaching notes to address records, 79–80
  attaching notes to To Do items, 93–94
  deleting a note from address record, 85–86
  deleting a note in To Do List, 103–104
Novatel Wireless Modem, 261, 274
numbers in Graffiti
  on Help screen, 36
  tricks for making, 41
  writing area for, 34
numeric keypad, 45
NY CrossTown 1.5, 258

• O •

occupations, add-on software for different
  architects, 253–254
  athletic coaches, 254
  bartenders, 254, 255
  couch potatoes, 254
  electrical engineers, 255
  help desk technicians, 255–256
  lawyers, 256
  managers, 256, 257
  ministers, 256
  molecular biologists, 257
  musicians, 257–258
  New York City taxi drivers, 258
  parents, 258–259
  physicians, 259
  pilots, 259–260
  psychics, 260
  salespeople, 261
  stockbrokers, 261
  teachers, 261–262
  telemarketers, 262
  travel agents, 262
  writers, 263
OligoCalc, 257
On The CD icon, 7
on-screen keyboard, 44–45
Open Archive dialog box
  returning archived item to PalmPilot with, 221
  viewing archived items with, 220
opening applications in PalmPilot
  Address Book, 73–74
  with application hard buttons, 14–15
  with Applications soft button, 20–21
  Date Book, 121
  Expense application, 211
  HotSync Manager, 178–179
  Memo Pad, 109–110
  Preferences application, 47–48
  Security application, 56–57
  To Do List, 90
operating system, defined, 244
operating system, Palm
  finding out which version of Palm OS you have, 244–245
  installing new version of, 245–246

Options menu commands
  Options➪About command, 245
  Options➪Font, 118
  Options➪HotSync Options, 158–159
  Options➪Mail Server, 237
  Options➪Phone Lookup, 106
  Options➪Preferences, 86
  Options➪Recent Calculations, 25
  Options➪Rename Custom Fields, 87
organization of this book, 3–5
organizational tools on the CD-ROM
  Action Names, 299
  Actioneer, 279–280, 299
  AreaCoder, 299
  BrainForest, 263, 299
  BugMe!, 299
  PhoneLog, 299
  Punch List, 253–254, 299
  TealGlance, 299
  ThoughtMill, 263, 300
  TimeReporter, 300
  World Time, 300
organizing memos, 118–119
Outlook, Microsoft, 171, 179
Outlook 98 For Dummies, Microsoft, 283, 284

• P •

pager phone numbers, 76, 77
Palm III
  beaming a business card with, 66, 81
  beaming memos with, 120
  beaming To Do items with, 98–99
  checking the time with, 66
  defined, 2
  deleting applications on, 216
  FlashBuilder III for, 277, 300
  front and back of, 13
  infrared (IR) port on, 4, 81
  power button, 16
  upgrading, 248–250
Palm III beaming feature
  defined, 137–138
  future of, 144
  for memos, 120
  receiving an application, 143
  receiving a category, 141–142
  receiving an item, 139–140
  sending an application, 142–143
  sending a category, 140–141
  sending an item, 138–139
  for To Do items, 98–99
  turning off, 53
Palm Central Web site
  defined, 286
  downloading free Area Codes database from, 262
  downloading free copy of Bible from, 256
  downloading free Drinks from, 254, 255
  downloading free OligoCalc from, 257
  Tarot Assistant available at, 260
Palm Desktop, installing, 167–171
Palm Desktop 3.0
  defined, 168
  upgrading to, 251
Palm Desktop Address Book
  adding new entries to, 189–191
  attaching note to address record, 191–192
  deleting name in, 193
  editing address records in, 191
  finding name in, 192
  setting up custom fields in, 193–194
Palm Desktop Date Book
  adding appointments in, 185
  Day view of, 183–184
  deleting appointments in, 188–189
  Month view of, 184
  private appointments in, 188

repeating appointments in, 186–187
Week view of, 184
Palm Desktop Expense program, 210–211
Palm Desktop interface
 defined, 182
 Expense icon, 183
 Install icon, 183
 menu bar, 182
 toolbar, 182
Palm Desktop memos
 categorizing, 207–208
 deleting, 210
 editing, 207
 entering, 204–206
 printing, 206–207
 private, 208–209
 reading, 206
Palm Desktop screen, 182–183
Palm Desktop To Do List
 assigning categories to items, 195–196
 assigning due date to item, 199–200
 attaching notes to items, 201–202
 creating new categories in, 196–197
 creating To Do items, 194
 deleting categories in, 197–198
 deleting To Do items, 202–203
 marking an item private, 200–201
 renaming categories in, 198–199
 setting preferences in, 203–204
 setting priority for items, 194–195
 viewing items by category, 202
Palm Install Tool, 213–214
Palm OS 3.0, 244
Palm OS 3.01, 244
Palm OS upgrade, 244–246
Palmeta Mail, 298
PalmOS.com, 286
PalmPilot
 batteries, 30–31
 contrast wheel, 16
 display area, 17–19

Graffiti area, 23
hard buttons, 14–15
HotSyncing, 29–30
keyboard, 44–45
power button, 16
versus regular computer, 15
Reset button, 16–17
soft buttons, 19–23
standard applications on, 24–29
turning off, 290
versions, 23–24
versus Windows CE, 12
PalmPilot 1000, 24
PalmPilot 5000, 24
PalmPilot accessories
 Brain Wash screen-cleaning system, 272
 business card scanners, 273, 280–281
 cases, 274
 Karma Cloth, 272
 Minstrel wireless modem, 274
 styluses, 272
 SuperPilot Memory Board, 250, 273
 Tripmate GPS receiver, 273–274, 280
 UniMount, 273
 WriteRight Screen Enhancements overlays, 271–272
PalmPilot Address Book
 accessing, 73–74
 attaching note to address record, 79–80
 defined, 25
 deleting a name from, 84–85
 deleting a note from address record, 85–86
 editing an address record, 78–79
 entering names into, 74–77
 finding name in, 82–84
 hard button, 14, 73–74
 marking business card, 81–82
 setting preferences in, 86–87
 setting up custom fields, 87–88

PalmPilot Date Book
  adding appointments to, 125–128
  alarms, 128–130
  button, 14, 121
  defined, 25–26
  deleting appointments in, 133–134
  dragging and dropping, 68–69, 123–124
  icon for, 20
  private appointments in, 132
  purging appointments in, 136
  repeating appointments in, 130–132
  setting preferences in, 134–135
  uncluttering screen in, 68
  views, 122–125
PalmPilot Mail program
  creating a message in, 147–149
  customizing, 158–163
  defined, 26, 146
  deleting a message in, 153–154
  desktop mail program needed for, 146
  forwarding a message in, 152–153
  icon for, 20
  purging deleted messages in, 154–155
  reading a message in, 149–150
  replying to a message in, 150–151
  saving drafts in, 155
  sending a blind copy, 155–156
  signatures, 161–162
  sorting messages in, 157
PalmPilot Memo Pad
  beaming memos, 120
  categorizing memos, 114
  changing fonts in, 118
  creating new memos, 110–111
  defined, 3, 28
  deleting memos, 116–117
  editing memos, 112–113
  faxing messages from, 240, 281–282, 301
  hard button, 14, 15, 109–110
  private memos, 115–116
  reading memos, 111–112
  setting preferences for, 118–119
  viewing memos by category, 117–118
PalmPilot Modem
  batteries, 224
  browsing the Web with, 239–240
  connecting to Internet with, 232–235
  cost of, 223
  faxing with, 240
  outside North America, 224
  performing a Modem HotSync, 227–232
  sending e-mail with, 146
  setting up, 224–225
  setting up PalmPilot to use, 225–227
PalmPilot Personal, 24
PalmPilot Professional
  defined, 24
  deleting applications on, 217
  infrared port (IR), 81
  Note screen, 94
  text sizing with, 118
PalmPilot To Do List
  attaching notes to items, 93–94
  beaming To Do's, 98–99
  changing To Do's, 99–101
  creating a To Do item, 90–91
  defined, 28
  deleting a note in, 103–104
  deleting a To Do List item, 102–103
  entering details for item, 91–93
  hard button, 14, 15, 90
  marking completed To Do's, 102
  purging completed To Do items, 107
  recurring To Do items, 269–270
  setting preferences for, 104–106
  undoing mistakes in, 101
  viewing items by category, 95–98
PalmPilot Web Ring, 285
PalmPilot Web site
  downloading latest version of Palm Desktop for Windows, 251
  for more information, 252

Index

Palm OS 3.01 on, 244
Palm OS patches on, 245–246
PalmPower Magazine, 287
PalmPrint IR program, 144, 301
PalmProject program, 256, 257
parents, add-on software for, 258–259
Parker, Calvin, 285
password
  deleting forgotten, 58–59
  setting, 57–58
Password dialog box, 57–58
patches, Palm OS, 245–246
PC serial ports, 169
PCs For Dummies, 5, 294
PDA Dash Web site, 287
Pen dialog box, 70
Pendragon Forms, 278
periods in Graffiti, 40
periods in ShortCut names, 62
persistent state quality, 16
Personal Digital Assistants, 287
personal information manager (PIM) programs, 3
pet keychains, 258
phone lines
  analog, 225
  digital, 225
  plugging phone line into modem, 224–225
Phone Number Lookup feature, 106–107
PhoneLog, 299
photographs on PalmPilot, 298
physicians, software for, 259
piano keyboard, on-screen, 257–258
Pilot Desktop 1.01 for the Mac, 168, 172
Pilot Desktop for Macintosh
  installing, 172–178
  upgrading, 251–252
Pilot Gear HQ
  EE Toolkit from, 255
  Web site, 287
Pilot Zone Web site, 288

Pilots, 2
PocketMirror for Outlook 97, 282
PocketSynth, 257–258
Pogue, David, 294
popularity of PalmPilot, 1
power button, 16
preferences, setting PalmPilot
  accessing General Preferences screen, 29, 47–48
  Auto-off interval, 50–51
  beaming, 53
  for buttons, 53–54
  date, 49–50
  format, 55–56
  sound volume, 51–52
  time, 48–49
Preferences application
  defined, 20, 28
  launching, 47–48
preferences for PalmPilot Address Book, 86–87
preferences for PalmPilot Date Book, 134–135
preferences for PalmPilot memos, 118–119
preferences for To Do List
  in Palm Desktop, 203–204
  in PalmPilot, 104–106
pre-installed programs on PalmPilot, 3
  Address Book, 25, 73–88
  Calculator, 25
  Date Book, 25–26, 121–136
pre-installed programs on PalmPilot
  defined, 24
  Expense, 26, 27, 210–211
  Giraffe game, 26, 27
  HotSync, 20, 26. *See also* HotSyncing
  Mail, 26, 145–163
  Memo Pad, 28, 109–120
  Preferences, 28, 29, 47–56
  Security, 28, 30, 56–60
  To Do List, 28, 89–107

printer port, Mac, 172–173
printing memos from Palm Desktop, 206–207
priority of a To Do item
  changing, 100
  setting, 91–92
  Show Priorities option, 105
  sorting by, 104–106
private appointments, 132
private memos, 115–116
problems, PalmPilot
  beaming failures, 291
  blank screens, 289
  "Fatal exception" error, 292
  Graffiti misunderstandings, 290–291
  hard buttons that stick, 290
  menu buttons that don't work, 290
  PalmPilots that won't start, 291
  PalmPilots that won't turn off, 290
  screen taps that don't work, 289
  too dark screen, 291
professions, add-on software for different
  architects, 253–254
  athletic coaches, 254
  bartenders, 254, 255
  couch potatoes, 254
  electrical engineers, 255
  help desk technicians, 255–256
  lawyers, 256
  managers, 256, 257
  ministers, 256
  molecular biologists, 257
  musicians, 257–258
  New York City taxi drivers, 258
  parents, 258–259
  physicians, 259
  pilots, 259–260
  psychics, 260
  salespeople, 261
  stockbrokers, 261
  teachers, 261–262

  telemarketers, 262
  travel agents, 262
  writers, 263
PROFS-AutoPilot synchronization tool, 300
programs
  beaming, 142–143
  deleting, 215–217
  installing add-on, 213–215
  opening, 14–15, 20–21
programs available for PalmPilot
  Action Names, 299
  Actioneer, 279–280, 299
  AirCalc, 259
  for airplane pilots, 259–260
  Amicus Attorney, 256
  AportisDoc, 143, 298
  for architects, 253–254
  Area Codes database, 262
  AreaCoder, 299
  Athlete's Calculator, 254
  Auto Doc, 259
  AvantGo, 297
  AvCheck, 259–260
  for bartenders, 254, 255
  BlackJack, 296
  BrainForest, 263, 299
  BugMe!, 299
  CardScan, 280–281
  on the CD-ROM, 12, 295–301
  for coaches, 254
  for couch potatoes, 254
  Delorme Street Atlas, 274, 280
  Desktop to Go, 283, 300
  DietLog, 254
  DigiPet, 258–259
  Drinks, 254, 255
  EE Toolkit, 255
  for electrical engineers, 255
  Eliza, Pilot Psychologist, 296
  FCPlus Professional, 295
  financial tools on CD-ROM, 295

Flash!, 261, 262
FlashBuilder III for Palm III, 277, 300
forms programs, 277–279, 301
games on CD-ROM, 296
HandFax, 240, 281–282, 301
HandStamp Pro, 297
HandWeb, 297
for help desk technicians, 255–256
Image Viewer, 298
Internet tools on CD-ROM, 297–298
Jpack, 296
JTutor, 261, 296
King James version of the Bible, 256
Klondike, 296
language dictionary, 296
for lawyers, 256
MakeDoc, 301
for managers, 256, 257
for ministers, 256
Mobile Medical Data, 259
for molecular biologists, 257
for musicians, 257–258
for New York City taxi drivers, 258
NY CrossTown 1.5, 258
OligoCalc, 257
organizational tools on CD-ROM, 299–300
Palmeta Mail, 298
PalmPrint, 144, 301
PalmProject, 256, 257
for parents, 258–259
PhoneLog, 299
for physicians, 259
PocketSynth, 257–258
by profession, 253–263
PROFS-AutoPilot, 300
for psychics, 260
Punch List, 253–254, 299
QuickSheet, 276–277
Qmate, 295

Remedy Help Desk, 255–256
Reuters Market Clip, 261
for salespeople, 261
Satellite Forms, 278–279, 301
Small Talk, 262, 281
standard pre-installed applications, 24–29
for stockbrokers, 261
synchronization programs, 282–283
synchronization tools on CD-ROM, 300
T9, 46, 276
Tarot Assistant, 260
for teachers, 261–262
TealEcho, 301
TealGlance, 299
TealMagnify, 301
TealPaint, 298
for telemarketers, 262
ThoughtMill, 263, 300
Time Expense Auto Keeper (TEAK), 295
TimeReporter, 300
for travel agents, 262
UnDupe, 300
utilities on CD-ROM, 300–301
Words Per Minute, 296
World Time, 300
for writers, 263, 299, 300
ProxiWeb (web browser), 240
proxy server, defined, 240
psychics, software for, 260
Psychologist, Pilot, 296
Puma Technology, 283
Punch List program, 253–254, 299
punctuation in Graffiti, 40
Purge Deleted Message dialog box, 154
purging
 appointments in Date Book, 136
 completed To Do items, 107
 deleted e-mail, 154–155

• Q •

Qmate, 295
Quicken, 295
Quicklist category, 84
QuickSheet, 276–277
Quinn, Jaime, 261

• R •

Rathbone, Andy, 294
reading e-mail, 149–150
reading memos
  on Palm Desktop, 206
  on PalmPilot, 111–112
reassigning a hard button, 67
rechargeable batteries, 31
recharging batteries, 268
reconfiguring modem, 225–227
Record menu commands
  Record⇨Attach Note, 79
  Record⇨Beam, 99, 138
  Record⇨Delete Event, 133
  Record⇨Delete Item, 39, 103
  Record⇨Purge, 107
  Record⇨Select Business Card, 81–82
recording voice notes, 269
recurring To Do items, 269–270
religious text, downloading, 256
Remedy Help Desk, 255–256
Remember icon, 7
remembering your password, 58–59
Rename Custom Fields dialog box, 87–88
renaming categories
  in Palm Desktop To Do List, 198–199
  in PalmPilot To Do List, 97–98
repeating appointments
  in Palm Desktop Date Book, 186–187
  in PalmPilot Date Book, 130–132
Reply Options dialog box, 150–151
replying to e-mail message, 150–151
Reset button, 16–17
resources on the Internet
  Calvin's PalmPilot FAQ, 285
  InSync Online, 286
  newsgroups, 286
  Palm Central, 286
  PalmOS.com, 286
  PalmPilot newsgroups, 286
  PalmPilot Web Ring, 285
  PalmPower Magazine, 287
  PDA Dash, 287
  Pilot Gear H.Q., 255, 287
  Pilot Zone, 288
  3Com, 288
restoring PalmPilot data, 218–219
return character, Graffiti, 37–38
Reuters Market Clip, 261
Revolv Design Company, 273
RhinoSkin case manufacturer, 274
right-clicking, defined, 6
Road Warriors Web site, 224
romantic movies, 146

• S •

sales of PalmPilot, 1
salespeople, software for, 261
Satellite Forms, 278–279, 301
Save Draft dialog box, 155
saving batteries with Auto-off, 50–51
saving e-mail drafts, 155
scanners, business card, 273, 280–281
scratching the screen, 34, 66
screen
  backlight for reading, 16
  blank, 289
  Brain Wash screen-cleaning system, 272
  display area, 17–19
  Graffiti area of, 23
  Karma Cloth for, 272
  scratches, 34, 66
  soft buttons, 19–23

WriteRight Screen Enhancements overlays, 271–272
screen taps that don't work, 289
Scroll buttons, 14, 15
Seapoint Software, 260
searching and replacing text (no can do), 268
Security program
  accessing, 56–57
  defined, 20, 28
  deleting forgotten password, 58–59
  hiding private items, 59–60
  screen, 30, 57
  setting password, 57–58
selecting, defined, 6
sending e-mail directly from PalmPilot, 146
serial ports
  Mac, 172, 174
  PC, 169
Set Date dialog box, 49–50
Set Time dialog box, 48–49
setting an alarm, 128–130
setting password, 57–58
setting preferences for PalmPilot
  accessing General Preferences screen, 29, 47–48
  Auto-off interval, 50–51
  beaming, 53
  for buttons, 53–54
  date, 49–50
  format, 55–56
  sound volume, 51–52
  time, 48–49
setting preferences for PalmPilot Address Book, 86–87
setting preferences for PalmPilot Date Book, 134–135
setting preferences for PalmPilot memos, 118–119
setting preferences for To Do List
  in Palm Desktop, 203–204

  in PalmPilot, 104–106
setting time on your PalmPilot, 48–49
shareware
  on the CD, 275
  defined, 253
shift character in Graffiti, 38
ShortCut Entry dialog box, 61
Shortcut icon, 7
ShortCuts, Graffiti, 43–44
ShortCuts, setting up, 60
  accessing ShortCuts screen, 61
  adding a new ShortCut, 61–62
  deleting a ShortCut, 63
  editing a ShortCut, 62–63
ShortCuts as timesavers, 66
Show Options dialog box, 157
signatures on e-mail, 161–162
Small Talk electronic phrasebook, 262, 281
Smartcode Software
  HandFax from, 240, 281–282, 301
  HandMail from, 239
  HandWeb Web browser from, 240
soft buttons
  Applications soft button, 19–21
  Calculator soft button, 19, 21–22
  defined, 6, 19
  Find soft button, 19, 22–23
  Menu soft button, 19, 21
soft reset, 17, 290
SoftCare Clinical Informatics, 254
SoftMagic Corp., 278
software available for PalmPilot
  Action Names, 299
  Actioneer, 279–280, 299
  AirCalc, 259
  for airplane pilots, 259–260
  Amicus Attorney, 256
  AportisDoc, 143, 298
  for architects, 253–254
  Area Codes database, 262
  AreaCoder, 299

software available for PalmPilot *(continued)*
   Athlete's Calculator, 254
   Auto Doc, 259
   AvantGo, 297
   AvCheck, 259–260
   for bartenders, 254, 255
   BlackJack, 296
   BrainForest, 263, 299
   BugMe!, 299
   CardScan, 280–281
   on the CD-ROM, 12, 295–301
   for coaches, 254
   for couch potatoes, 254
   Delorme Street Atlas, 274, 280
   Desktop To Go, 283, 300
   DietLog, 254
   DigiPet, 258–259
   Drinks, 254, 255
   EE Toolkit, 255
   for electrical engineers, 255
   Eliza, Pilot Psychologist, 296
   FCPlus Professional, 295
   financial tools on CD-ROM, 295
   Flash!, 261, 262
   FlashBuilder III for Palm III, 277, 300
   forms programs, 277–279, 301
   games on CD-ROM, 296
   HandFax, 240, 281–282, 301
   HandStamp Pro, 297
   HandWeb, 297
   for help desk technicians, 255–256
   Image Viewer, 298
   Internet tools on CD-ROM, 297–298
   Jpack, 296
   JTutor, 261, 296
   King James version of the Bible, 256
   Klondike, 296
   language dictionary, 296
   for lawyers, 256
   MakeDoc, 301
   for managers, 256, 257
   for ministers, 256
   Mobile Medical Data, 259
   for molecular biologists, 257
   for musicians, 257–258
   for New York City taxi drivers, 258
   NY CrossTown 1.5, 258
   OligoCalc, 257
   organizational tools on CD-ROM, 299–300
   Palmeta Mail, 298
   PalmPrint, 144, 301
   PalmProject, 256, 257
   for parents, 258–259
   PhoneLog, 299
   for physicians, 259
   PocketSynth, 257–258
   by profession, 253–263
   PROFS-AutoPilot, 300
   for psychics, 260
   Punch List, 253–254, 299
   QuickSheet, 276–277
   Qmate, 295
   Remedy Help Desk, 255–256
   Reuters Market Clip, 261
   for salespeople, 261
   Satellite Forms, 278–279, 301
   Small Talk, 262, 281
   standard pre-installed applications, 24–29
   for stockbrokers, 261
   synchronization programs, 282–283
   synchronization tools on CD-ROM, 300
   T9, 46, 276
   Tarot Assistant, 260
   for teachers, 261–262
   TealEcho, 301
   TealGlance, 299
   TealMagnify, 301
   TealPaint, 298
   for telemarketers, 262
   ThoughtMill, 263, 300
   Time Expense Auto Keeper (TEAK), 295

TimeReporter, 300
for travel agents, 262
UnDupe, 300
utilities on CD-ROM, 300–301
Words Per Minute, 296
World Time, 300
for writers, 263, 299, 300
sorting e-mail messages, 157
sorting memos alphabetically, 118–119
sorting tasks, 104–106
sound volume, setting, 51–52
space character, Graffiti, 37
spreadsheet program, QuickSheet, 276–277
standard programs on PalmPilot
  Address Book, 25, 73–88
  Calculator, 25
  Date Book, 25–26, 121–136
  defined, 24
  Expense, 26, 27, 210–211
  Giraffe game, 26, 27
  HotSync, 20, 26. *See also* HotSyncing
  Mail, 26, 145–163
  Memo Pad, 28, 109–120
  Preferences, 28, 29, 47–56
  Security, 28, 30, 56–60
  To Do List, 28, 89–107
starting applications in PalmPilot
  Address Book, 73–74
  with application hard buttons, 14–15
  with Applications soft button, 20–21
  Date Book, 121
  Expense, 211
  HotSync Manager, 178–179
  Memo Pad, 109–110
  Preferences, 47–48
  Security, 56–57
  To Do List, 90
Stevens Creek Software
  Athlete's Calculator program from, 254
  PalmPrint from, 144, 301

stockbrokers, software for, 261
Strata Systems, 254
Street Atlas, Delorme, 274, 280
stylus
  defined, 34
  finger versus, 66
  writing Graffiti letters with, 34–35
styluses, new and improved, 272
subscripts, 269
SuperPilot Memory Board, 250, 273
superscripts, 269
surfing the Internet 239–240
  with HandWeb (on CD-ROM), 240, 297
  with Microsoft Internet Explorer, 297
  with ProxiWeb, 240
synchronization programs
  on CD-ROM, 300
  commercial, 282–283
system sounds, 51

• T •

T9 system for entering text, 46, 276
tapping, defined, 6
taps that don't work
  on Menu soft button, 290
  screen taps, 289
Tarot Assistant program, 260
teachers, add-on software for, 261–262
TealEcho program, 301
TealGlance, 299
TealMagnify program, 301
TealPaint program, 298
Technology Resource Group (TRG), 213
  FlashBuilder III from, 277
  SuperPilot memory board, 250, 273
Tegic Communications
  T9 system from, 276
  Web site, 46
telemarketers, software for, 262
telephone lines, 225

things you *can't* do with PalmPilot
  assigning multiple categories to one
      item, 270
  categorizing dates, 270
  creating an appointment spanning two
      or more dates, 269
  creating recurring To Do items,
      269–270
  linking items between programs, 268
  recharging batteries in the cradle, 268
  recording voice notes, 269
  running on AC power, 267
  searching and replacing text, 268
  using superscripts and subscripts, 269
  viewing two programs at the same
      time, 268
3Com Corporation, 249
  technical support phone number, 290
  Web site, 168, 172, 285, 288
time
  checking the, 66
  setting the, 48–49
  World Time program on CD, 300
Time Expense Auto Keeper (TEAK), 295
time stamp ShortCuts in Graffiti, 43, 66
TimeReporter, 300
timesavers
  application, 67–69
  general, 65–67
  Graffiti, 70
TinySheet, 276
Tip icon, 7
To Do Item Details dialog box, 91–93
To Do List, Palm Desktop
  assigning categories to items, 195–196
  assigning due date to item, 199–200
  attaching notes to items, 201–202
  creating new categories in, 196–197
  creating To Do items, 194
  deleting categories in, 197–198
  deleting To Do items, 202–203
  marking an item private, 200–201
  renaming categories in, 198–199
  setting preferences in, 203–204
  setting priority for items, 194–195
  viewing items by category, 202
To Do List, PalmPilot
  attaching notes to items, 93–94
  beaming To Do's, 98–99
  changing To Do's, 99–101
  creating a To Do item, 90–91
  defined, 28
  deleting a note in, 103–104
  deleting a To Do List item, 102–103
  entering details for item, 91–93
  hard button, 14, 15, 90
  marking completed To Do's, 102
  purging completed To Do items, 107
  recurring To Do items, 269–270
  setting preferences for, 104–106
  undoing mistakes in, 101
  viewing items by category, 95–98
To Do List hard button, 14, 15, 90
To Do Plus, 90
To Lookup screen, 147
touch-sensitive screen, 15
travel agents, software for, 262
traveling with PalmPilot
  cases to carry PalmPilot in, 274
  outside North America, 224
  UniMount for your car, 273
TRG (Technology Resource Group)
      company, 213
  FlashBuilder III from, 277
  SuperPilot memory board, 250, 273
triangles
  downward-pointing, 77
  left- and right-pointing, 150
Tripmate GPS receiver, 273–274, 280
troubleshooting tips
  for beaming failures, 291
  for blank screens, 289
  for "Fatal exception" errors, 292

Index 327

for Graffiti problems, 290–291
for hard buttons that stick, 290
for menu buttons that don't work, 290
for PalmPilots that won't start, 291
for PalmPilots that won't turn off, 290
for screen taps that don't work, 289
for too dark screen, 291
True North, Inc., 258
Truncate Options dialog box, 163
truncating options for e-mail, 162–163
turning off beaming feature, 53
turning off PalmPilot, 290
undoing mistakes in To Do List program, 101

• U •

UnDupe program, 300
UniMount for your car, 273
upgrading
   Palm III, 248–250
   Palm Desktop for Windows, 251
   PalmPilot, 243–244
upstroke command, Graffiti, 70
user interface, 15
user name, 170, 175, 222
utilities on CD-ROM, 300–301

• V •

versions of Palm OS
   finding out which version of Palm OS you have, 244–245
   installing new, 245–246
versions of PalmPilot, 23–24
   Palm III, 2. *See also* Palm III
   PalmPilot 1000, 24
   PalmPilot 5000, 24
   PalmPilot Personal, 24
   PalmPilot Professional, 24. *See also* PalmPilot Professional

viewing
   archived items, 220
   different dates, 67–68
   To Do items by category, 95–98
   two programs at the same time (no can do), 268
voice recording, 269

• W •

Warning icon, 7
warranty, PalmPilot's, 290
Web browsing, 239
   with HandWeb (on CD-ROM), 240, 297
   with Microsoft Internet Explorer, 297
   with ProxiWeb, 240
Web sites
   Calvin's PalmPilot FAQ, 285
   InSync Online, 286
   Palm Central, 286
   PalmOS.com, 286
   PalmPilot Web Ring, 285
   PalmPilot Web site, 244, 245–246, 251, 252
   PalmPower Magazine, 287
   PDA Dash, 287
   Pilot Gear H.Q., 255, 287
   Pilot Zone, 288
   Stevens Creek Software, 144
   3Com, 288
Week view, Palm Desktop Date Book, 184
Week view, PalmPilot Date Book, 123–124
Weingarten, Jan, 284
Windows 3.1, 168
Windows 3.11 For Dummies, 4th Edition, 294
Windows 95, 244
Windows 95 For Dummies, 2nd Edition, 294

Windows 98, 244
Windows 98 For Dummies, 5, 294
Windows CE versus PalmPilot, 12
Windows operating system, 12, 244
Wireless Modem, Novatel, 261
Word, Microsoft
  dragging memos into, 207
  icon on Palm Desktop, 211
Words Per Minute (in Graffiti), 296
WorkPad, IBM, 2–3, 24
World Time, 300
World Wide Web
  browsing, 239–240, 297
  resources, 4–5, 285–288. *See also* Web sites
WriteRight Screen Enhancements overlays, 271–272
writers, software for
  BrainForest, 263, 299
  ThoughtMill, 263, 300
writing in Graffiti
  alphabet for, 34–36
  backspace character, 37
  capital letters, 38–39
  versus entering data through Palm Desktop, 182
  fish loop, 42–43
  Help screen, 35–36
  letters and numbers, 34–36, 41
  on PalmPilot screen, 23
  punctuation, 40
  return character, 37–38
  ShortCuts, 43–44
  space character, 37
  timesavers for, 70
  whiz secrets for, 40–41
  Words Per Minute program for, 296
  writing area, 34

SPECIAL OFFER FOR IDG BOOKS READERS

FREE GIFT!

FREE
IDG Books/PC WORLD CD Wallet
and a Sample Issue of
PC WORLD

THE #1 MONTHLY COMPUTER MAGAZINE
How to order your sample issue and FREE CD Wallet:

- ✉ Cut and mail the coupon today!
- ☎ Call us at 1-800-825-7595 x434
  Fax us at 1-415-882-0936
- ☞ Order online at
  www.pcworld.com/resources/subscribe/BWH.html

ORDER TODAY!

...For Dummies is a registered trademark under exclusive license to IDG Books Worldwide, Inc., from International Data Group, Inc.

FREE GIFT/SAMPLE ISSUE COUPON

Cut coupon and mail to: PC World, PO Box 55029, Boulder, CO 80322-5029

YES! Please rush my FREE CD wallet and my FREE sample issue of PC WORLD! If I like PC WORLD, I'll honor your invoice and receive 11 more issues (12 in all) for just $19.97—that's 72% off the newsstand rate.

NO COST EXAMINATION GUARANTEE.
If I decide PC WORLD is not for me, I'll write "cancel" on the invoice and owe nothing. The sample issue and CD wallet are mine to keep, no matter what.

Name _____
Company _____
Address _____
City _____ State _____ Zip _____
Email _____

PC WORLD

Offer valid in the U.S. only. Mexican orders please send $39.97 USD. Canadian orders send $39.97, plus 7% GST (#R124669680). Other countries send $65.97. Savings based on annual newsstand rate of $71.88.   7BXJ0

SPECIAL OFFER FOR IDG BOOKS READERS

Get the Most from Your PC!

Every issue of PC World is packed with the latest information to help you make the most of your PC.

- Top 100 PC and Product Ratings
- Hot PC News
- How Tos, Tips, & Tricks
- Buyers' Guides
- Consumer Watch
- Hardware and Software Previews
- Internet & Multimedia Special Reports
- Upgrade Guides
- Monthly @Home Section

YOUR FREE GIFT!

As a special bonus with your order, you will receive the IDG Books/PC WORLD CD wallet, perfect for transporting and protecting your CD collection.

...For Dummies is a registered trademark under exclusive license to IDG Books Worldwide, Inc., from International Data Group, Inc.

SEND TODAY
for your sample issue
and FREE IDG Books/PC WORLD CD Wallet!

How to order your sample issue and FREE CD Wallet:

✉ Cut and mail the coupon today!
   Mail to: PC World, PO Box 55029, Boulder, CO 80322-5029

☎ Call us at 1-800-825-7595 x434
   Fax us at 1-415-882-0936

☞ Order online at www.pcworld.com/resources/subscribe/BWH.html

PC WORLD

SPECIAL OFFER for owners of *PalmPilot For Dummies*!

Try Intellisync® for PalmPilot Connected Organizers FREE for 30 Days!

Your copy of *PalmPilot For Dummies,* by Bill Dyszel, includes a CD containing a FREE, 30-day trial version of Intellisync for PalmPilot Connected Organizers — the best way to ensure your 3Com connected organizer is current anytime, anywhere.

Intellisync for PalmPilot Connected Organizers keeps you up-to-the-minute with simultaneous synchronization between your Palm III or PalmPilot organizer and such popular PC applications as Microsoft Outlook 97/98 and Schedule+, ACT!, Lotus Organizer and Notes,

and many more. Whether you're on the road or at your desk, one-touch synchronization with Intellisync means you'll never be overbooked, out of date, or out of touch.

Try the **30-day trial version of Intellisync for PalmPilot Connected Organizers on the enclosed CD.** Then take advantage of a special offer, exclusively for owners of *PalmPilot For Dummies.*

As an owner of *PalmPilot For Dummies,* by Bill Dyszel, you qualify to purchase Intellisync for PalmPilot Connected Organizers at the special price of $49.95 — a $20 savings off the retail price.

Call 1-800-774-PUMA,

or visit our Web site at **www.pumatech.com/ppfd,** to purchase Intellisync for PalmPilot Connected Organizers for the special price of just **$49.95**.

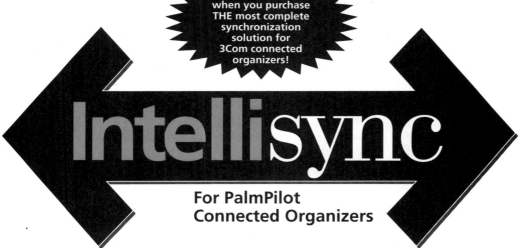

SAVE $20 when you purchase THE most complete synchronization solution for 3Com connected organizers!

Key Features of Intellisync for PalmPilot Connected Organizers

Easy, one-button synchronization
Just push the HotSync button on your device's cradle and Intellisync updates the information on your Palm III or PalmPilot with all of the PC applications on your desktop — automatically.

Works with popular PC applications
- Microsoft Outlook 97/98
- Microsoft Schedule+
- Symantec ACT!
- Lotus Organizer
- Lotus Organizer Premium Edition
- Lotus Notes
- Novell GroupWise

- Day-Timer Organizer 98
- GoldMine
- Eudora Planner
- ON Technology Meeting Maker

Check www.pumatech.com for the latest application support.

Powerful filtering
Quickly synchronize even large databases by using filters to select only the exact information you need updated.

Full conflict resolution
When changes are made to the same record on your 3Com organizer and desktop PC,

Intellisync detects and resolves the conflict automatically, or makes changes based on the customized controls you've selected.

Complete customization
Choose the applications you want to synchronize, then use advanced capabilities like intelligent field mapping and date range support for complete control over your information.

Integrated e-mail sync
Import, export, and synchronize e-mail messages between your PC and 3Com organizer. (Currently available for Outlook, Exchange.)

©1998 Puma Technology, Inc. All rights reserved. Puma Technology, the Puma Technology logo, Intellisync, the Intellisync logo, DSX Technology, and the DSX Technology logo are trademarks of Puma Technology, Inc., that may be registered in some jurisdictions. All other company and product names are trademarks of their respective owners.

™ Patented Data Synchronization Extensions Technology (DSX Technology™) is the core of Puma's Intellisync family of products.

IDG Books Worldwide, Inc., End-User License Agreement

READ THIS. You should carefully read these terms and conditions before opening the software packet(s) included with this book ("Book"). This is a license agreement ("Agreement") between you and IDG Books Worldwide, Inc. ("IDGB"). By opening the accompanying software packet(s), you acknowledge that you have read and accept the following terms and conditions. If you do not agree and do not want to be bound by such terms and conditions, promptly return the Book and the unopened software packet(s) to the place you obtained them for a full refund.

1. **License Grant.** IDGB grants to you (either an individual or entity) a nonexclusive license to use one copy of the enclosed software program(s) (collectively, the "Software") solely for your own personal or business purposes on a single computer (whether a standard computer or a workstation component of a multiuser network). The Software is in use on a computer when it is loaded into temporary memory (RAM) or installed into permanent memory (hard disk, CD-ROM, or other storage device). IDGB reserves all rights not expressly granted herein.

2. **Ownership.** IDGB is the owner of all right, title, and interest, including copyright, in and to the compilation of the Software recorded on the CD-ROM ("Software Media"). Copyright to the individual programs recorded on the Software Media is owned by the author or other authorized copyright owner of each program. Ownership of the Software and all proprietary rights relating thereto remain with IDGB and its licensers.

3. **Restrictions on Use and Transfer.**

    (a) You may only (i) make one copy of the Software for backup or archival purposes, or (ii) transfer the Software to a single hard disk, provided that you keep the original for backup or archival purposes. You may not (i) rent or lease the Software, (ii) copy or reproduce the Software through a LAN or other network system or through any computer subscriber system or bulletin-board system, or (iii) modify, adapt, or create derivative works based on the Software.

    (b) You may not reverse engineer, decompile, or disassemble the Software. You may transfer the Software and user documentation on a permanent basis, provided that the transferee agrees to accept the terms and conditions of this Agreement and you retain no copies. If the Software is an update or has been updated, any transfer must include the most recent update and all prior versions.

4. **Restrictions on Use of Individual Programs.** You must follow the individual requirements and restrictions detailed for each individual program in Appendix C of this Book. These limitations are also contained in the individual license agreements recorded on the Software Media. These limitations may include a requirement that after using the program for a specified period of time, the user must pay a registration fee or discontinue use. By opening the Software packet(s), you will be agreeing to abide by the licenses and restrictions for these individual programs that are detailed in Appendix C and on the Software Media. None of the material on this Software Media or listed in this Book may ever be redistributed, in original or modified form, for commercial purposes.

5. **Limited Warranty.**

   (a) IDGB warrants that the Software and Software Media are free from defects in materials and workmanship under normal use for a period of sixty (60) days from the date of purchase of this Book. If IDGB receives notification within the warranty period of defects in materials or workmanship, IDGB will replace the defective Software Media.

   (b) **IDGB AND THE AUTHOR OF THE BOOK DISCLAIM ALL OTHER WARRANTIES, EXPRESS OR IMPLIED, INCLUDING WITHOUT LIMITATION IMPLIED WARRANTIES OF MERCHANTABILITY AND FITNESS FOR A PARTICULAR PURPOSE, WITH RESPECT TO THE SOFTWARE, THE PROGRAMS, THE SOURCE CODE CONTAINED THEREIN, AND/OR THE TECHNIQUES DESCRIBED IN THIS BOOK. IDGB DOES NOT WARRANT THAT THE FUNCTIONS CONTAINED IN THE SOFTWARE WILL MEET YOUR REQUIREMENTS OR THAT THE OPERATION OF THE SOFTWARE WILL BE ERROR FREE.**

   (c) This limited warranty gives you specific legal rights, and you may have other rights that vary from jurisdiction to jurisdiction.

6. **Remedies.**

   (a) IDGB's entire liability and your exclusive remedy for defects in materials and workmanship shall be limited to replacement of the Software Media, which may be returned to IDGB with a copy of your receipt at the following address: Software Media Fulfillment Department, Attn.: *PalmPilot For Dummies,* IDG Books Worldwide, Inc., 7260 Shadeland Station, Ste. 100, Indianapolis, IN 46256, or call 800-762-2974. Please allow three to four weeks for delivery. This Limited Warranty is void if failure of the Software Media has resulted from accident, abuse, or misapplication. Any replacement Software Media will be warranted for the remainder of the original warranty period or thirty (30) days, whichever is longer.

   (b) In no event shall IDGB or the author be liable for any damages whatsoever (including without limitation damages for loss of business profits, business interruption, loss of business information, or any other pecuniary loss) arising from the use of or inability to use the Book or the Software, even if IDGB has been advised of the possibility of such damages.

   (c) Because some jurisdictions do not allow the exclusion or limitation of liability for consequential or incidental damages, the above limitation or exclusion may not apply to you.

7. **U.S. Government Restricted Rights.** Use, duplication, or disclosure of the Software by the U.S. Government is subject to restrictions stated in paragraph (c)(1)(ii) of the Rights in Technical Data and Computer Software clause of DFARS 252.227-7013, and in subparagraphs (a) through (d) of the Commercial Computer–Restricted Rights clause at FAR 52.227-19, and in similar clauses in the NASA FAR supplement, when applicable.

8. **General.** This Agreement constitutes the entire understanding of the parties and revokes and supersedes all prior agreements, oral or written, between them and may not be modified or amended except in a writing signed by both parties hereto that specifically refers to this Agreement. This Agreement shall take precedence over any other documents that may be in conflict herewith. If any one or more provisions contained in this Agreement are held by any court or tribunal to be invalid, illegal, or otherwise unenforceable, each and every other provision shall remain in full force and effect.

Installation Instructions

The *PalmPilot For Dummies* CD offers valuable PalmPilot software that you won't want to miss. To use the CD, follow these steps:

Windows

1. **Double-click and read the file called License.txt.**
2. **Double-click and read the file called Readme.txt.**
3. **Double-click the folder for the software you are interested in.**
4. **Find the file called Setup.exe or Install.exe, or something similar, and double-click on that file.**

   The program's installer walks you through the process of setting up your new software.

Mac OS

1. **Insert the CD into your computer's CD-ROM drive.**
2. **Double-click the CD icon to show the CD's contents.**
3. **Double-click and read the Read Me First icon.**
4. **Open your browser.**
5. **Click File➪Open and select the CD entitled *PalmPilot For Dummies*.**
6. **Some programs come with installer programs — with those you simply open the program's folder on the CD and double-click the icon with the words *Install* or *Installer*.**

For more information on using this CD, see Appendix C.

Discover Dummies Online!

The Dummies Web Site is your fun and friendly online resource for the latest information about ...For Dummies® books and your favorite topics. The Web site is the place to communicate with us, exchange ideas with other ...For Dummies readers, chat with authors, and have fun!

Ten Fun and Useful Things You Can Do at www.dummies.com

1. Win free ...For Dummies books and more!
2. Register your book and be entered in a prize drawing.
3. Meet your favorite authors through the IDG Books Author Chat Series.
4. Exchange helpful information with other ...For Dummies readers.
5. Discover other great ...For Dummies books you must have!
6. Purchase Dummieswear™ exclusively from our Web site.
7. Buy ...For Dummies books online.
8. Talk to us. Make comments, ask questions, get answers!
9. Download free software.
10. Find additional useful resources from authors.

Link directly to these ten fun and useful things at
http://www.dummies.com/10useful

For other technology titles from IDG Books Worldwide, go to www.idgbooks.com

Not on the Web yet? It's easy to get started with *Dummies 101®: The Internet For Windows® 98* or *The Internet For Dummies®, 5th Edition*, at local retailers everywhere.

Find other ...*For Dummies* books on these topics:

Business • Career • Databases • Food & Beverage • Games • Gardening • Graphics • Hardware
Health & Fitness • Internet and the World Wide Web • Networking • Office Suites
Operating Systems • Personal Finance • Pets • Programming • Recreation • Sports
Spreadsheets • Teacher Resources • Test Prep • Word Processing

The IDG Books Worldwide logo and Dummieswear are trademarks, and Dummies Man and ...For Dummies are registered trademarks under exclusive license to IDG Books Worldwide, Inc., from International Data Group, Inc.

IDG BOOKS WORLDWIDE BOOK REGISTRATION

We want to hear from you!

Visit **http://my2cents.dummies.com** to register this book and tell us how you liked it!

- Get entered in our monthly prize giveaway.
- Give us feedback about this book — tell us what you like best, what you like least, or maybe what you'd like to ask the author and us to change!
- Let us know any other ...*For Dummies*® topics that interest you.

Your feedback helps us determine what books to publish, tells us what coverage to add as we revise our books, and lets us know whether we're meeting your needs as a ...*For Dummies* reader. You're our most valuable resource, and what you have to say is important to us!

Not on the Web yet? It's easy to get started with *Dummies 101*®: *The Internet For Windows*® *98* or *The Internet For Dummies*®, 5th Edition, at local retailers everywhere.

Or let us know what you think by sending us a letter at the following address:

...*For Dummies* Book Registration
Dummies Press
7260 Shadeland Station, Suite 100
Indianapolis, IN 46256-3945
Fax 317-596-5498

BESTSELLING BOOK SERIES FROM IDG